RORTY & PRAGMATISM

THE VANDERBILT LIBRARY OF AMERICAN PHILOSOPHY

The Vanderbilt Library of American Philosophy, under the general editorship of Herman J. Saatkamp, Jr., is a series devoted to past and current issues in American philosophy. The series offers interpretive perspectives focusing on both the historical roots of American philosophy and present innovative developments in American thought, including studies of values, naturalism, social philosophy, cultural criticism, and applied ethics.

OTHER TITLES IN THE SERIES

RORTY
& PRAGMATISM

The Philosopher Responds to His Critics

EDITED BY

HERMAN J. SAATKAMP, JR.

VANDERBILT UNIVERSITY PRESS • NASHVILLE & LONDON

This publication is made from recycled paper and meets the
minimum requirements of American National Standard for
Information Sciences—Permanence of Paper for Printed Library
Materials. ⊚

Library of Congress Cataloging-in-Publication Data

Rorty and pragmatism: The philosopher responds to his critics /
edited by Herman J. Saatkamp, Jr. —1st ed.
                      p.   cm. — (Vanderbilt library of
                           American philosophy)
Each article includes a response by R. Rorty.
Includes bibliographical references and index
Contents: Dewey between Hegel and Darwin / Richard Rorty —
Rorty's pragmatism and farewell to the age of faith and
enlightenment / Charles Hartshorne — America and the
contestations of modernity / Thelma Lavine — American
pragmatism / Richard Bernstein / What is the legacy of
instrumentalism? / James Gouinlock — Pragmatism as naturalized
Hegelianism / Allen Hance — Vulgar pragmatism / Susan Haack
— Rorty and the antirealism / Frank B. Farrell — Philosophy and
the future / Richard Rorty.
ISBN 0-8265-1263-1 (alk. paper)
1. Rorty, Richard.   I. Rorty, Richard.   II. Saatkamp, Herman
J.   III. Series.
B945.R524R67   1995   94-47580
191—dc20   CIP

CONTENTS

PREFACE

I want to express my thanks to those who contributed to this volume. The authors of the articles on Richard Rorty's philosophy have placed themselves in the unusual position of inviting a direct response by Rorty. Such dialogue decidedly promotes philosophical discussion, and it also requires a high level of maturity and scholarship. And I am grateful to Richard Rorty for his responses to each article, which clearly enhance the level of communication in philosophy and also present an *apologia* of his outlook.

I am particularly grateful to Dan Unger, a graduate student at Texas A&M University, for his assistance in scanning and editing much of the material. His knowledge of philosophy and his good will have been of considerable value in the preparation of this volume. The members of the editorial board of the Vanderbilt Library of American Philosophy have offered wise counsel, and the staff of Vanderbilt University Press have provided clear and thoughtful guidance.

Herman J. Saatkamp, Jr.

INTRODUCTION

THE VANDERBILT LIBRARY OF AMERICAN PHILOSOPHY

Rorty and Pragmatism is one of the first volumes in the Vanderbilt Library of American Philosophy. The series focuses on the origins and boundaries of American thought, its roots and edges, and joins an understanding of past philosophical inquiries with the pressing issues of current philosophical investigations. Concentrating on American philosophy is a pragmatic strategy that provides an intellectual baseline for considerations radiating far beyond North America. Philosophy, after all, is a discipline that is neither parochial nor national in outlook. The purpose of the Vanderbilt Library of American Philosophy is to advance philosophy by enhancing our knowledge of the past and by providing a body of inquiry for future generations.

RORTY AND PRAGMATISM

Richard Rorty's challenge to traditional forms of philosophical inquiry has brought accolades and criticisms. He argues that philosophy cannot become a strict science and that the traditional view of philosophy as the pursuit of eternal truth must be abandoned in a temporalized world.[1] To assume that philosophy is at the top of the hierarchy of disciplines is a mistake. Rather, philosophy should be understood from a pragmatic, interpretive, and historicist perspective that undermines the centrality of basic, foundational questions in philosophy of mind and epistemology.[2] Clarity and precision are not to be eschewed, but clarity is a matter of familiarity, not an intrinsic property of certain locutions.

Rorty's anti-essentialist philosophy is in the lineage of Wittgenstein's "philosophical therapy" in which pseudo-problems are resolved or, better, dissolved.[3] But in this volume he is more hesitant to deride these problems as meaningless or nonsense, and he focuses more sharply on the utility of the essentialist tradition.

> I have sometimes used Wittgensteinian pejoratives like "nonsense," "meaningless," etc., but I regret having done so. I think Wittgenstein was wiser when he said that you can give anything a sense if you want to. Epistemologists have given various questions sense in the same way as astrologers and theologians gave their questions sense: by embed-

ding them in a coherent language-game. But questions about the utility of all three language-games persist. (223, note 1)

Rorty's analysis of the philosophical enterprise has generated many criticisms, some impassioned and others more thoughtfully forceful. In this volume, Rorty responds to several of his most prominent and thoughtful critics:
Hartshorne, Lavine, Bernstein, Gouinlock, Hance, Haack, and Farrell.
These critics represent a wide range of philosophical backgrounds and concerns, but each raises significant questions about Rorty's philosophical outlook. Whether one agrees with Rorty's responses or not, the replies are
consequential. They provide insight into Rorty's thought, its development,
and his sense of the future of philosophy. They further the discussion of the
role of philosophy and of its contributions to society.

RORTY AND DEWEY

Richard Rorty's approach to philosophy is Janus-faced, looking both at the
history and the future of philosophy.[4] His most articulated historical ties are
to John Dewey, whom he views as a teacher and leader but not as the ultimate arbiter.

Rorty's exegesis of Dewey's pragmatism returns philosophy, and
American thought, to a set of original insights holding substantial promise
for contemporary concerns. But his exegesis goes beyond explication.
Dewey's voice is filtered through Rorty's view of the role of philosophy, and,
as quickly as Rorty notes his discipleship to Dewey, he marks his differences.
He jettisons Dewey's notions of *experience* and of *scientific method*, arguing
that each contributes little and leads to considerable confusion if taken seriously. His critics argue that Rorty throws the baby out with the bathwater,
and they often reject his analysis of Dewey and also his account of pragmatism's implications for current discussions.

In this volume, Rorty argues that pragmatism is a historicist way of
"avoiding the conflict between science and the religious or moral consciousness," substituting "'utility' for 'accuracy' or 'concreteness' as a term of epistemic approbation" (4). He is concerned that philosophy advance rather
than impede inquiry, and he views this concern as providing a specific role
for philosophy: "the particular charge of philosophy is to make sure that old
philosophical ideas do not block the road of inquiry—that continued use of

the normative language employed in the social and moral strifes of an earlier day does not make it harder to cope with contemporary problems" (14).

Some of these old philosophical ideas are found in Dewey, while others infect contemporary philosophical methodology where the spirit (not the letter) of Dewey's pragmatism can serve as a corrective. Rorty agrees with Hilary Putnam that much of analytic philosophy degenerates into quarrels among differing "intuitions" of the philosophical professoriate, often about questions "far from having either practical or spiritual significance" (202). And he maintains that Dewey's approach makes pragmatism more useful in philosophical investigations.

> Dewey would have been pleased by the fact that the twentieth century has spent increasingly little time talking about the nature of ultimate reality. In part this has been because increasing prominence of Language as a topic, accompanied by an increasing recognition that one can describe the same thing in different ways for different purposes, has helped to make pragmatism, as a doctrine of the relativity of normative judgments to purposes served, more palatable. More important, perhaps, is that lots of different developments in our century— Freudian accounts of inner moral conflicts, ethnographic descriptions of alternative forms of social life, experimentalism in literature and the arts—have made it steadily easier for us to substitute Deweyan questions like Which communities' purposes shall I share? and What sort of person would I prefer to be? for the Kantian questions What should I do? What may I hope? What is man? (15)

RORTY AND THE FUTURE OF PHILOSOPHY

In the concluding essay of this volume, "Philosophy and the Future," Rorty's optimism about philosophy's ongoing future will surprise some, and others will question his decided endorsement of democracy as central to the philosopher's role. But both perspectives are integral strands in the thread of Rorty's temporalized intellectual world.

For Rorty, the future of philosophy is secure as long as there are social and cultural changes: "[P]hilosophy cannot possibly end until social and cultural change ends. . . . In free societies, there will always be a need for their [philosophers'] services, for such societies never stop changing, and hence never stop making old vocabularies obsolete." The new challenges of the temporalized intellectual world are freedom and time. No longer servants of truth but "servants of democracy," philosophers should prize the freedom "to be honest with one another and not be punished for it." Abandoning hope for certainty and eternal perspectives, philosophers also should abandon the insistence that their intuitions are more than contingent historical products. "Truthfulness, like freedom, is temporal, contingent, and fragile. But we can recognize both when we have them." Philosophers should see their roles as historicized:

> If we stop preening ourselves on our position at the top of the hierarchy of disciplines, stop identifying our professional practices with "rational thought" or "clear thought," we shall be in a better position to grant Dewey's point that our discipline is no more able to set its own agenda than is engineering or jurisprudence. Such an admission would help us dispense with the idea that scientific or political developments require "philosophical foundations"—the idea that judgment must remain suspended on the legitimacy of cultural novelties until we philosophers have pronounced them authentically rational. (201)

The philosophical task is in accord with Dewey's remarks that "philosophy can proffer only hypotheses, and that these hypotheses are of value only as they render men's minds more sensitive to the life about them."[5] This new philosophical goal is the creation of a sensitivity to life rather than the production of new knowledge.

RORTY'S RESPONSES TO HIS CRITICS

Richard Rorty responds with care to the articles in this volume, often analyzing and replying to specific arguments and criticisms. Some may fault the accuracy and adequacy of his responses, but he clearly takes his critics' assessments seriously, and his rejoinders are not mere ripostes. His replies not only reveal his arguments and leanings in philosophical debate; they also disclose personal interests and biographical details. The following comments and quotes are mere adumbrations of the range and articulation of Rorty's responses.

It is fitting that the first critique is by Charles Hartshorne, who was Rorty's first teacher of philosophy. There is a charm to Rorty's response, that of a highly regarded student replying to his highly regarded mentor: "Charles Hartshorne was the first teacher to excite in me a genuine enthusiasm for philosophy. I had wandered into a philosophy major without any clear idea of what awaited me, and I should probably have wandered out again had I not started to take courses with Hartshorne" (29). His study with Hartshorne led to his early considerations of contingency and time: "I was also impressed by Hartshorne's citation of Bergson's remark 'if time is not real, nothing is real,' a remark which keeps coming back to me as I write yet another panegyric to historicity and contingency" (29). And even his first philosophical article is recalled:

> The first philosophical article I ever wrote was an attempt to ally Wittgenstein with Peirce—to view them both as temporalistic critics of Platonism, necessity, eternity, and Carnap. (It was, of course, the Peirce of Evolutionary Love, rather than the Peirce of the Logic of Relatives, whom I admired most.) Thirty-some years down the road, I am still on the same temporalistic kick, and still have pretty much the same reactions to reading Hartshorne (and, for that matter, Carnap) as I did back then. (30–31)

Although clear in his criticisms of Hartshorne, Rorty also is gracious in his praise.

> I have pulled no punches in saying how sharply I disagree with Hartshorne's central philosophical convictions. I should like to balance this by being equally frank about my admiration for Hartshorne as a teacher and as a human being. A nineteen-year-old trying to decide what to do with his life is bound to be influenced by the role models he happens to encounter. In the course of studying with Hartshorne, it struck me that if this sort of person was a philosophy professor, then becoming a philosophy professor was probably not such a bad idea. I do not think that I managed to live up to his example, either of intellectual passion or of generosity of spirit, but I am very proud to have been Hartshorne's student. (36)

This dialogue between former student and professor provides a model for the best of scholarly relationships, and surely Rorty's focus on creating a sensitivity to freedom and time is consonant with much of Hartshorne's teaching.

Rorty's encounter with his critics has other gracious moments as when he says that he agrees with "almost everything" in Bernstein's paper. And of Hance he writes: "I am grateful to Allen Hance for having read widely in my writings and for giving a very accurate account of my view of the history of modern philosophy. In writing about that history, I have never been happy with what I have said about Hegel. Much of Hegel remains mysterious to me. In particular, I cannot read *The Science of Logic* with interest, or pleasure, or understanding, or to the end" (122). And of Farrell's *Subjectivity, Realism, and Postmodernism—The Recovery of the World*: "It is the sort of book I hope we get more of—one that moves easily back and forth between Hegel and Davidson, and between Dennett and Derrida, while maintaining a consistent point of view and developing a strong, focused line of argument. I particularly admire Farrell's thoughtful and original use of Blumenberg's account of the Ockhamite origins of Bacon, Descartes, and the modern world" (189). But Rorty's amiable appraisals of some of his critics do not mask areas of strong disagreement. Lavine and Gouinlock call to question Rorty's account of Dewey and his allegiance to pragmatism. Their concerns spark the following responses: "Every disciple of a great philosopher has a duty to his or her master to distinguish the spirit from the letter of his or her teachings. This duty arises from the fact that not everything the great philosopher says convinced everybody. He or she was not, it always turns out, the Last Philosopher—the one who got everything straightened out, sorted things out so well that no further philosophy is needed" (52) and "The trouble with the kind of treatment which Dewey gets from Lavine and Gouinlock, it seems to me, is that these commentators stick so closely to the letter that they can make no concessions to current audiences" (53).

Haack sees Rorty as "probably the most influential critic of the epistemological enterprise in contemporary English-speaking philosophy" (126) and couples Rorty with Stich because both "repudiate the idea that criteria of justification should be judged by their truth-indicativeness. Rorty thinks the idea makes no sense; Stich, that it is narrow-minded and parochial." Haack calls both "vulgar pragmatists," challenging their claim to the lineage of classical pragmatism (joining Lavine and Gouinlock), a challenge she explicitly argues within her article. A sample of Rorty's response follows: "Haack is more or less right in suggesting that I am prepared to turn sociologist of knowledge (139). . . . But I should prefer to say 'historian, sociologist, and moralist of knowledge,' where 'moralist' means something like 'somebody with suggestions about the costs and benefits of changing your sense of relevance in specific ways.' A 'moralist of knowledge' in this sense is pretty much the same thing as what is sometimes called a 'culture critic'" (225, note 11). And of his more fundamental difference with Haack he writes:

> One of the disagreements between Haack and myself is that she thinks that epistemology is a natural and obvious topic of reflection, whereas I think that it survives nowadays only because some philosophy professors still think it important to take epistemic skepticism seriously—a spiritual exercise I find profitless. Once you get rid of the skeptic (in the way, for example, in which Michael Williams gets rid of Barry Stroud in the former's *Unnatural Doubts*), then I think you have little motive for waxing epistemological (unless you get a kick out of refuting once again, as Haack seems to me to do successfully, the foundationalists, the reliabilists, and the reductionists). I see James and Dewey (and even Peirce at his best—in the anti-Cartesian "Capacities" papers—despite the empty bombast of passages like the one Haack quotes at 147) as having done an especially good job of dissuading us from taking the skeptic seriously. They do so by asking us to worry more about relevance and less about rigor (or, *pace* Lavine and Gouinlock, more about consequences than about method). (225–26, note 14)

Farrell writes that his motive for initiating his book was a belief that Rorty has given an "unreliable account of recent philosophy, that he gets certain figures wrong, Davidson in particular (see "Rorty and Antirealism"). Rorty responds to the reliability of his reading of Davidson, and also writes: "The realistic intuitions which he [Farrell] defends seem to me to have no practical function, and his insistence on them seems to have a purely spiritual function. If we both got off our 'religious' high horses we might be able to agree that nobody's language has ever been or ever will be unconstrained by the world, and also that nobody will ever be able to be interestingly specific about what these constraints are and how they work" (194). At several points in his replies Rorty notes developments in his own thought, as when he responds to Farrell:

> I think that Farrell is right to criticize that paper ["The World Well Lost"], and various other papers of mine, for suggesting that the only alternatives are a radical subjectivism in which the self projects schemes

out upon a featureless reality (what Putnam has satirized as "the cook-ie cutter view") on the one hand, and an unknowable noumenon on the other. . . . But "The World Well Lost" was written twenty-three years ago. Lately I have been trying to mark out a position that does not take sides between subject and object, mind and world, but that instead tries to erase the contrast between them. I have, so to speak, been trying to lose *both* us and the world. Whereas Farrell reads me as trying to glorify us at the expense of the world, and hopes to rectify the balance with a "modest realism," I want to stop using the us-world contrast, and thus to get rid of the realism-antirealism issue. (191)

The above sampling provides a taste of the articles and responses in this volume, but they do not reveal the rich detail or the rigor and depth of thought found in them. I leave those delights for the reader to discover. Rarely do we have the chance to examine in one volume some of the best critiques of a major philosopher alongside his or her own direct responses. *Rorty and Pragmatism* provides us that opportunity, and in Rorty's terms, enlarges and enhances our own set of philosophical vocabularies:

I think of the course of human history as a long, swelling, increasingly polyphonic poem—a poem that leads up to nothing save itself. When the species is extinct, "human nature's total message" will not be a set of propositions, but a sct of vocabularies—the more, and the more var-ious, the better. Nobody will get this message, I suspect, since I still find no reason to agree with James and Hartshorne that "the best things are the more eternal things." But I do not see why eternity, or the silence of the infinite spaces, should matter. (33–34)

RORTY & PRAGMATISM

1

DEWEY BETWEEN HEGEL & DARWIN

Richard Rorty

James Kloppenberg sees Dewey as one of the philosophers of "the via media," a *via media* between idealism and empiricism. The second chapter of his *Uncertain Victory* is entitled "The Radical Theory of Knowledge." The heart of that theory, as Kloppenberg tells the story, consists in a new, nonatomistic conception of experience—a conception that is the least common denominator of Dilthey's notion of *Erlebnisse* and James's notion of "a world of pure experience." In Kloppenberg's account, this new conception of experience has a pragmatist account of truth as a corollary.[1]

Like Kloppenberg, David Hollinger emphasizes the connections between pragmatism and radical empiricism in William James.[2] Both Kloppenberg and Hollinger see James and Dilthey's talk about the inner life and the flux of experience—talk that is continuous with Bergson's and Whitehead's talk of misplaced concreteness—as an important part of what Hollinger calls "a cluster of assertions and hopes about the basis for culture in an age of science."[3] They both see what Hollinger calls James's "shift toward the panpsychism of the idealists" as an important part of the contribution of German idealism to American pragmatism. Kloppenberg rightly says that Dewey's claim that experience "carries principles of connection and organization within itself" is an "echo" of Green and Hegel.

I have no wish to challenge the claim that this sort of panpsychism, and this rejection of Humean atomism, loomed large in James's and Dewey's minds. A survey of the most interesting and original philosophers of the year 1900 would indeed show, as Kloppenberg suggests, that most of them wanted to close the epistemological gap between subject and object by some form of the panpsychist claim that the two are continuous. For panpsychism seemed an obvious way to perform what Kloppenberg calls "the marriage of Hegel and Darwin." Bracketing these two men under the rubric "evolutionary thought"—something Dewey did constantly—is helped considerably if one can answer to the question *What* evolves? with "experience," and if one can manage to treat that term and the term *nature* as quasi-synonymous. Insofar as there was an emerging consensus in philosophy in 1900, it was that we could get beyond the sterile arguments of the philosophical tradition only if we became able to see nature and experience as two descriptions of the same thing. Peirce spoke for the best philosophical thought of his time when he said: "All the creations of our mind are but patchworks from experience. So that all our ideas are but ideas of real or transposed experience."4

But if one looks at the end of the twentieth century rather than at its beginning, one finds pragmatism enjoying something of a renascence but no similar renascence of panpsychism.5 The philosophers of today who speak well of James and Dewey tend to speak ill of Dilthey and Bergson. They tend to talk about *sentences* a lot but to say very little about ideas or experiences, as opposed to such sentential attitudes as beliefs and desires. They would reject the question Are relations given immediately in experience? as presupposing a notion of "givenness" that is just one more "dogma of empiricism." Following Sellars, they would deny that they do not think *anything* is "given immediately in experience." They are enthusiastic about Peirce's claim that "my language is the sum total of myself,"6 and about the passages in which Peirce distinguishes sharply between cognitions and sensations—between sentential attitudes and mental states that can be described without reference to sentences. But they regret that these are passages to which neither James nor Dewey, nor even Peirce himself, paid much attention.7

In short, contemporary philosophers who profess sympathy with pragmatism show little sympathy with empiricism—they would rather forget empiricism than radicalize it. Donald Davidson speaks for many when he rejects—as one more hangover of Hume's attempt to be the Newton of the mind—Quine's notion of "stimulus meaning"(stated in terms of such nerve endings as the retina). Davidson substitutes a "distal" theory of meaning formulated in terms of public external objects; his philosophy of language has no use for Lock's and Hume's specifically psychic terrain, intermediate between physiology and linguistically formulated beliefs.[8]

As an alternative to Dewey's own self-understanding of his relation to Hegel and Darwin—a self-understanding accurately presented by Kloppenberg—I want to suggest an account of this relation that emphasizes Hegel's historicism rather than his idealism, and Darwin's affinities with positivism rather than with vitalism. So I shall be describing what Dewey might have and, in my view, should have said, rather than what he did say. I shall be constructing a hypothetical Dewey who was a pragmatist without being a radical empiricist, and a naturalist without being a panpsychist. The point of constructing such a Dewey is to separate what I think is living and what I think is dead in Dewey's thought, and thereby to clarify the difference between the state of philosophical play around 1900 and at the present time.

When thinking about Dewey, it pays to begin by thinking about Hegel. Charles Taylor has helped us see Hegel as having brought Kant together with Herder and Humboldt—as having combined transcendental idealism with a sense of historical relativity—the same sense of relativity that C. I. Lewis urged in his *Mind and the World-Order.* Manfred Frank, in his important book *What is Neostructuralism?* has helped us see "the fundamental insight of all post-Hegelian philosophy" as the abandonment of a "claim to a transhistorical frame of orientation beyond linguistic differen tiality."[9] Frank speaks of this insight as "perhaps the fundamental insight of postclassical philosophy in its entirety, insofar as it participates in the *linguistic turn.*"[10] In Frank's account, the sense of historical relativity, the sense of relativity to available linguistic resources, the sense of human finitude, and the sense that "it is not possible to interpret our world from an Archimedean point"[11] are at bottom the same. Frank thinks that the linguistic turn was first taken by Herder and Humboldt, thinkers who made it possible, as Frank puts it, to think of "transnational and transhistorical 'reason'" as an "'image of the world' inscribed in a linguistic order."[12]

Frank's account suggests a new way of viewing Dewey as a "philosopher of the via media." From this angle, the extremes between which Dewey hopes to navigate are not idealism and empiricism, but rather historicism and scientism. By *historicism* I mean the doctrine that there is no relation of "closeness of fit" between language and the world: no image of the world projected by language is more or less representative of the way the world really is than any other. By *scientism* I mean the doctrine that natural science is privileged above other areas of culture, that something about natural science puts it in closer touch with reality than any other human activity.

If one wishes to wed historicism and scientism, then one will marry Hegel and Darwin not by finding a holistic, panpsychist way of describing the relations between experience and nature, but rather by finding a historicist, relativist way of describing Darwin's claim upon our attention. By a historicist and relativist way, I mean a way of seeing natural science, and Darwin in particular, as simply one more description of the world to be placed alongside others, rather than as offering the *one* image that corresponds to reality. Whereas Kant, Fichte, and Hegel had had to condemn natural science's image of the world to the realm of "appearance" in order to avoid conflict with our common moral consciousness—had had to say that natural science did not, appearances to the contrary, *really* coincide with reality as it was in itself—a historicist way of avoiding this conflict cannot invoke an appearance-reality distinction. Nor can it resort to notions of misleading abstraction and misplaced concreteness, for *concrete* implies a special relation of closeness to reality for which historicism has no room. In a historicist account, there is no description either of nature or experience that is more or less accurate or concrete than some rival (unless "more accurate" and "more concrete" are construed pragmatically, as "more useful for the following purposes . . .").

In the interpretation of Dewey that I want to suggest, the point of the pragmatist theory of truth is to provide such a nonidealistic, historicist way of avoiding the conflict between science and the religious or moral consciousness. That theory substitutes *expediency* for *accuracy* or *concreteness* as a term of epistemic approbation. But the pragmatist theory of truth, notoriously, comes in two distinct forms, only one of which will do for my interpretation of Dewey. This is the form embodied in James's claim that "'the true' . . . is only the expedient in the way of our thinking, just as 'the right' is only the expedient in our way of behaving."[13]

This statement of the theory of truth is quite distinct from James's unfortunate claim that "ideas (which themselves are but parts of our experience) become true just in so far as they help us get into satisfactory relation with other parts of our experience."[14] This is unfortunate for two reasons. First, it runs together the truth of a sentence (which, unless it contains a reference to a time, is eternally true or eternally false and cannot "become" true) with the expediency of believing a sentence to be true. Second, it runs together sentences with experiences—linguistic entities with introspectible entities.

James and Dewey usually spoke as if these two formulations came to much the same thing—as if anyone who accepted the first would be inclined to accept the second. But whereas the former statement of the pragmatist theory points in the direction of Herder, Humboldt, and a historicist sense of truth as a property of linguistic entities, the latter does not. The first formulation can easily be made compatible with the linguistic turn, but not the second. The second, but not the first, contains the germ of panpsychism and radical empiricism. "Getting into satisfactory relation with other parts of our experience" will be acceptable as an account of true beliefs only if the distinction between the propositional and the nonpropositional, and the distinction between properties of the agent and properties of her environment, are blurred in the way in which Dewey went on to blur them in *Experience and Nature*.

One way of highlighting the difference between the first and the second formulation is to reflect on pragmatism's relation to Darwin. Darwinism requires that we think of what we do and are as continuous with what the amoebae, the spiders, and the squirrels do and are. One way to expound this continuity is suggested by the second formula: we may think of these members of other species as sharing with us something called experience—something not the same as consciousness or thought, but something of which consciousness or thought are more complex and developed forms. This way of obtaining continuity is illustrated by Locke's attempt to tell a story about how we get from the baby's mind to the adult's—by adding in more simple ideas and then joining them up to produce complex ideas. This way of procuring continuity blurs the distinction that Peirce draws between cognitive and noncognitive mental states—between, for example, sensations and beliefs. As I have argued in my *Philosophy and the Mirror of Nature*, it also blurs the distinction between the question What causes our beliefs? and the question What justifies our beliefs?—a blurring that is essential for any representationalist theory of knowledge.

This blurring is characteristic both of British empiricism and of British idealism. All that the "radical empiricism" side of pragmatism did was to blur things further by denying that relations between ideas are "contributed by the mind" rather than being "given" in the way in which qualia are purportedly "given"—denying that, as Green put it, "only thought relates." As Dewey said, "Unless there is breach of historic and natural continuity, cognitive experience must originate within that of a noncognitive sort."[15] Because Dewey was committed to such blurring, he refused to separate intentionality and intelligence from consciousness in the manner of contemporary philosophers who (like Daniel Dennett) have gotten on intimate terms with intelligent but insensate machines. Even as late as *Experience and Nature,* a book in which language gets considerable play, we find Dewey saying, "Sentiency in itself is anoetic . . . but nevertheless it is an indispensable means to any noetic function."[16]

The problem with this way of obtaining continuity between us and the brutes is that it seems to shove the philosophically embarrassing discontinuity back down to the gap between, say, viruses and amoebae. But why stop there? Only by giving something like experience to protein molecules, and perhaps eventually to quarks—only a full-fledged panpsychism—will eliminate such embarrassments. But when we invoke panpsychism in order to bridge the gap between experience and nature, we begin to feel that something has gone wrong. For notions like "experience," "consciousness," and "thought" were originally invoked to *contrast* something that varied independently of nature with nature itself. The philosophically interesting sense—the only sense relevant to epistemology—of experience is one that goes back to *ta phainomena* rather than to *empeiria*, to a realm that might well be "out of touch" with nature because it could vary while nature remained the same and remain the same when nature varied. Much of Dewey's work was a desperate, futile attempt to get rid of the *phainomena* versus *onta onta*, appearance versus true reality, distinction, and to replace it with a distinction of degree between less organized and directed and more organized and directed *empeiria*. This attempt was futile because his fellow philosophers insisted on language in which they could discuss the possibility of our being "out of touch with reality" or "lost in a realm of mere appearance." Dewey often rejoined by insisting that we replace the appearance-reality distinction by a distinction between beliefs useful for some purposes and beliefs useful for others. If he had stayed with *that* rejoinder he would have been on firm ground. But unfortunately he also rejoined that his opponents had "misdescribed experience." This rejoinder was utterly ineffectual.

In his "Empirical Survey of Empiricisms," Dewey said that we needed "a new concept of experience and a new type of empiricism"—one that invoked neither the Greek contrast of experience and reason nor the atomistic sensationalism of Hume, Mill, and Russell. But he admitted that "this third view of experience . . . is still more or less inchoate."[17] Most of Dewey's critics felt that it was not only inchoate but confused and disingenuous. For it seemed to them that any sense of *experience* that did not acknowledge a possible divergence between experience and nature merely blurred the issues that a theory of knowledge ought to discuss.[18] So they saw Dewey not as presenting what Kloppenberg calls a "radical theory of knowledge" but as dodging hard epistemological questions by redefining the terms in which they had been raised.[19]

I think that these critics were justified, and that the force of the pragmatist theory of truth was blunted by Dewey's unpersuasive redefinitions. James and Dewey never, alas, made up their minds whether they wanted just to forget about epistemology or whether they wanted to devise a new improved epistemology of their own. In my view, they should have opted for forgetting. Dewey should have dropped the term *experience* rather than redefining it and should have looked elsewhere for continuity between us and the brutes. He should have agreed with Peirce that a great gulf divides sensation and cognition, decided that cognition was only possible for language users, and then said that the only relevant break in continuity was between non–language-users (amoebae, squirrels, babies) and language users.

He could then have gone on to note that the development of linguistic behavior—of social practices that used increasingly flexible vocal cords and thumbs to produce longer and more complex strings of noises and marks—is readily explicable in naturalistic, Darwinian, terms. We can tell as good stories about the success of species that gradually developed such practices as we can about the success of species that developed practices of migrating or hibernating. How meaning became a property of certain strings of marks and noises is as unmysterious as how tableness became a property of batches of molecules. So, my alternative Dewey would have said, we can construe "thinking" as simply the use of sentences—both for arranging cooperative enterprises and for attributing inner states (beliefs, desires) to our fellow humans. If we have thinking in this sense—the ability to have and ascribe sentential attitudes—we can see it as something that has nothing in particular to do with "experiences of a non-cognitive sort." To be sure, there is a *causal* continuity between experience as what Dewey called "a matter of functions and habits, of active adjustments and readjustments, of co-ordinations and activities"[20] and thinking, but for that matter there is a causal continuity between nutrition and thinking. Such continuity does not require us to find a sort of proto-intentionality in the amoeba.

The point of these last paragraphs may be summed up as follows: Dewey's and James's attempt to give a "more concrete," more holistic, and less dualism-ridden account of experience would have been unnecessary if they had not tried to make "true" a predicate of experiences and had instead let it be a predicate of sentences. For then they would not have thought of "ideas (which are themselves but parts of our experience)" *becoming* true or being *made* true. They would not have set themselves the bad question, Granted that truth is *in some sense* the agreement or correspondence of experiences with reality, what must experience and reality be such that they can stand in such relations?"

Asking this question made James and Dewey think that the cause of the endless disputes about subject and object, mind and body, was a misunderstanding of the nature of experience or reality or both. But this was not the cause. The cause was the idea that truth is a matter of a certain relation between subject and object, mind and the physical world—a relation of "agreement" or "correspondence." James and Dewey agreed that this relation could not be a matter of "copying"—of features shared by the experience and the reality. But they thought they had to find a substitute for *copying* and asked what *agreement* might mean instead.[21] James said that it must mean "verification" in the sense of "agreeable leading" from one bit of experience to another. "Truth *happens* to an idea," James said, when it succeeds in marrying new experience to old experience.[21] Again, "To 'agree' in the widest sense with a reality, *can only mean to be guided either straight up to it or into its surroundings, or to be put into such working touch with it as to handle either it or something connected with it better than if we disagreed.*"[23] Dewey's version of this goes as follows:

> . . . the pragmatist holds that the relation in question is one of correspondence between existence and thought; but he holds that correspondence instead of being an ultimate and unanalyzable mystery, to be defined by iteration, is precisely a matter of correspondence in its plain, familiar, sense. A condition of dubious and conflicting tenden-

cies calls out thinking as a method of handling it. This condition produces its own appropriate consequences, bearing its own fruits of weal or woe. The thoughts, the estimates, intents, and projects it calls out, just because they are attitudes of response and of attempted adjustment (*not* mere "states of consciousness") produce their effects also. The kind of interlocking, or interadjustment that then occurs between these two sorts of consequences constitutes the correspondence that makes truth.[24]

These redefinitions of *agreement* and *correspondence* would be harmless enough if they were simply ways of saying "truth is what works"—if they were simply restatements of what I previously called "the first formulation" of the pragmatist theory of truth. But James and Dewey thought of them as more than that, and that is why they were led down the garden path of radical empiricism. It is why they ran together an insistence on what Kloppenberg calls "the contingent quality of our most basic categories of thought" with the claim that we needed what he calls "a new conception of immediate lived experience."[25]

Much of what I have been saying can be summarized as the claim that Dewey and James thought that an appropriate philosophical response to Darwin required a kind of vitalism—an attempt to coalesce the vocabulary of epistemology with that of evolutionary biology. This was the attempt whose most notorious products were the jargons of *A Pluralistic Universe, Creative Evolution, Process and Reality, Experience and Nature,* and *Knowing and the Known.* But in his "Influence of Darwin on Philosophy" Dewey suggests another, better alternative. This is that we see Darwin as showing us how to naturalize Hegel—how to have Herderian historicism without Kantian idealism, how to hold on to a Hegelian narrative of progress while dispensing with the claim that the real is the rational.

One problem with wedding Hegel and Darwin has always been that Hegel seems to say that human civilization just *couldn't* casually be wiped out by a plague or a comet, and that language-using beings just *had* to emerge from the evolutionary process so that the Idea could finish off Nature and get started on Spirit. He seems to say that there really is a power, not ourselves, which is more like us than it is like amoebas or squirrels—or, more precisely, a power of which we are better manifestations than they are. So the purely mechanical account of biological evolution offered by a synthesis of Darwin with Mendel, though commending itself to atheists, seems antithetical to a philosophy built, as Hegel's was, around the idea of the Incarnate Logos.[26]

The nice thing about purely mechanical accounts of nature, from an atheist's point of view, is that they tell us that there are no purposes to be served save our own, and that we serve no purposes except those we dream up as we go along. As Dewey said in his Darwin essay: "The classic [Greek] notion of species carried with it the idea of purpose. . . . Purposefulness accounted for the intelligibility of nature and the possibility of science, while the absolute or cosmic character of this purposefulness gave sanction and worth to the moral and religious endeavors of man."[27] Dewey argued that Darwin had finished the job that Galileo began—the job of eliminating from nature any purpose that transcends a particular organism's needs in a particular situation.[28] But once purpose leaves nature, then there is no longer a philosophical problem about the "possibility of science" (or, more generally, of knowledge). For there is no longer a problem of reconciling the subject's purposes with the object's—of getting the two on the same wavelength. The object becomes an object of manipulation rather than the embodiment of either a *telos* or a *logos*, and truth becomes "the expedient in the way of thinking." The contrast between the pursuit of truth and the pursuit of expediency goes when the notion of truth as "agreement" or "correspondence" with something that has purposes of its own goes.

In other words, if one *wholeheartedly* adopts the first formulation of the pragmatist theory of truth, one will feel no need to follow it up with the second formulation. So one will feel no need to ask about what experience is *really* like, as opposed to the way in which the Greeks or the British empiricists described it, nor to ask whether nature is better described in vitalistic or mechanistic terms. For all descriptions of experience, nature, and their relation to one another will be evaluated *simply* in terms of expediency—of suitability for accomplishing the purpose at hand. That is how Dewey wanted the pragmatic theory of truth evaluated: "Naturally, the pragmatist claims his theory to be true in the pragmatic sense of truth; it works, it clears up difficulties, removes obscurities, puts individuals into more experimental, less dogmatic, and less arbitrarily skeptical relations to life; aligns philosophy with scientific method; does away with self-made problems of epistemology; clarifies and reorganizes logical theory, etc."[29]

Consider the claim that the pragmatist theory of truth "aligns philosophy with scientific method" in the light of Dewey's impish remark that Hegel is the "quintessence of the scientific spirit."[30] His point is that whereas Kant's transcendental idealism "starts from the accepted scholastic conception of thought,"[31] Hegel's absolute idealism broke free of the idea of the notion of "a special faculty of thought with its own peculiar and fixed forms."[32] Hegel, Dewey says, "denies the existence of any faculty of thought which is other than the expression of fact itself."[33] He holds that "the only possible thought is the reflection of the significance of fact."[34]

The terms *expression of fact* and *significance of fact* are not very perspicuous, but it seems fair to interpret them as meaning "the significance of what is going on for the purposes of the community of inquirers doing the thinking." More generally, it seems fair to interpret the individuous contrast Dewey draws between Kant and Hegel in terms of the invidious contrast between a pre-Darwinian attachment to the idea of purposes not our own and a post-Darwinian ability to see inquiry as continuous with practical deliberation.[35] It seems fair, in short, to interpret Dewey as seeing the opposition between Kant and Hegel as an opposition between a non-pragmatic and a proto-pragmatic view of inquiry.

Once one starts to look for pragmatism in Hegel, one finds quite a bit to go on. In particular, one can capitalize on Hegel's remark that "philosophy is its time apprehended in thought"—a remark that might serve as a motto for Dewey's attempts to see the changing problematics of the philosophers as reflections of sociocultural developments. The more one pursues the theme of *embodiment* in Hegel—explores what Taylor calls the "anti-dualist" implications of the "expressivist" line of thought that Hegel took over from Herder[36]—the more one wants to brush aside the ontology of Absolute Idealism, and the insistence that the real is the rational. One finds oneself trying to wean Hegel away from the Idea, just as Hegel (and later Peirce) tried to wean Kant from the Thing-In-Itself. To succeed in doing so would be to get Hegel to stop talking about human communities as expressions of something greater than themselves—stages in the realization of some purpose greater than they themselves could envisage. Then one could just see such communities "expressivistically," in terms of their own local needs. But this shift would lead Hegel, and us, to describe our own community, and our own philosophical views, in terms of parochial, temporary, contingent needs.

It would lead one, for example, to put forward an account of truth not as something that clears up all difficulties or removes all obscurities connected with the topic, but as something useful in clearing up *our* difficulties and removing *our* obscurities. If one claims that one's theory of truth works works better than any competing theory, one will be saying that it works better by reference to *our* purposes, *our* particular situation in intellectual history. One will not claim that it was what it would have paid, always and everywhere, to have thought of truth as, but simply as, as James says, what it would be better for *us* to believe about truth. Taken as part of an overall philosophical outlook, such a theory would be part of an attempt to hold *our* age in thought.

I can describe this area of overlap between Hegel and Dewey in another way by considering a standard objection to pragmatist theories of truth. This objection is that pragmatism tells you that truth is what works, but doesn't answer the question Works for what? It doesn't tell you what purposes to have; its ethics is situational at best. So, of course, was Hegel's ethics, and that was another reason why Dewey consistently preferred Hegel to Kant. The dualism of "ought" and "is," of categorical and hypothetical imperatives, was for Dewey one more symptom of Kant's "scholastic" presuppositions.[37]

Dewey's fundamental contribution to moral philosophy has always been taken as his insistence on a "means-end-continuum"—that is, as the claim that we change our notions of the Right and of the Good on the basis of the particular mixture of success and failure produced by our previous efforts to act rightly and do good. From the point of view I am adopting, this insistence can be seen as one more consequence of his historicism. The historicism that Taylor and Frank find in Herder and Humboldt is one that insists that the language of moral deliberation, and of moral praise or blame, is a function of the needs that a society hopes to fulfill. Societies evolve into other societies, therefore, by finding that the moral language they have been using brings with it consequences they do not like—just as species evolve into other species by finding that some of the habits their ancestors developed for coping with one environment have become liabilities in coping with a changed environment. To say that moral progress occurs is to say that the later societies are more complex, more developed, more articulate, and above all more flexible than their predecessors. It is to say that later societies have more varied and interesting needs than earlier ones, just as squirrels have more varied and interesting needs than amoebae.

If one asks why flexibility, articulation, variety, and interestingness are worthy ends to pursue—why they are morally relevant ends for individuals or societies—Dewey has nothing more to tell you than "so act as to increase the meaning of present experience."[38] "We do not," he says, "require a revelation of some supreme perfection to inform us whether or not we are making headway in present rectification."[39] It is as futile for human communities to ask "Is our recent political history, the one we summarize in a narrative of gradual progress, taking us in the right direction?" as it would be for the squirrels to ask whether their evolution from shrews has been going in the right direction. The squirrels do what is best by their lights, and so do we. Both of us have been moving in the direction of what seems, by our respective lights, more flexibility, more freedom, and more variety.

In this attitude toward morality, it seems to me, we get a genuine marriage of Darwin with a de-absolutized Hegel. Just as, in the case of truth and knowledge, we had to introduce a seemingly un-Darwinian discontinuity between language and sentience in order to get an unparadoxical account of truth and to capture the point of Hegel's distinction between Nature and Spirit, so here we have to introduce a seemingly un-Hegelian sense of irrationality and contingency in order to get a suitably Darwinian account of morality. But just as in the previous case we can give a naturalistic account of the difference of kind between the intentional and the nonintentional (by viewing the social practices that make language and intentionality possible as continuous with those that made cooperative tiger-hunting possible), so here we can give a more or less teleological account of seemingly irrational accident. We can say that a given irrational and accidental event (for example, the decline of the dinosaurs, the desire for gold on the part of bigoted and fanatical sixteenth-century monarchs) in fact contributed to an admirable result (the anthropoids, the United States of America), not because world-historical Reason was cunning, but just by good luck.

Teleological thinking is inevitable, but Dewey offers us a relativist and materialist version of teleology rather than an absolute and idealist one. Whereas Hegel had held that the study of history brings over from philosophy the thought that the real is the rational, the Hegel-Darwin synthesis Dewey proposes must de-ontologize this claim and make it simply a regulative, heuristic principle. Narratives of historical progress are legitimized not by the philosopher's explanation that the slaughter-bench of history is where the Incarnate Logos is redemptively tortured, but because the nature of the historian's craft requires her to discern what Hegel called "the rose in the cross of the present." It requires her to tell her community how they are now in a position to be, intellectually and morally, better than predecessor communities, thanks to their knowledge of the struggles of those predecessors. As the saying goes, we know more than our ancestors because they are what we know; what we most want to know about them is how to avoid their mistakes.[40]

I said earlier that the most Dewey can claim is that truth as what works is the theory of truth it now pays us to have. It pays us to believe this because we have seen the unhappy results of believing otherwise—of trying to find some ahistorical and absolute relation to reality for truth to name—and we must now try to do better. Similarly, the theory that, as Dewey said, "growth itself is the only moral end" is the moral theory it now pays us to have, for we have seen the unhappy results of trying to divinize and eternalize a given social practice or form of individual life.[41] In both epistemology and moral philosophy, in short, we have seen the unhappy results of trying to think of normative terms like *true* or *good* or *right* as signifying relations of "agreement" or "correspondence" between something human and something nonhuman.

From this perspective, the question Does Dewey give us a satisfactory theory of the true, the good, and the right? presupposes an answer to the question What, at the present moment in history, is the function of such theories? Dewey thought that the function of all philosophical theories was the same: not to "deal with ultimate reality" but to "clarify men's ideas as to the social and moral strifes of their own day."[42] This function is, however, that of high culture in general, rather than of philosophy in particular. So I think it would have been a bit more precise to say that the particular charge of philosophy is to make sure that old *philosophical* ideas do not block the road of inquiry—that continued use of the normative language employed in the social and moral strifes of an earlier day does not make it harder to cope with contemporary problems.

Dewey thought that the reductionist use of Darwin and the rationalist use of Hegel had produced some normative language that was, in fact, blocking our road. Darwin's scientist followers (those who emphasized what he had in common with Hobbes rather than what he had in common with St. Francis) had suggested that there was an underlying reality—the struggle for survival—which high culture is a conspiracy to conceal. Hegel's rationalist followers (those who read him as a historicized Spinoza rather than a metaphysicized Herder) had suggested that there was an underlying reality called the Absolute—a reality that somehow validated our religious and moral aspirations. The nineteenth century spent a lot of time dithering between these alternative conceptions of what "ultimate reality" or "human nature" was really like, and thus between traditional and scientistic ways of describing the moral and political choices it faced.

Dewey would have been pleased by the fact that the twentieth century has spent increasingly little time talking about the nature of ultimate reality. In part this has been because the increasing prominence of Language as a topic, accompanied by an increasing recognition that one can describe the same thing in different ways for different purposes, has helped to make pragmatism, as a doctrine of the relativity of normative judgments to purposes served, more palatable. More important, perhaps, is that lots of different developments in our century—Freudian accounts of inner moral conflicts, ethnographic descriptions of alternative forms of social life, experimentalism in literature and the arts—have made it steadily easier for us to substitute Deweyan questions such as, Which communities' purposes shall I share? and What sort of person would I prefer to be? for the Kantian questions, What Should I Do? What May I Hope? What is Man?

2

RORTY'S PRAGMATISM & FAREWELL

TO THE AGE OF

FAITH & ENLIGHTENMENT

Charles Hartshorne

The pragmatist . . . can only say, with Hegel, that truth and justice lie in the direction marked by the successive stages of European thought. This is not because he knows some "necessary truths." . . . It is simply that the pragmatist knows no better way to explain his conviction than to remind his interlocutor of the position they both are in, the contingent starting points they both share, the floating, ungrounded, conversations of which they are both members.—Richard Rorty

Richard Rorty admits that judgments may differ concerning the "direction" European thought has taken. He knows only circular arguments for or against the view of Plato that philosophy should seek to "escape from time and history," in other words, to find eternal, necessary truths; or (with Hegel, as Rorty interprets Hegel) should regard this search as "doomed and perverse. All we can do is to "read the history of philosophy and draw the moral."[1]

My first comment is that Rorty has here constructed a somewhat mythical court of final appeal. There is no single, accessible, unitary thing called European thought or history of philosophy and no single set of starting points, the same for all of us. Moreover, I suspect that we are here confronted, after all, with the correspondence view (which in general Rorty seems to reject) of *historical* truth at least. Or was there no actual Plato or Hegel with whom our attributions to these writers are intended to agree? I hold that there was (and in a genuine sense is) an actual Plato and an actual

Hegel and that each of us has real though limited access to their ideas; also that we are not all equally well equipped to find out what they thought. I hold also that some very important aspects of the actual thoughts of past philosophers are omitted from most standard reference works, and in some cases the very names of some of those whose thoughts they were are scarcely to be found in those works. I do agree with Rorty (and Hegel) that a basic test of our philosophies is the light they throw on intellectual history.

Another comment is that I think, as Hegel already did, that we need to be less provincial than the limitation to *European* suggests. I think it is time that at least the Buddhist tradition should be taken seriously into account. I have argued for years that there are indeed non-European ideas that can serve "our European purposes better." But then it is notable that one (somewhat Americanized) European philosopher, Alfred North Whitehead, has arrived, probably independently, at some central Buddhist insights, and that two Americans, William James and Charles Peirce, partly anticipated him in this.

Rorty's dismissal of metaphysics, defined as search for necessary truths, is not justified by a careful consideration of the historical facts about what has happened in metaphysics from the pre-Socratics to Peirce, Whitehead, and the present writer. Finding necessary truths is not the same as "escaping from time and history." Eternity, absolute necessity, according to the dominant metaphysics of recent times, can only be the most abstract aspect of becoming and cosmic history. A truth is necessary and eternal if it characterizes becoming as such, otherwise not. This is the point of the "ultimacy" which Whitehead assigns to "creativity." Furthermore, our human knowledge of the ultimate is not itself ultimate in the same sense. If we manage to arrive at a correct view of the necessary, this is a contingent achievement; and it is conditioned by historical factors. Mistakes can be made even in arithmetic, much more in metaphysics (including theories of the eternal and necessary aspects of deity). Knowledge of necessary truths is not infallible knowledge of them except in the divine knowing, which is infallible whether it is about necessary or contingent truths. Human knowledge is fallible in both aspects. And one needs to make use of intellectual history in seeking necessary truths and in evaluating claims to have found them.

Whether or not we can know necessary truths, the question seems logically in order. Do not the following three propositions exhaust the possibilities? (1) There are no necessary truths; (2) there are necessary truths, but we cannot in any reasonable sense know them, or sensibly seek to know them; and (3) there are necessary truths, and we can (to some extent, or with whatever qualifications as to precision or certainty) sensibly seek to find them.

If one accepts (1), then the principle of contrast can be invoked to justify the criticism that "contingent" loses its meaning if "necessary" has no application. Moreover, the necessary is easily explicated as what all possibilities have in common (or what will obtain no matter which possibilities are actualized). It seems extravagant to suggest that they have nothing whatever in common.

If one accepts (2), one is by implication admitting that when we speak of contingent (in contrast to necessary) truths we do not know what we are talking about. Similarly, with the idea of eternity, if we have no understanding of that, then "temporal" is not adequately understood either. What all possible times have in common must either be sheer nothing or whatever it is that is eternal.

Of the three options the third seems to me the most credible. One reason this is difficult for some to see is that the role of the necessary or eternal has been badly misconceived by many philosophers and theologians. The purely eternal has been taken to be the "most real," whereas it is an extreme abstraction, by implication of its very logic as set forth first by Leibniz (with some mistakes about the meaning of *possible*). In ethics the attempt has often been to make the most abstract principles of good or right (which alone can be necessary) do all the work of ethics or, at any rate, to expect more from them than they could logically deliver. Another confusion is the one already dealt with between the necessity of the proposition and the certainty of our knowledge of it. Connected with this error is the failure to take adequately into account the semantic problem of expressing necessary truths in language, which primarily evolved and is primarily used for discussing contingent truths, that is to say, all truths other than the most abstract or universal, applicable to all possible existents, or, in ethics or logic, to all rational beings.

That the method of reason is the method of "conversation" or discussion, mutual criticism, is an acceptable view common to Rorty and Popper. Discussion about necessary truths is one form of the general discussion. Success in this special form is of course no guarantee of success in other forms. That is not its value. It is a logical truism that contingent truths are not deducible from necessary ones alone. Metaphysics is not "foundational" in that sense. Neither is mathematics. Yet both may have their uses. What all possibilities have in common may yet distinguish them all from various seeming possibilities that are really verbal confusions. And certain ideas often supposed impossible may in truth be among the common aspects of all genuine possibilities. Thus freedom as at least minimal transcendence of causal necessities may be a requirement of all possible occurrences. If Einstein had accepted (as Bergson and Peirce did) the metaphysical truth of the essentially creative aspect of becoming as such, his last decades might have taken a more constructive turn, more congenial to his scientific colleagues in quantum physics.

Metaphysical truth cannot dictate any more specific truth, but it might (for those who claim to know it) forbid certain negative extremes such as the absolute absence of emergence in becoming or of mind as such in the lower levels of nature. Such negative absolutes are unobservable, and a veto upon them need not hamper observational science.

Since (unconditionally) necessary truths are strictly universal, what makes them true must be in everything. They must be implicit in all ideas. How far it is important for a given purpose that the implicit metaphysical content of beliefs, any beliefs, be made explicit depends on the purpose and the situation. Scientists have long ago absorbed at least part of the metaphysics they need and may do well much of the time to let others worry about formulating that part. They embody it in their practice. On the other hand, extreme crises, such as those that have been produced by the difficulties of combining relativity physics with quantum and particle physics, may make it worth while to pay attention to metaphysical issues—about the asymmetry of time and the independence of earlier from later events, or about the place of mind as such in the cosmos, or the relations between continuity and discreteness, or the finitude or infinity of the spatial aspect of reality, or the mutual independence of contemporaries.

Theologians have tried periodically to do without metaphysics and have repeatedly found that they cannot do so. The Barthians tried it in one way and some positivistic theologians—Van Buren, for example—have tried it in another way. The success of either approach is problematic. So is that of the Marxist version of, or substitute for, religion.

Whether the renunciation of metaphysics is a viable human option for an entire culture, Rorty admits he does not know. I salute his candor on this point. But even if it is culturally viable I fail to see that it represents our best or most intelligent option. Why should we give up all efforts to satisfy such natural curiosity as that about the eternal or necessary aspects of reality, in contrast and relation to which the contingent and emergent aspects alone have their full sense and definition? To what extent we shall ever reach a consensus on these topics is not itself a metaphysical question. An absolute consensus is hardly possible in any science or human inquiry; but we can sensibly strive to minimize misunderstandings and do our best to persuade one another of what truths we think we discern.

Always there have been both more and less speculative minds in philosophy. Some periods give the critics of speculation more prominence and attention than others. Ours is a somewhat antimetaphysical culture, except that the skepticism of academics and intellectuals is balanced by waves of popular religiosity and superstition suggesting that the human species is not about to accept a merely positivistic or merely anthropocentric view of things.

It is amusing to think of Peirce or James reading Rorty. It is perhaps hard to say which of them would have liked his views least. Probably it is Peirce, for whose pragmaticism the conceivable practical import defined meaning but not truth. Moreover, in developing his categories Peirce was looking for necessary truths. As Rorty well knows, James was seeking a way to justify some ethical and religious beliefs, especially in freedom transcending causal determinism and in some form of theism—however qualified in the attributes assigned to deity. One might say that in Rorty, James's "will (or right) to believe" becomes a will or right to disbelieve. There is at least a very sharp difference of emphasis.

In Rorty's thinking there is much subtlety and a wide acquaintance with contrasting philosophies. However, in dealing with some topics of interest to me, also to Peirce and James, he becomes crude or dogmatic. Determinism, rejected for carefully analyzed reasons by both the founding pragmatists, is apparently acceptable to Rorty, as is materialism, of which Peirce said that it "leaves the world as unintelligible as it finds it." Rorty holds that only science can inform us about nature. Science is now telling us that chance is a real factor in all process, that the valid laws are statistical, not absolute. And Rorty tells us next to nothing about the recent history of this problem, whether in metaphysics or in physics.

In the preface to his *Philosophy and the Mirror of Nature*, Rorty admirably explains how six teachers, of whom I was one, brought him to the conviction "that a 'philosophical problem' was a product of the unconscious adoption of assumptions built into the vocabulary in which the problem was stated—assumptions which were to be questioned before the problem itself was to be taken seriously."[2] Dewey has said that philosophy should not be a method of solving problems invented by philosophers, but a method, cultivated by philosophy, for dealing with problems of ordinary people. Of course, either way one is using a vocabulary. I have long accepted the view that metaphysical mistakes do consist in part of misusing terms but have argued against the view that such misuse is the very definition of metaphysics. The ultimate source of metaphysical concern is not merely terminological. Human mortality presents us with the question How do we adjust ourselves to the certainty of our own eventual death and, for all we can know, even the eventual extinction of our species? Conflicts of purpose with other human beings, or even more generally with nonhuman animals, present us with the question How do we relate concern for our own welfare or advantage to concern for that of others? Are Buddhists right or wrong in their criticism of the idea of personal identity, taken as final in ethics and religion? Conflicting religious and antireligious beliefs and attitudes present us with questions about immortality, or at least about the permanence or lack of it of our achievements, and about God, or other allegedly superhuman beings. The progress of scientific explanations of events through their causes presents us with the question Are our choices or decisions mere links in a causal chain in which what happens is in each case the only thing that then and there could have happened, *or* is causality less determining, so that at each moment there is at least a small range of possibilities, an indeterminate but determinable potentiality that only our deciding makes determinate? In more technical terms, are there antecedently *sufficient* as well as necessary conditions for decisions, or only necessary conditions? The vocabulary in which this is stated does not produce the problem that is presented by the scientific tradition and successes. It arises from the mathematics of classical physics and astronomy. Quantum physics has a new mathematics that changes the problem somewhat. But even before quantum physics a few philosophers and scientists were advocating, stimulated by the laws of gases, a nonclassical view of natural laws.

I find in Rorty a dearth of interest in the kinds of problems hinted at above. He focuses rather on "epistemological" problems. With Gustav

Bergmann, I hold that epistemology is merely the metaphysics (he says ontology) of knowing, rather than a propaedeutic of metaphysics. Rorty also talks much about "foundationalism," a jargon term for which I see no great need. I do doubt that I am a foundationalist or that Whitehead was. On the whole, I think Rorty is overconcerned about problems invented by philosophers and too little concerned about problems of human beings, who are aware, unlike other animals, of their mortality, and are aware also that their choices are largely predetermined by the past, yet with the sense of these choices as really determining what was previously somewhat undetermined.

In the indexes of Rorty's two books the words *determinism, freedom, choice,* and *decision* do not occur. Nor do the words *time, past, future; contingency, modality, possibility; potentiality, actuality; abstract, concrete; relation; universal, particular; infinite, finite; absolute, relative, becoming, creativity,* and other similarly abstract terms. Nor, finally, does the word *metaphysics* appear in the index, although it occurs in the text. *Mind,* with many entries, is indexed in *The Mirror,* but not *matter* or *physical.* And not *God. Necessary* occurs but is explicated (mistakenly) as the highest degree of noncontroversiality, not in terms of its relation to possibility and contingency, or to becoming and the openness of the future. The Aristotelian and Peircean ideas of the future as modally different from the past and of the unconditionally necessary as what is, without first coming to be, are ignored. The really enduring philosophical problems are not discussed.

Rorty mentions my and Whitehead's panpsychism (which I usually term psychicalism). He astonishes me by saying panpsychists reject the statement "Neural processes are physical events." Rorty also says that materialists deny that "mental" and "physical" are incompatible predicates. I also deny it. If physical means, as in Descartes, extended, and if what is localized but not punctiform is extended, then I hold that physical things are all either aggregates or, if singular—for example, nerve cells or some of their constituents—then they at least feel. Whitehead says they also have at least minimal forms of what he technically terms mentality, that is, some sense, however limited, of the contrast between actual and possible, or past and future.

Rorty also says that my or Thomas Nagel's "panpsychism tends to merge with neutralism," defined as the doctrine that "the mental and physical are two 'aspects' of some underlying reality which need not be described further." This recalls Spinoza more than it does anything I have ever said or meant. I hold that the physical is simply the psychical considered only in its aspects of causal and spatio-temporal relations or structures, abstracting from nonstructural, qualitative aspects.

In his essay "Mind As Ineffable" in *Mind in Nature*, Rorty clarifies further his conception of the psychical. He tries to show that *mind* has no distinctive meaning, no special character as contrasted to physical realities. If this means that a psycho-physical dualism is unfounded, then I grant it. Psychicalism is precisely the view that the psychical as such is not a special kind of reality but is reality itself or as such. Concrete and singular realities at least feel or sense, however little they may think; abstract realities are abstract aspects of the psychical, aggregate realities are groups of sentient singulars; subhuman realities, if singular, are subhuman psyches; superhuman realities are superhuman psyches. The difference between reality or actuality and the psychical or mind in the most generalized sense is that the second set of words gives positive content to the terms by expressing them in relation to our experience or knowledge. What we experience is itself experience in some form, what we feel is itself feeling in some form. *Mere* stuff or *mere* matter is not positively experienced or felt but only seems to be because of the low levels, or radically nonhuman forms, of its feeling quality.

The reason for psychicalism is not to escape a skepticism generated "by the naive metaphysics of common sense." The basic reason is that the notion of mere physical stuff or process is not self-explanatory, let alone explanatory of mind. Mind, as Peirce said, is self-intelligible and the explanation of all things, so far as they are open to explanation. It is mind that knows (other) mind, experience that discloses (other) experience. Mere matter is an empty negation that explains nothing. Matter or the physical in ordinary language is simply sentience on low levels that we can experience only indistinctly. It is mind, the psychical, that we must deal with; what we need matter for is adequately furnished by appropriately nonhuman forms of mind. Otherwise, it is an idle, superfluous term. In Rorty I find no evidence for a need to abandon this position.

An oddity of Rorty's *Philosophy and the Mirror of Nature* is that, although he says that we may expect a philosophy to throw some light on belief in God, what he says on the subject suggests that he knows next to nothing about the form this belief has more and more been taking for several centuries in theology and philosophy. Rightly, he holds that if deity is equated with infinity, it is an empty idea, devoid of religious value. This objection is as old as Carneades; the reply to it is as old as Socinianism and is entirely in harmony with some of the most influential forms of philosophical theology today. That "divine" and "infinite" say the same thing does not harmonize with Barth's or Whitehead's beliefs, to mention two of many recent writers of prominence. Berdyaev is another. From Hegel to the writer of this book those really conscious of the history of theism and the metaphysics of religion are not likely to take for granted that worshipping God is the same as adoring the idea of infinity—or mere unlimitedness, or mere eternity, or mere absoluteness, or any other single one-sided abstraction of this kind. In some sense, the Hegelian saying, "truth [at least, metaphysical truth] is the unity of contraries" is widely accepted in theology.

Vaguely generalized metaphysical agnosticism like Rorty's may be fashionable. But I do not see what other reason those of us interested in metaphysics have for allowing this fashion to deter us from trying to arrive at reasonable metaphysical beliefs. We will not convince everyone to share our beliefs. Neither will Rorty do that with his unbeliefs.

A very neat expression of his attitude is Rorty's remark that we deal with things not by knowing what they are but by "coping, merely coping" with them. One reply might be that the insects cope quite well; we, however, are creatures that find meaning in life partly by thinking we can come to know at least approximately, or with whatever qualifications, what things are. We want to participate in what Wordsworth deliberately called "the life of things." Scientists want to participate in the beautiful causal structures of the world, patterns embodied in one way in scientists' thoughts and in another way in nature generally. What natural science does not try to do, at least at present, is participate in the qualities of feeling in nonhuman animals and perhaps in plants and in all nature. The correspondence sought in science is purely intellectual, not emotional or sentient. Yet Darwin and doubtless most biologists have attributed feelings (of perhaps not humanly knowable kinds) to all animals. Darwin seriously wondered if plants were to be excluded in this connection.

Rorty perceptively realizes that religious people and scientists have in common a greater faith in the objective validity of our thinking, its correspondence with reality, than he has. To be religious, he suggests, is to find, or hope to find, a "connaturality" of ourselves with the rest of reality. I agree, and I think that scientists are at heart religious in this sense. Some of the greatest among them have been conscious of this. I also hold with Peirce and others that to understand is in principle to succeed in the endeavor to find analogies between ourselves and other realities.

A teapot (an example of Wittgenstein's) is scarcely analogous at all to a human being. But the molecules and atoms into which physics analyzes teapots are not nearly so different in certain essential respects from ourselves. They, and not the teapot, share with us self-activity; they, and not the teapot, are partly unpredictable in their actions, as (*pace* some psychologists) are we. Also, the inclusive physical cosmos is more like us than like a teapot. The teapot has no unique principle of order; its chemical atoms behave according to the laws of their kind in the teapot's environment. But the inclusive cosmos, in comparison with other conceivable universes, has its unique laws pervading all its parts; and each of us, unless an identical twin or quintuplet, has a unique gene structure which gives us a specialization of chemical capacities not shared with any other. Even an identical twin has a uniquely developed nervous system influencing and orchestrating all its activities. Thus you and I, or a cell of one of our bodies, or, more problematically perhaps, a molecule or atom, or at the opposite extreme, the universe are all dynamic singulars in a sense in which teapots are not. Before Leibniz no one was nearly so clear as he came to be about this distinction between dynamic singulars and aggregates. Perhaps he actually made too much of it in some ways. Whitehead was, on the main point, a neo-Leibnizian, as am I.

Is human thinking a mirror of nature? If what is meant by mirror is a medium reflecting with absolute distinctness and precision, then of course the human mind is no mirror. (Nor is an ordinary mirror that.) But if the criteria for mirroring are suitably relaxed, why is one's mind not analogically a mirror? I find no very impressive argument in Rorty on this point. Consider a geographical map. It is not correspondent to its region with infinite precision or without qualification. But it is roughly, and for some purposes sufficiently, thus correspondent. Things more or less like maps are important elements in human thinking. They are merely the most obvious examples of the validity of the (suitably qualified) correspondence theory of truth. I am somewhat mystified by those who seem unwilling to grant this.

Rorty says that the success of our predictions does not prove the (strict?)

correspondence truth of the theories from which the predictions are derived. Popper says this, too, and with emphasis. But Popper also says (with some wavering and apparent inconsistency) that we can reasonably hope on the whole to achieve some partial or approximate correspondence with things as they are and to keep increasing this correspondence. We cannot simply capture the "essences" of things; but still we eliminate erroneous views of them and thus make our pictures of the world more nearly correspondent with the realities. The two extremes—we know exactly what things are, and we know nothing of what they are—are both unjustified. If Rorty's view is not the second extreme, it is not easy to see the distinction.

Some people set great store by the goal of not believing too much, others on not believing too little. Here, as everywhere, I am chronically a moderate and distrust extremes. My admiration for Popper arises partly from his avoidance of at least many extremes. In distrust of metaphysics he is less extreme than the positivists but still too extreme for my taste.

The metaphor of the mirror is not ultimately necessary. What is necessary is prehension as feeling of (others') feeling, by which not only the relation of experience to what is experienced is explained but also the relations of effects to causes, or subsequent results from earlier conditions. Among the essential results of modern, also of much older Asiatic, metaphysical thinking, neglected or dismissed by Rorty, are the criticisms of substance or genetic identity by Hume and the Buddhists and the alternative analysis of (partial) identity in change by Buddhists and, most clearly, by Whitehead. Rorty's analysis of internal and external relations in the *Encyclopedia of Philosophy* misses the basic point partially explicated by Peirce in his concept of Secondness, more precisely implied by Whitehead in his definition of prehension, and emphasized by me in many writings, that is, the point that the basic relations are internal for one term and external for the other. These relations hold not between substances or individuals taken as identical but between momentary actualities whose sequences constitute in many cases the careers or the concrete actualities of enduring individuals. Physics has come in this century to conceive the world in terms of "events, not things." Peirce wavered and never achieved full clarity on the question, hampered by his overextended doctrine of continuity-ism or synechism. Whether becoming is continuous or quantized is another of the essential and not artificial problems of metaphysics that are ignored by Rorty. The issue is not wholly new with quantum physics or Whitehead but was suggested by some Islamic as well as all Buddhist thinkers long ago, and by Hume more recently.

On one point neoclassical metaphysics can agree with Rorty. According to him the only metaphysical synthesis that could conceivably fulfill the traditional philosophical ambition of significantly supplementing and completing the account of reality given by science is idealism. But idealism, Rorty insists, has collapsed and is not likely to win acceptance again. However, what has collapsed is what was called idealism at the turn of the century, and this, as I have repeatedly argued, is a mixture of genuinely idealistic motifs (meaning ways of using the idea of mind or experience to explain reality as such, including physical reality or matter) with motifs which not only do not follow from the idealistic one but are implicitly incongruous with it. Examples are: the denial of the reality of becoming, the classical deterministic view of causality, and the notion of physical objects as insentient not only as wholes but in all their constituents. In addition, historical idealists tended to blur or deny the distinction between eternal, necessary, metaphysical truths and contingent, empirical ones. Rorty knows, I presume, that the idealism of Peirce and Whitehead, and, still more explicitly, my own contrasts rather sharply with the views taken as definitive of historical "idealism." He goes so far as to say that this historical world-view is believed nowadays by "no one." Perhaps so, but nothing, or not a great deal, follows from this concerning the future prospects of an idealism purified from the far from small mistakes or contaminations referred to.

Perhaps the most useful thing Rorty has done (in *The Consequences of Pragmatism*) is to survey the variety of activities going under the name of philosophy today. He finds fantastically diverse things. One possible conclusion that I am tempted, but not ready, to draw is that what some of us are still doing, that is, trying to reflect rationally on metaphysical questions concerning necessary truths (those with which any conceivable experience is at least compatible) may in the near future be carried on as much or more by liberal theologians as by those calling themselves philosophers. After all, in considering the history of philosophy many of us study Philo, Augustine, Anselm, Aquinas—all very definitely theologians, but theologians who saw an important role for philosophy as well as for science. Antiscientific, unphilosophical theology—fundamentalism—is a different matter. However, in an age facing threats of nuclear, biological, and chemical warfare, who dares to make predictions about our human future?

My ethics, which has a metaphysical aspect, tells me that, despite these awful dangers, we are obligated to do the best we can with a situation one would not have chosen to be in, but which has been brought about by freedom, the source of both good and evil. There seems no way in which giving up the metaphysical quest would lessen the dangers and some possibility that pursuing the quest would increase our powers to avoid them. It is heartening that the Catholic bishops of this country (with at least many of whom I would have grave disagreements about some matters) are moving to counteract the enthusiasm of some for increasing our stores of nuclear weapons at the cost of doing less and less for social justice to millions of unfortunates, huge budgetary deficits, and yet with no clear relation to the professed goal of saving us all from utter nuclear catastrophe, or with the implausible claim that damage done by nuclear war could be kept within reasonable bounds. (The genuine experts seem far from encouraging on this subject.) Perhaps theologians and scientists may prove akin in these matters also.

RESPONSE TO CHARLES HARTSHORNE

Charles Hartshorne was the first teacher to excite in me a genuine enthusiasm for philosophy. I had wandered into a philosophy major without any clear idea of what awaited me, and I should probably have wandered out again had I not started to take courses with Hartshorne. In one of those courses, he took us through *Process and Reality*. Reading that book led me to write my M.A. thesis (under Hartshorne's supervision) on Whitehead's theory of eternal objects. I argued that it was hard to reconcile that theory with the claim that Creativity is "the category of the ultimate." The eternal objects, perfectly determinate and immune from change, seemed to me out of tune with the rest of Whitehead.

Despite my instinctive sardonic, juvenile atheism, I was moved by Whitehead's description of God as "the fellow-sufferer who understands." I was impressed by Hartshorne's description of the orthodox theistic tradition as insisting on "paying pointless metaphysical compliments to God," especially in respect to his infinity. I decided that if I could ever get myself to believe in God, it would certainly be a finite God of the sort described by Mill, James, Whitehead, and Hartshorne. I was also impressed by Hartshorne's citation of Bergson's remark "if time is not real, nothing is real," a remark which keeps coming back to me as I write yet another panegyric to historicity and contingency (see "Philosophy and the Future").

Nevertheless, when I read Hartshorne's *Divine Relativity*, I was put off by all the attempts at demonstration, all the stuff about modality, all the talk of necessary metaphysical truth. I vaguely felt that both Whitehead and

Hartshorne were trying to mix oil and water—trying (as Pogson-Smith said about Spinoza) to "bind the spirit of Christ in the fetters of Euclid," or, more precisely, to bind the spirit of Wordsworth in the fetters of *Principia Mathematica*. It seemed to me that both were too fond of logic, just as both Plato and Whitehead had been too fond of mathematics. The eternal objects, like those necessary metaphysical truths that Hartshorne kept offering us, seemed to me the wrong sort of companions for a suffering deity, a deity subject to contingent afflictions.

Looking back on those days at Chicago, I recall that Rudolf Carnap and Hartshorne had formed a kind of alliance. Both men, I imagine, felt marginalized in a philosophy department dominated by Richard McKeon and his students.[1] But there was much more to the alliance than mere academic politics, or a sense of shared oppression. Hartshorne used to rephrase his own and Whitehead's metaphysical doctrines in terms of Carnap's notion of "true in all possible state-descriptions." The two men shared a taste for the formal and for the necessary. Both liked the idea that time and change were contained within a logical structure, a permanent matrix beyond the reach of contingency.

I did not. I wrote a paper for Carnap against the very idea of analytic truth at the same time that I was writing my thesis against the very idea of eternal objects for Hartshorne. When Quine's "Two Dogmas" came out I embraced it with glad cries. When, a few years after that, I read the sentence "Why did we think that logic was something sublime?" in the *Philosophical Investigations*, I felt that everything was going my way. Like many other innumerate, mathematically handicapped students (the kind who find the history parts of the M.A. and Ph.D. exams in philosophy easy, and the logic parts terribly hard) I rather resented logic, formalism, and everything that smacked of eternity—everything that refused to be put up for contingent grabs. The turn away from formalism which Wittgenstein initiated seemed to me to make (what we then called) "linguistic philosophy" a lot more exciting than it had been in Carnap's hands.

The first philosophical article I ever wrote was an attempt to ally Wittgenstein with Peirce—to view them both as temporalistic critics of Platonism, necessity, eternity, and Carnap.[2] (It was, of course, the Peirce of Evolutionary Love, rather than the Peirce of the Logic of Relatives, whom I admired most.) Thirty-some years down the road, I still have the same temporalistic focus, and still have pretty much the same reactions to reading Hartshorne (and, for that matter, Carnap) as I did back then. So, though I am delighted to have an occasion to respond to Hartshorne's "Rorty's Pragmatism and Farewell to the Age of Faith and Enlightenment," what I shall be saying may be rather predictable.

In a few pages, Hartshorne covers a very large number of topics. I shall try to deal only with the most important—the ones about which we disagree most sharply.

THE DISTINCTIVELY HUMAN

Hartshorne says that, unlike the insects, who merely cope, we humans "find meaning in life partly by thinking that we can come to know at least approximately, or with whatever qualifications, what things are." This has certainly been true of most human beings so far, and it is certainly, as Hartshorne goes on to say, what ties scientists and religious people together in a sense of the "connaturality" of ourselves with the rest of reality. Nevertheless, I am not sure that this is how we *should* find meaning in life.

Hartshorne, like James and Dewey, often uses Wordsworth to give himself a sense of participation in "the life of things." I use Wordsworth to give myself a sense of participation in the life of Wordsworth, and that seems to me use enough. I should like to avoid the question of whether Wordsworth got the life of things right—whether he knew, at least approximately, what things are. Wordsworth's nature poems bring back to me, as doubtless they do to most of his readers, private memories of "the hour/Of splendor in the grass, of glory in the flower." But since I do not know how to answer the question of whether Wordsworth or Democritus gets closer to the way things are in themselves, I turn pragmatist and deplore the question. I argue that there is no way things are in themselves, and no issue about whether we are more connatural with utterly inanimate bits of stuff or with birds.[3] I argue that we would be better off without the notion of "the intrinsic nature of reality," and thus better off without metaphysics—without attempts to determine whether Hartshorne is right, or pathetically fallacious, when he says that "what we experience is itself experience in some form."

Hartshorne, like the early Heidegger, takes our concern with our own mortality to be at the center of the impulses which drive us to metaphysics. But I think that Heidegger was right in suggesting, in his later work, that metaphysics was not as good a way to express this concern as poetry. So I think of Wordsworth as not needing to be backed up by metaphysical argument—as not benefiting by Coleridgean philosophical footnoting—but as complete in himself. More generally, I think of metaphysicians as footnotes to poets—as people who must rest content, for the most part, with rearranging previously-existing language rather than creating new language. I agree with Heidegger that "Was aber bleibet/Stiften die Dichter."[4] I think that, as footnotes to Wordsworth go, Whitehead and Hartshorne write the best ones. But I prefer Wordsworth unfootnoted.

To sum up: Hartshorne wants to make the world safe for Wordsworth metaphysically, and I want to do the same thing metaphilosophically. He wants to argue that some of what Wordsworth said is literally, philosophically, metaphysically true—that Wordsworth got something right. I want to argue that we can get the most out of Wordsworth by not asking whether he got anything right.

SCIENCE AND OBJECTIVITY

"Religious people and scientists," Hartshorne rightly says, have in common a greater faith in the "objective validity of our thinking, its correspondence with reality," than I do. That seems to me the problem with religious people and scientists. I agree with many German *Geisteshistoriker* that natural science is the Enlightenment version of religion—that post-Enlightenment intellectuals think that science will do for them what religion promised to do, viz., put them in touch with Ultimate Reality, the Way Things Really Are. By contrast, I tend to view natural science as in the business of controlling and predicting things, and as largely useless for philosophical purposes. Whereas Hartshorne views phenomena like quantum indeterminacy as a tip-off to metaphysical truth, I suspect that science will not converge to agreement with either panpsychists or materialists.[5] Rather, it will blithely and indifferently throw off encouragement to both sides as it proceeds in its merry way, inventing whatever gimmicks it needs to get on with its task of "taking hold of bodies and pushing them."[6]

My utopia, as I have often said, is one in which poets rather than scientists or priests or religious prophets are thought of as the cutting edge of civilization, and are the heroes and heroines of the culture. The reason I think such a culture would be ideal is that it would have given up the presupposition common to Carnap and Hartshorne—that everything we do take place within an eternal, unchangeable framework, and that discerning this framework is an important human task. Such a poeticized culture would take for granted, with Sellars, that "all awareness is a linguistic affair," and that there can be no such thing as an ideal language that pictures the way reality is in itself. So the inhabitants of such a culture would be more interested in the proliferation of languages, tasks, and forms of human life than in the convergence of scientific and metaphysical opinion to a single set of propositions.

It may be true, as Hartshorne says, that Peirce and James would deplore most of my views. I cannot, indeed, think of any of those views which Peirce might endorse, except maybe my anti-Cartesianism and my Sellarsian exaltation of language. But I should like to think that the utopian vision I have just outlined might have some attraction for James, who wrote that "the divine can mean no single quality, it must mean a group of qualities, by being champions of which in alternation, different men may all find worthy missions. Each attitude being a syllable in human natures' total message, it takes the whole of us to spell the meaning out completely. So 'a god of battles' must be allowed to be the god for one kind of person, a god of peace and heaven and home, the god for another."[7] If one puts this sort of ultimate pluralism together with Santayana's poetasting conception of the function of metaphysicians, then one can say that the convergence to a single set of metaphysical or religious opinions is about the *last* thing we want. Just as we do not want the god of battles to erase the god of home, or conversely, so we want both ever new Lucretiuses and ever new Wordsworths, both ever new Whiteheads and ever new J. J. C. Smarts. We want both ever new variations on "the atoms of Democritus/and Newton's particles of light," and ever new variations on Hartshorne's rejoinder that such things are only "the psychical considered only in its aspects of causal and spatio-temporal relations or structures."[8]

I think of the course of human history as a long, swelling, increasingly polyphonic poem—a poem that leads up to nothing save itself. When the species is extinct, "human nature's total message" will not be a set of propositions, but a set of vocabularies—the more, and the more various, the better. Nobody will get this message, I suspect, since I still find no reason to agree with James and Hartshorne that "the best things are the more eternal things." But I do not see why eternity, or the silence of the infinite spaces, should matter. If there really is an eternal fellow-sufferer who understands (or even a non-eternal but long-lived race of sympathetic Galactics), so much the better. But I think James (and, perhaps even more readily, Whitman) would have agreed that we can carry on perfectly well even if we suspect there is not.

To sum up: I think the problem with religious people and scientists is that they think it important not simply to create, but to get something right. I should like to free Whitehead's Category of the Ultimate[9] not just from the theory of eternal objects, but from the fetters of the correspondence theory of truth, and from the idea that we need a super-science called metaphysics.

FREEDOM AND DETERMINISM

Hartshorne is right that I have nothing to say about free will. This is because I am one of those who, on reading Hume's chapter on the subject early in life, became instantly converted to compatibilism and never looked back. When I began to think of myself as a pragmatist, I began to think of that chapter in Hume as a sort of proto-pragmatism. I read Hume as saying that you can do lots of different things with language, and that they do not have to be fitted together in a single neat package. You can use it to assign responsibility for actions, as in the criminal law, and you can use it to predict what people will do, as in the fine-grained psychoneurology we hope lies ahead. You can do both without creating what Sellars, alas, thought of as the problem of reconciling the "manifest" with the "scientific" image of man.

That seems a pseudo-problem to me, as do a lot of other problems which Hartshorne takes seriously. What I initially liked best about the pragmatists was the attack on metaphysical pseudo-problems early on in James's *Pragmatism*. I still think that the greatest contribution of pragmatism to culture is not, as Hartshorne believes, the support which Peirce and James give to panpsychism and indeterminism, but the support which James and Dewey give to the enterprise which Wittgensteinians call "philosophical therapy." I agree with Hartshorne that metaphysics cannot be dismissed as "misuse of language,"[10] but I also agree with James that a metaphysical difference can safely be neglected if we cannot tie it in with a difference in practices.[11]

I take Kant's claim that we are free from the point of view of practical reason but determined from that of the understanding to be just another way of saying, like Hume, that we can use different languages for different purposes, without trying for a third language which synthesizes them. I take the early Hegel of the *Phenomenology* to acknowledge the fact that not all languages need to be commensurated, brought together into a unified *Wissenschaft*.[12] Following Arthur Danto, I take Nietzsche's perspectivalism as a hyped-up version of pragmatism—though, following Davidson, I would urge that the ocular metaphor of different perspectives on a single reality is misleading.[13] In other words, I linguisticize as many pre–linguistic-turn philosophers as I can, in order to read them as prophets of the utopia in which all metaphysical problems have been dissolved, and religion and science have yielded their places to poetry.

To sum up: whereas Hartshorne thinks it important to defend indeterminism as a metaphysical truth, I think that reassurance on this metaphysical point has nothing to contribute to the development of an ever freer, more creative, more interesting culture. I agree with Hume and Kant that we are going to carry on as if we were free, regardless of whether physics is currently siding with the determinists or the indeterminists. I do not think it matters whether we accept "the essentially creative aspect of becoming" as long as we keep trying to create ever more open space for the play of the human imagination. I see cultural politics, rather than metaphysics, as the context in which to place everything else.

NECESSARY TRUTH

Hartshorne says that we should explicate *necessary* in terms of its relation to possibility and contingency rather than "as the highest degree of uncontroversiality." Quine and Wittgenstein have suggested that we should stick to uncontroversiality when explicating necessity. More generally, they have suggested that we think of modality as a function of human practice, not as a feature of the universe apart from our practices. Here Hartshorne is on the side of Saul Kripke and David Lewis, who would like there to be real modalities which are not simply a function of epistemic ones.

My preference for the Quine-Wittgenstein way of thinking about modality is, once again, due to a preference for making human history the measure of all things. I want to use that history—that swelling, unfinished poem—as my ultimate context, rather than placing it within a still wider, metaphysical context. Because I think of *God* as primarily a name for that wider context, I am inclined to proclaim myself an atheist. But that term is not much more than an abbreviation for suspicion of what Heidegger called "the onto-theological tradition"—a tradition to which the logician in Whitehead remained loyal, but with which the Wordsworthian in Whitehead might, it seems to me, have dispensed.

The post-Kantian form of the onto-theological tradition, a form which Heidegger's own *Being and Time* still exemplifies, is the attempt to be transcendental—to find conditions of possibility as well as of actuality. I see transcendental philosophy as an attempt to confine contingency and creativity within fixed limits. So my favorite traditions of post-Kantian philosophy are the specifically anti-Kantian ones, and of these pragmatism seems to me the most promising. As I say in discussing Hance's article, below, I think of the urge for transcendentality as a result of the quest for certainty. I think the same of the urge to find necessary truths and real modalites.

To sum up: Hartshorne defines a necessary truth as one "with which any conceivable experience is at least compatible." My objection is that we do not yet have any idea what is and what is not a conceivable experience. Because I think of the enrichment of language as the only way to enrich experience, and because I think that language has no transcendental limits, I think of experience as potentially infinitely enrichable. The attempt to find necessary truths by applying a conceivability test seems to me capable of giving us only a pallid summary of our present linguistic practices.

I have pulled no punches in saying how sharply I disagree with Hartshorne's central philosophical convictions. I should like to balance this by being equally frank about my admiration for Hartshorne as a teacher and as a human being. A nineteen-year-old trying to decide what to do with his life is bound to be influenced by the role models he happens to encounter. In the course of studying with Hartshorne, it struck me that if this sort of person was a philosophy professor, then becoming a philosophy professor was probably not such a bad idea. I do not think that I managed to live up to his example, either of intellectual passion or of generosity of spirit, but I am very proud to have been Hartshorne's student.

3

AMERICA & THE CONTESTATIONS

OF MODERNITY:

BENTLEY, DEWEY, RORTY

Thelma Z. Lavine

I. DEWEY AND BENTLEY

John Dewey's proclivity to be intellectually and emotionally stimulated by persons who project creative vitality and goal-driven energy lasted throughout his life. One such object of Dewey's fascination had ventured to write to Dewey from the small town of Paoli, Indiana, in 1932 enclosing a copy of his book, *Linguistic Analysis of Mathematics*. Two and one-half years later, having finally read the book at the urging of Ernest Nagel, Dewey replied:

New York, May 22, 1935

Dear Mr. Bentley:

Some time ago I received a copy of your *Linguistic Analysis of Mathematics* I fear I didn't acknowledge it. . . . Recently I have read it and am still re-reading it. It has given me more enlightenment and intellectual help than any book I have read for a very long time. I have been engaged during this year in trying to get my ideas on logical theory into systematic shape for publication, and I cannot put into words how much your book has meant to me in this process.[1]

Dewey's delight in finally reading Arthur Bentley's *Linguistic Analysis of Mathematics* is understandable. Here was a forceful informative attack on foundationalism in mathematics which confirmed the principal argument of

Dewey's own projected *Logic: The Theory of Inquiry*, that the logical "foundations" of inquiry are not external to inquiry but contained within its own practices. After this first exchange of letters there was a lapse of three years. The correspondence between Dewey and Bentley resumed in 1938 after *Logic: The Theory of Inquiry* was published. It reached a peak of daily and weekly exchanges as their collaboration progressed, tapering off after 1949 with their publication of *Knowing and the Known*. Arthur Bentley had entered the "life-career" of John Dewey, and Bentley would remain a significant personal and intellectual presence for Dewey throughout those years.

Dewey is soon writing to Bentley: "I don't feel a lot of your positions are divergent from mine. I think our different modes of approach complement each other. I hadn't expected at my age (I'm 85 in October) to get a 'refresher course' that really refreshed. I feel I've got it through this contact with you."[2]

Bentley's own scholarly career stretched from *The Process of Government*, published in 1908 and which became a classic in the field of political science, to *Knowing and the Known*, 1949, written in collaboration with Dewey, which has become a classic text in the history of American pragmatism. Bentley's achievements occurred in the course of a life-history marked by severe psychological depressions, discontinuities, withdrawals, and returns. The joint effort with Dewey appears to coincide with one of his sustained periods of productivity.

The two men share the spirit of the American cultural revolution that occurred at the turn of the century. There is a Hegelian deposit in the thought of both; both hold to a holistic process philosophy and accordingly are anti-dualistic, anti-foundationalist, anti-abstractionist, anti-formalist, and, in opposition to positivism and empiricism, both tend to be interpretivist. Dewey and Bentley share as well a naturalistic, organism-environment frame; a rejection of traditional metaphysics and epistemology; an opposition to a legislative function for mathematics and logic in inquiry; and a behavioral approach to the social sciences.

But from the start there were differences. In *The Process of Government* Bentley had written as a process theorist in the social sciences; the raw material, he argues, is the group in its meaningful activity—each group in process, each classifiable by systems of classification which are themselves in process. Mental-physical, inner-outer, individual-social, subjective-objective are not discrete elements, but are dissolved into interactional (transactional) phases of group activity. Bentley presents this boldly imaginative picture of one great moving process of human activity, knowable as an intersection of multiple, unprioritizable perspectives which are themselves in process, in the following dramatic metaphor of process cosmology: "We have one great moving process to study, and of this moving process it is impossible to state any fact except as valued in terms of the other facts."[3]

Bentley next pursues the philosophy of science in *Behavior, Knowledge, Fact* with a scientific construct of a terrestrial celestial cosmos, in which all sciences are seen as modes of local knowledge stretching backward and forward across time and space, circular, foundationless, and in process of change. "Against this world view," he says, "no construction built up in terms of some pin-point 'mind of a moment' has any hope for consideration." This is what Bentley describes as his "floating cosmology." And he adds:

> I can deeply sympathize with anyone who objects to being tossed into such a floating cosmology. . . . The firm land of "matter" or even of "sense" or "self" is pleasanter if only it stands firm. . . . But . . . our firmest spots of conventional departure themselves dissolve in function. When they have so dissolved . . . there is no hope of finding refuge in some chance island of "fact" which may appear. The continents go, and the islands.[4]

Already there begins to emerge the intractable, devastating logic of a process philosophy which functions as a solvent for structures. Historically, the familiar form of the logic of process in philosophy is the sensory process with which Hume dissolved the necessity of the new causal laws of Enlightenment science. Repetition of the radical logic of process was mounted by Bentley in the 1930s, with Dewey a reluctant fellow-traveler. Now, in the last decades of this century, the logic of process is repeated in the sweeping historicist process with which Richard Rorty has undertaken to dissolve the structures of Western philosophy.

Differences between Bentley and Dewey surface first with Bentley's being shocked by Dewey's concern with the "life-career" of the individual human being instead of with the immense patternings of the temporal-spatial cosmos. As they continue to correspond, Bentley pursues his process cosmology, driving the logic of process, which Dewey shares with him, to its extreme implications, and challenging the views which Dewey does not share with him. As the *Correspondence* and *Knowing and the Known* show, Deweyan pragmatism, which is itself a type of process philosophy, is not reflectively immunized against its own dissolving techniques. Dewey is thus vulnerable to the force of Bentley's proddings, and he falters as the dissolving operation of his own pragmatism is turned against itself. The end result is a pragmatism *in extremis*, the dissolution of the structure that Dewey required for his own longstanding philosophical agenda: to reconstruct philosophy in relation to the problematic situation of his time, and to ameliorate the problems of society by bridging the gap between science and morality. Bentley had, however, already warned of this outcome in the extract quoted above: "Our firmest spots of conventional departure themselves dissolve in function. When they have so dissolved . . . there is no hope of finding refuge in some chance island of 'fact' which may appear."

The intellectual collaboration that eventuated in *Knowing and the Known* undertook three interrelated projects: a critique of formal logicians in defense of Dewey's *Logic: The Theory of Inquiry*; a critique of logical positivism, now perceived to threaten pragmatism; and the construction of a new language for pragmatism and the behavioral sciences. The Bentleyan cosmic process of local knowledge ranging across time and space, which is glimpsed in *Knowing and the Known*, receded as the project of linguistic reform became the central issue. As for Dewey, the project of linguistic reform produced serious problems. As natural events, knowings and knowns are to be investigated by the methods successful in the natural sciences. Knowing through *naming* is the initial problem; the search for a *"firm list of names*," scrutinized for vagueness, traditional residues, interactionism, transactionism, specification. The search for firm names inevitably led to the loss of names and relationships in Deweyan pragmatism, which was vulnerable to these new structures. Rejected names include: reality, naturalism, experience, individual, subject-object, problematic situation, concept, meaning, knowledge. Dewey registered protests, arguments followed, and Dewey characteristically conceded. On reality, Bentley says: "You hedge. Hedging has brought us nowhere. I am against any more of it. On subject-object, Bentley states: "You indicate you have no need for the subject; however, you indicate the object is needed." Dewey replies: "I doubtless have used the word object in a pre-organism sense."[6]

The question of dominance has understandably been raised about this important intellectual collaboration, especially since it is accessible, not only in the completed product but in the making, through a voluminous correspondence.

What begins as a "refresher course" under the tutelage of Bentley evolves into the dominance of the energetic, creative vitality of Bentley even in the early stages of the collaboration. At the end it may be seen that the entire conceptual apparatus with which *Knowing and the Known* attempts to construct a theory of language for pragmatism and behavioral science has come from Bentley's *Behavior, Knowledge, Fact*. Postulation, behavior, observation, naming, specification, fact, self-action/interaction/transaction, circularity, the cosmos of knowledge—for all of these, Bentley drew upon his own text. At least in respect to the production of *Knowing and the Known*, Bentley succeeded in his ambition to provide, with the collaboration of Dewey, the next step in the development of pragmatism. The next step, in short, would be Bentley's.

Ironically, the mission of *Knowing and the Known*—to provide a language for pragmatism and the behavioral sciences, to combat the foundationalism of formal logicians and the looming hegemony of logical positivism—is fulfilled in none of these goals. Beset by logical foundationalism and by the rising logical positivism, *Knowing and the Known*, the historic collaborative effort of two pragmatist process philosophers, emerges astonishingly as a mirror (despite some differences) of the logical positivism it opposes. It offers its own rigorous scientific language of transactionalism, its own formal language of naming; it affirms the exclusive legitimacy of science as a mode of knowledge and frame of reference; and it denies cognitive significance to metaphysics and ethics, and any connection between science and commonsense.

The radical process logic of Bentley and the defensive turn to the formal language of scientific transactionalism in *Knowing and the Known* leave John Dewey's philosophic constructions hopelessly undermined—the great unifying Darwinian/Hegelian frame of nature, aesthetically and humanly perceived in its precariousness and stability, the linkage of science, democracy, and morality, the overdetermined life-career of the modern individual, and the problematic situation, key to the recognition and resolution of difficulties. Hopelessly undermined also is the austerely magnificent Bentleyan floating cosmology spanning millennia in time and space. After the project ended, a disappointed Dewey returned to writing about means and consequences, common sense and science. He died in 1951, two years after *Knowing and the Known* was published.

II. DEWEY AND RORTY

A generation later, in 1979, came Richard Rorty's *Philosophy and the Mirror of Nature*. In this and in subsequent voluminous writings exhibiting masterful philosophical scope and subtlety, Rorty engaged in undermining (along with other philosophic quarry) the philosophy of John Dewey, even while proclaiming himself a Deweyan. Rorty is the Oedipal son, a rival superbly equipped, indefatigably energetic, mockingly deferential, postmodernist in the jouissance of displacing the philosopher-father. How would Dewey, given his proclivity for goal-driven creative people, have responded to this embodiment of Oedipal energy who is goal-driven against Dewey himself? Rorty is Harold Bloom's strong poet, energetically creating himself by opposing and displacing the predecessor poet. How does this play out?

Rorty is not without reason in announcing himself a Deweyan. If Rorty is as he describes himself, presenting a historicist view of philosophies as constructed in specific historical contexts and in response to specific changing conditions, and if he then concludes that philosophy has no claim to be providing an unchanging foundation for knowledge, his Deweyan credentials are established. For does not Dewey, drawing continuously upon Hegelian, Darwinian, Spencerian, historicist modes of change, view process as the primary trait of all philosophical constructions? Does Dewey not then conclude that claims to fixed, absolute philosophic foundations for knowledge are abhorrent? If this is where Dewey stands, how far away is the rivalrous, competitive Oedipal son? It is, moreover, Dewey who has taken his readers and followers from the bold perception of the reflex arc as model for the concept of the problematic situation (the key concept of *Logic: The Theory of Inquiry*) to see inquiry in a new and Hegelian way, as called into existence by an indeterminate, disunified quality in a situation. The Hegelian function of inquiry is to effect a resolution, to convert, reconcile, transform the elements of the original situation into a unified whole. The problematic situation presents a model for inquiry which permits no finalities, no fixities or absolutes, but only hypotheses that change as new situations present new materials to be resolved. It is a model that relativizes all elements to the particular situation and thus permits no universals, no general principles, no theoretical certainties. It is Dewey's model for science and democracy. Philosophy itself, Dewey tells us repeatedly, is conceived on this model; its origin is in some particular perplexity, for which organizing, clarifying hypotheses are framed to bring about a readjustment of the situation.

Dewey constructs various specific models for using the general pattern of inquiry in social inquiry. The two most successful he identifies as "the genetic method" and "means and consequences." The genetic method functions within a situational logic of the time-bound, culture-bound character of problematic situations and the responses they evoke. A response adequate to a past situation is doubtful, problematized in respect to its adequacy in a changed situation.

Means and consequences focuses on change introduced by human agency. Here Dewey reaffirms his view of process as the primary trait of reality, and its function as a universal solvent. Every existence is an event. Transactions of events are in process in physical nature and in organic adaptations. Structures are events in which the rate of change is slow or regular. The attempt on the part of philosophical, political, or religious conceptions to introduce fixity and order into the world is an error. All such fixed beliefs are themselves functions of local and changing events. The means introduced by human agency can relate only to an end-in-view that is correlated with the means which have been introduced. Such ends are only hypotheses, changing with new situations. There are no fixed ends. Process as universal solvent dissolves theories of fixed human nature, the fixed and obsolete curricula of public education, and the religious certitudes of the established churches. But Dewey is most energized to attack and dissolve the fixities of political philosophies, and specifically the American sacralization of individualism and unalienable rights as set forth in the Declaration, as well as the structures of separation of powers, representative democracy, and recurring elections as set forth in the Constitution—all of these he rejected as retrograde survivals of past situations, false pretensions to intuitive reason, and obstructions to change.

With this account of the scope and detail of Dewey's historicism, Dewey's own undermining of absolutisms and foundational claims in every domain of philosophy, where, then, can Rorty, the historicist Oedipal son, strike? He can strike from a source unavailable to Dewey: the linguistic philosophy of the late Wittgenstein and the notion of a plurality of nonprioriti-zable languages ("language-games") linked to a plurality of "forms of life." But now a further step is taken, with the aid of the linguistic philosopher Donald Davidson: languages (vocabularies) are to be seen as tools which help us cope with specific situations and specific times. They are the contingent product of the specific circumstances with which they cope. But this particularized function is their only significance. They are not means of representing or expressing anything, and no neutral criterion exists by which one vocabulary can be preferred or prioritized over another.

By delegitimating, leveling-down scientific method, knowledge, and technology as one of the many vocabularies coping with specific contingent situations without representing anything other than this contingency, Rorty has now delivered a fatal blow to the philosopher-father: scientific method is Dewey's central concept. Dewey means by scientific method the pattern of inquiry finally formulated and elaborated in *Logic: The Theory of Inquiry*—the Hegelian working out of the conflictual problems of the problematic situation, most significantly in the testing of the proposed solution by its experiential outcomes. This pattern of inquiry is not only the method for all inquiry: it is also Dewey's procedure for scientific testing by valid prediction or by falsification; it is Dewey's realism; it is his form of the correspondence theory of knowledge; it is his form of the reality principle; it is Dewey's prescription for sanity against the flux of sensations, cosmic perspectives, or vocabularies. By seeing the method of inquiry as the reflective intervention by action into the problematic complex of events, in which the intervention is tested by its outcomes, Dewey breaks out of radical historicism and linguisticism.

In fact, Dewey was an Enlightenment enthusiast for advances in scientific knowledge and technology, which he valued for their potential to ameliorate the human condition and for their strengthening of industrial productivity as much as for their expansion of human horizons. Dewey would have been excited by NASA and the technology of space exploration, which he would see as yielded by the working through of macro- and micro-problematic situations, and by repetitions of testing, falsifying, and retesting, on a transactional data base of enormous complexity. He would be excited by the developments moving toward a unified theory in physics, by the genome project and its medical potentialities, and by the beginnings of molecular biology. Dewey would see these developments not as vocabulary changes but changes in our ability to make predictable transactions with our natural world. Even viewed as vocabularies, these developments are highly prioritizable in their predictive capacities.

Despite the pervasiveness of historicist process theory in his philosophy, neither science nor democracy is dissolved in process for Dewey. Scientific method and democratic process are the processes which critique, control, and enhance process, but they are not themselves dissolved by it. (Dewey specifically distinguished democratic group process from political democracy, which he regarded as a "nexus of ideals and institutions"—that is, as fixities.) The same pattern of inquiry, seeking a testable resolution of a Hegelian, contextual problematic situation, which is operative in scientific method, is operative also in democratic process. Here the pattern of inquiry avoids ideological disputation and adjudicates difficulties by giving each viewpoint a voice in the quasi trial and error of debate until a resolution in the form of consensus is achieved. Both procedures, scientific and democratic, are experimental, tied to action and to change. James Gouinlock has pointed out that *both* science and democratic process share (for Dewey) not only the same pattern of inquiry, the "method of intelligence," but also the same moral virtues: a willingness to question, to search for clarity and evidence, to hear and respect the views of others, to consider alternatives impartially, to change one's views as a consequence of inquiry and communication.

If the sacred can be defined as that which a historicist viewpoint is unwilling to subject to historicist dissolution, then Dewey's philosophy may be seen to rest upon the sacralization of scientific method and democratic process. This immunization of scientific method and democracy from historicist undoing and dissolving is as close to sacralization as Dewey's naturalism could permit him to go. If he did not claim scientific method, the pattern of its inquiry, and democratic process (which shares the pattern) as sacred, he saw them as normative for America and for the modern world. These are Dewey's islands. But they also identify the structures which constitute the cognitive and cultural framework of modernity. More than any of the other classical American philosophers, Dewey perceived the contestation within the framework of modernity between the Enlightenment tradition deriving from Locke and Newton and the Counter-Enlightenment Romantic tradition deriving from Rousseau, and the Romantic and Idealist German, English, and American poets and philosophers.

Each of the conflicting structures has its own thought-style. The Enlightenment thought-style includes universal human reason as the source of scientific and political truth; unalienable natural rights of the individual to life, liberty, property and the pursuit of happiness; government by consent of the governed; the rule of law and equality under the law; liberation by reason from myth, dogma, tradition, and prejudice; and the sustaining of a civil society of free and open social and economic relations.

Romantic Counter-Enlightenment ideas oppose, reject, scorn, and fear the power of Enlightenment thought and practices to discredit and displace traditional economic, political, religious and ethnic modes of cultural and personal life. The Counter-Enlightenment thought-style stands in opposition to abstract reason, arguing for the greater human significance of spirit, will, imagination; in opposition to objective science, asserting that the path to truth lies in subjectivity, the arts, and culture; in opposition to the political autonomy of the individual and natural rights democracy, holding that politics has its source in the group and is sustained by a statism of left or right; in opposition to the self-interest of the individual, asserting the primacy of the needs and aspirations of the community. In opposition to the achievement of a civil society and technological modernization, the concern of the Counter-Enlightenment is for the victims of Enlightenment civil society and modernization—the marginalized, the oppressed, the poor, minorities, rebels, revolutionaries, martyrs.

Dewey's perception of the contestations that constitute the framework of Modernity can be seen in his effort to integrate them, to synthesize the two cognitive modes, Enlightenment and Counter-Enlightenment, for an America whose national and social identity was rooted in Enlightenment truths. His integrative effort reflects the social and intellectual drama in response to which classical American philosophy came into being. The social and political upheavals in the post–Civil War decades were widely seen as the product of economic monopoly and political corruption, underwritten by the Declaration and the Constitution. These changes called forth critical questioning of the pillars of Enlightenment America and precipitated the turn of thoughtful Americans to new European winds of doctrine—Hegelian, Schopenhauerian, Darwinian, Marxist, Nietzschian, Bergsonian, Freudian—all appealing in this time of troubles, all at odds with the Enlightenment conceptions upon which the nation was founded.

Dewey's own philosophic quest led from his Vermont

Congregationalism to Hegel and to the interpretive mode of Romantic Counter-Enlightenment. His long philosophic career can be seen as an attempt to interpret and appropriate these conflicting modes of modernity. As I have elsewhere tried to show, his crucial philosophical constructions follow the pattern of his theory of inquiry, combining elements from Enlightenment scientific procedures and Counter-Enlightenment Romantic and Hegelian themes.

Implicit in the project of Dewey's philosophy is the postulate that no one engaged in philosophical reflection in our time can escape the normativity of the Enlightenment and Counter-Enlightenment contesting paradigms, the priority of scientific and democratic procedures contested by the priority of self, community, and tradition. The normativity of these contesting paradigms, which have been in process of development for 300 years, can be seen as the foundations of the culture of modernity, foundations which we have not philosophically constructed, Cartesian-style, but which as traditions have constructed us, and our modes of understanding. Nor has Richard Rorty, Oedipal son and hero, escaped the dialectic of modernity. In his prescription for a postmodern liberal culture and his separation of the public life of conventional liberalism from the Romantic life available to the private self is evidence that the dialectic of the culture of modernity cannot be escaped, despite protestations that the contestations of modernity are to be seen as foundationless, contingent vocabularies.

In his attempt to provide philosophic support for the unification of a fragmenting nation by means of his integration of the normative structures of modernity and in his passion for a unified and progressive America, Dewey had little taste for or empathy with the personally alienated and the psychologically disenchanted. His philosophic focus was primarily directed to the macro level of the problems of modernity, and this enables his philosophy to continue to speak to issues of the present: the scientific realism which is asserting itself in the wake of advances in the natural sciences and the international issue of human rights that has asserted itself since 1989.

III. BENTLEY, DEWEY, RORTY

To affirm change in the form of a radical pre-Hegelian Humeian sensationalism, or in the form of a radical process cosmology (Bentley) or in the form of a radical process linguisticism (Rorty) is to leave us without the possibility of knowledge. Although both Dewey and Rorty employ a Romantic-Hegelian historicism, Dewey's historicism is linked with a naturalistic account of organism and environment and provides for the possibility of knowledge by the testing of proposed resolutions of problematic situations. Rorty's historicism, linked with a radicalization of Wittgenstein's language-games as contingencies lacking representation, tied to particular circumstances, is without the possibility of knowledge. He joins deconstructionist Derrida and postmodernist Lyotard in the jouissance of gleefully repudiating the entire "ensemble" of Enlightenment scientific method, objective knowledge, valid and testable truth, and universality.

What is the appeal of these philosophies, to what groups, in respect of what concerns? The Hegelian deposit in Bentley's thought led, as we have seen, to a cosmic process of perspectives without priorities, without any normative or teleological affirmations, without reference to problems of the existing historical situation. This abstract negativity failed to rally any troops, failed to excite any approbations or animosities. Bentley's floating cosmology has floated away, has left our horizon. By contrast, Dewey's philosophy appealed to many groups, rallied many different troops and in large numbers: social democrats, left-wing progressivists, economic and educational reformers, naturalists (including those opposing idealism or religion), antitraditionalists, antinativists. Many of these groups, under new designations, continue to be functional or, if dormant, are available for reactivation.

A generation later, Rorty's strong intellectual appeal is to those who, having been disaffected by the Wittgensteinian, analytic undoing of philosophy, are following on Rorty's more radical and interesting path of deconstruction and postmodernism. Rorty also rallies the troops of the disenchanted, the generation of the college-educated in America for whom the 1960s fervor has long since burned out; while the linguistic turn, pronouncing in their philosophy courses the death of philosophy, is itself deadended. Rorty's feisty negativity exerts a vast appeal to these troops, whose residue of negativity finds expression in the Rortian boredom of conventional liberalism and the futile Rortian quest for an enchanted private life. But Rorty's contingent vocabularies rally no Deweyan groups in pursuit of political, social, economic, social, educational, or ameliorative goals.

We return at the end to the story of Rorty the Oedipal son. Freud has taught us that in the family, as in the primitive tribe, the son, after the rivalrous attack upon the father, through either fear or remorse, concedes and accepts and internalizes the father's rules as binding. So also Rorty: I accept pragmatism, I am a good Deweyan pragmatist.

But Rorty accepts the father's rules by redescribing them. This Oedipal son tells the other sons (Deweyan philosophers) *what the father really said*, or *what he meant to say*, or *what he should have said*: that the father, Dewey, was "beyond scientific method," antirealist, anti-any correspondence claims for truth, antimetaphysical; and that he inclined toward a later Wittgensteinian view of language, even toward seeing philosophy as a genre of literature. *This is the last displacement of the father by the Oedipal son, a redescription of Dewey the father according to which what he meant to say as a philosopher becomes what Rorty has now said.*

But the philosophy of John Dewey the father has been widely accepted and internalized in the philosophic consciousness of America, and increasingly in Europe. The Deweyan philosophy survives as a moral commitment to interpret and resolve problematic situations within the horizon of the scientific and democratic modes of modernity. This is what Dewey meant to say, what he said, and what he did all his professional life. This is his bequest to us Deweyans and to the world.

RESPONSE TO THELMA LAVINE

Thelma Lavine sees me as cutting us off from "the possibility of knowledge" and as "gleefully repudiating the entire 'ensemble' of Enlightenment scientific method, objective knowledge, valid and testable truth, universality." So it is no wonder that she sees me as having betrayed Dewey. I of course find it hard to recognize my views in this description. But I realize that that is because I think you can have knowledge—objective knowledge—without representation, realism, or correspondence, and Lavine does not. It seems to me that Lavine and I disagree on two points: (1) Are the latter notions (representation, realism, correspondence) so closely linked to that of objective knowledge that when they go it does too? (2) Did Dewey think they were that closely linked?

I should have thought Dewey's polemics against "copy theories" were enough to distance him from the notions of representation and correspondence. In my view, Dewey's attempt to terminate what he called "the epistemology industry" took the form of a criticism of the picture of two things—language and the world, thought and reality, subject and object—united by just such problematic relations as those. Without the idea that there are not merely causal relations between organism and environment but also such noncausal relations as representation and correspondence, it is hard to formulate a position which can be called "realist."

Lavine shares the widely held view that one must find some way to save our realistic intuitions, for otherwise one will be imprisoned within the "radical historicism and linguisticism" that she sees me as advocating. I think that it is enough to preserve whatever is worth saving from those intuitions to give a causal account of our intentional states—to say, with Dewey, Davidson, and common sense, that our beliefs and desires are a product of interaction (sometimes, with luck, controlled interaction) between us and our environment, and to leave it at that. But Lavine thinks that "by delegitimating, leveling-down scientific method, knowledge, and technology as one of the many vocabularies coping with specific contingent situations without representing anything other than this contingency, Rorty has now delivered a fatal blow to his philosopher father." As I say below in reply to James Gouinlock, I do not think that Dewey ever said anything very clear about what "scientific method" was supposed to be. I certainly do not think he said enough to validate Lavine's claim that "scientific inquiry . . . is Dewey's realism, it is his form of the correspondence theory of knowledge; it is his form of the reality principle; it is Dewey's prescription for sanity against the flux of sensations, cosmic perspectives, or vocabularies" (44).

As I see it, all Dewey had in mind when he talked about "scientific method" was the familiar social practices of democratic communities when they are at their best—when they exemplify the moral virtues that Lavine lists ("a willingness to question, to search for clarity and evidence, to hear and respect the views of others," etc., 45). I am as fond of these practices as Lavine or Dewey, but I do not see that they are somehow rendered more intelligible, or somehow encouraged, by being called "scientific method," and I do not see that they are more widely distributed among scientists than among lawyers or philologists. It is true, as I have remarked in various papers, that communities of researchers in the natural sciences have often been paradigms of democratic consensus-building, and good exemplars of the virtues Lavine lists.[1] But I do not see what would be lost if, in Lavine's claim that "Dewey's philosophy may be seen to rest on the sacralization of scientific method and democratic process," the phrase "scientific method and" were omitted.

Another way of saying this is that I construe Dewey as saying that we have objectivity whenever we have intersubjective agreement on the beliefs which guide our actions. That means that objectivity comes in degrees, just as intersubjectivity does, but is none the worse for that. It also means that objectivity has nothing to do with relations of accurate representation. Lavine's insistence on realism, representation, and correspondence, as well as her suspicion of contingency and historicity, makes clear that intersubjectivity without such relations is not good enough for her, and that she thinks it was not good enough for Dewey.

I do not know how to settle the exegetical question of whether it was good enough for Dewey. Lavine can cite endless "realist" passages from Dewey, and I can cite endless antirepresentationalist passages. I shall construe the former in my sense and she will construe the latter in hers. The philosophical question, as opposed to the exegetical one, is currently in debate between, for example, Donald Davidson and Thomas Nagel, Hilary Putnam and Bernard Williams, Daniel Dennett and John Searle, Arthur Fine and Philip Kitcher, and many other participants in arguments about realism, antirealism, and whether we can get beyond realism and antirealism. These arguments are not going to be settled in the present space.

Lavine may be right in her claim that I am an "Oedipal son," at least to the following extent. I may have gotten in the habit of construing Dewey in my own sense, and thus putting words in his mouth that he would have eschewed. This is a bad habit, and I regret if I have indulged it to the point of misleading the rising generation about what Dewey actually believed (as Gouinlock fears I may have done). But if I had been more cautious and had more consistently done what Gouinlock describes as distinguishing between the "good Dewey" and the "bad Dewey," then I do not think Lavine's charge of patricide would be appropriate.

Every disciple of a great philosopher has a duty to his or her master to distinguish the spirit from the letter of his or her teachings. This duty arises from the fact that not everything the great philosopher says convinced everybody. He or she was not, it always turns out, the Last Philosopher—the one who got everything straightened out, sorted things out so well that no further philosophy is needed. So the followers have to explain why conviction was not unanimous—why everybody was not converted. The only way to do this is to say such things as: the master should have put his point this way rather than that; he should not have gotten hung up on shibboleths (for example, "scientific method"); he should have used another terminology than the somewhat antiquated one he in fact employed; he should not have confused a certain pseudo-problem with a certain real problem. All these critical things are said by disciples with an eye to keeping the master's thought alive, his image bright, his books read.

This is the sort of thing I say about Dewey all the time. It is the sort of thing that Norman Kemp Smith said about Kant all the time, the sort of thing that Charles Taylor says about Hegel all the time, the sort of thing that A. J. Ayer was always saying about the British empiricists, and, I think, the sort of thing that any admirer of a dead philosopher who wants to make that philosopher look good to a contemporary audience had *better* say.[2] The trouble with the kind of treatment which Dewey gets from Lavine and Gouinlock, it seems to me, is that these commentators stick so closely to the letter that they can make no concessions to current audiences. So they cannot help those audiences catch the spirit. They maintain purity of doctrine at the price of having to explain disagreement with Dewey, or refusal to take Dewey seriously, as a result of the sad degeneracy of the times, the prevalence of contemptible modern fads.

To be more specific: for the reasons given in "Dewey Between Hegel and Darwin," I think that the switch from talking about consciousness and experience to talking about language—what Bergmann called "the linguistic turn"—was a good thing and something that Deweyans should adjust to rather than defy (or view, as Lavine seems to, as an unfortunate fad.) So I should like to think of my attempts to de-methodize and linguistify Dewey—playing down the similarities between Dewey and science-worshipping positivists and playing up those between Dewey and postpositivist analytic philosophers—as an adaptation of his view to a changed and, to my mind, better philosophical environment. For all my doubts about analytic philosophy, I think that the linguistic turn was an instance of genuine philosophical progress.[3]

4

AMERICAN PRAGMATISM: THE CONFLICT OF NARRATIVES

Richard J. Bernstein

A tradition not only embodies the narrative of an argument, but is only recovered by an argumentative retelling of that narrative which will itself be in conflict with other argumentative retellings.—Alasdair MacIntyre

Recently, the question of narrative has been thrust into the foreground of philosophic controversy, and widely divergent understandings of narrative and its significance for philosophy have emerged. Thinkers as different as Hans-Georg Gadamer, Paul Ricoeur, Hannah Arendt, Charles Taylor, Alasdair MacIntyre, Martha Nussbaum, and Richard Rorty have argued that narrative and story-telling are central for any adequate philosophizing. What gives a critical edge to their claims is their battle against the bias of many modern philosophers who are still deeply suspicious of any philosophic use of narrative.

This suspicion, which has been so entwined with modern philosophy since Descartes, persists right up to the present. When I was a graduate student during the 1950s, the question was frequently asked: Do you *do* philosophy, or the history of philosophy? The underlying presupposition was that serious "tough-minded" types *did* philosophy. Those who were "tender-minded"—not good or original enough—focused on the history of philosophy (a study that presumably had little relevance for original creative philosophizing). Although there has been an explosion of excellent work in the history of philosophy during the past few decades, it would be naive to think that the prejudice against history and narrative is dead. In their heart of hearts, many of our philosophic colleagues still believe in some version of this rigid dichotomy.

Most recently, the question of narrative has been raised in a polemical fashion by Lyotard, who begins *The Postmodern Condition* by identifying as "modern" any discipline that seeks to legitimate itself by appealing to a grand metanarrative. "Postmodern" is a stance of thorough skepticism and incredulity toward metanarratives. Ironically, one of the reasons why Lyotard's provocative claims have been so widely discussed is because he so effectively sketches a grand narrative about the eruption of the "postmodern."

Let me declare here that I want to engage in the "argumentative retelling" of a metanarrative—literally a narrative about the narratives that we tell ourselves about the history and development of the American pragmatic movement. I have several objectives in undertaking this task. I hope to demonstrate the following points:

1. That what we call pragmatism is itself—to use a Kantian turn of phrase—*constituted* by the narratives that we tell about pragmatism.

2. That the history of pragmatism has always—from its "origins" right up to the present—been a conflict of narratives. Despite family resemblances among those who are labeled pragmatists, there have always been sharp—sometimes irreconcilable—differences within this tradition. There are (as a pragmatist might expect) a *plurality* of conflicting narratives.

3. That there is not only a conflict of narratives, but *a fortiori*, a conflict of metanarratives. There are better and worse narratives and metanarratives. And we can give good reasons in support of our claims for what is better. (I take this to be a cardinal principle of any pragmatic narrative.)

4. That when future philosophers tell the story of the development of philosophy in America from the late nineteenth century through the twentieth century, they will highlight its thematic continuity far more than is presently acknowledged. They will see it as a continuous series of explorations and controversies about persistent pragmatic themes.

After these preliminaries let me begin by taking the plunge into what may well be called "founding" narrative of pragmatism—the famous story that James sketches in his 1898 address at the University of

California. James begins by telling us that: "Philosophers are after all like poets. They are pathfinders." In his typically literary and nuanced manner, he develops an elaborate simile of "blazes made by the axe of the human intellect on the trees of the otherwise trackless forest of human experience. They give you a direction and a place to reach." Then James tells his story.

> I will seek to define with you merely what seems to be the most likely direction in which to start upon the trail of truth. Years ago this direction was given by an American philosopher whose home is in the East, and whose published works, few as they are and scattered in periodicals, are no fit expression of his powers. I refer to Mr. Charles S. Peirce, with whose existence as a philosopher I dare say many of you are unacquainted. He is one of the most original contemporary thinkers; and the principle of practicalism—or pragmatism as he called it when I first heard him enunciate it at Cambridge in the early '70's—is the clue or compass by following which I find myself more and more confirmed in believing we may keep our feet upon the proper trail. Peirce's principle, as we may call it, may be expressed in a variety of ways, all of them very simple. In the *Popular Science Monthly* for January 1878, he introduces it as follows: the soul and meaning of thought, he says, can never be made to direct itself towards anything but the production of belief, belief being the demi-cadence which closes a musical phrase in the symphony of our intellectual life.

James goes on:

Beliefs, in short are really rules for action; and the whole function of thinking is but one step in the production of habits of action. . . . Thus to develop a thought's meaning we need only determine what conduct it is fitted to produce; that conduct is for us its sole significance. . . . To attain perfect clearness in our thoughts of an object, then, we need only consider what effects of a conceivably practical kind the object may involve—what sensations we are to expect from it, and what reactions we must prepare. Our conception of these effects, then, is for us the whole of our conception of the object, so far as that conception has positive significance at all.

So much for what James calls "the principle of Peirce, the principle of pragmatism." James thinks it should be "expressed more broadly than Mr. Peirce expresses it."

> The ultimate test for us of what a truth means is indeed the conduct it dictates or inspires. But it inspires that conduct because it first foretells some particular turn to our experience which shall call for just that conduct from us. And I should prefer for our purposes this evening to express Peirce's principle by saying that the affective meaning of any philosophic proposition can always be brought down to some particular consequence, in our future practical experience, whether active or passive; the point lying rather in the fact that the experience must be particular, than in the fact that it must be active.[1]

I have cited passages from this address at such length for several reasons. It is, as I have already mentioned, the founding narrative—some might say "the founding myth"—of pragmatism. "Pragmatism" is not a word that Peirce used in the articles to which James refers. And it was only at the turn of the century that the word "pragmatism" spread—so much so that nine years later speaking of "Peirce's pragmatic principle," James wrote in his *Pragmatism*: "It lay entirely unnoticed by anyone for twenty years, until I, in an address before Professor Howison's philosophical union at the University of California, brought it forward again and made a special application of it to religion. By that date (1898) the times seemed ripe for its reception. The word 'pragmatism' spread, and at present it fairly spots the pages of the philosophic journals."[2]

For any close student of Peirce, however, we can understand the quip that pragmatism is the movement that began with James's misunderstanding of Peirce. For despite James's generous intentions toward his cantankerous friend Peirce, James runs together what Peirce so diligently sought to distinguish. Unlike James, Peirce carefully distinguishes questions of meaning and truth. James shows almost no sensitivity to Peirce's categories, especially the way in which Peirce distinguishes Secondness and Thirdness, action and conduct, the existent and the real, or the particular and the universal. This is not simply a matter of logical or conceptual finesse. James's understanding of what he calls "the principle of Peirce, the principle of pragmatism" is essentially nominalistic—it is a version of the type of nominalism that Peirce spent so much of his life opposing. It is little wonder that Peirce in his 1905 *Monist* article, "What Pragmatism Is," renamed his doc-

trine "'pragmaticism,' which is ugly enough to be safe from kidnappers"—
and went on to tell his own narrative about the emergence of pragmaticism.[3]

The primary issue that interests me is not: Did James get Peirce right?
The answer, I believe, is quite straightforward: No!—or, more cautiously,
not quite. It was James himself who taught us just how important temperament is for philosophizing. Temperament involves a complex set of attitudes, preferences, a sense of what is vital and important that is shaped by
one's personal history and education. It would be difficult to imagine any
two thinkers who differed more than Peirce and James in their philosophic
temperaments. It is not accidental that James, despite his dabbling in
experimental science, likens the philosopher to the poet while Peirce is
always holding before us his idealization of the experimental laboratory scientist. I do not think that James ever had any deep understanding or "feel"
for the importance of the role that logic, mathematics, and the exact sciences play in Peirce's philosophic speculations.

If we look at the contemporary scene and explore the recent resurgence
of pragmatism, the types of differences, tensions, and conflicts that we find
between James and Peirce have their echoes and parallels in the contested
differences between Rorty and Putnam—both of whom think of themselves
as working in, and carrying on, the pragmatic tradition. Indeed, many of
the differences between Rorty and Putnam revolve around the same set of
issues that divided James and Peirce—the question of the meaning and
philosophic status of "realism."

If one extends James's understanding of temperament to Dewey, then
the diversity of the pragmatic movement—as reflected in its "founding" figures—is stretched even further. Dewey lacked Peirce's logical finesse and
hands-on knowledge of the natural sciences. He also lacked James's grace
and nuanced powers of description. Dewey is America's preeminent
philosopher of democracy. At the center of his vision and philosophic concerns are the social and political issues of the individual in a democratic
community. Of all the pragmatists he comes closest to being what Gramsci
called an "organic intellectual." Returning to the contemporary scene, it is
not surprising that Cornel West, who also thinks of himself as a committed
pragmatist seeking to restore and extend the political and social significance
of pragmatism, takes Dewey to be his great "hero"—"the greatest of the
American pragmatists."

Let me return to Dewey's own narrative of pragmatism. *Pragmatism* is not a word that Dewey frequently used to characterize his own orientation. Insofar as he used an -ism term, he preferred *instrumentalism*—although what he meant by it has little to do with what logical empiricists meant by *instrumentalism* or what the Frankfurt critical theorists meant by *instrumental reason*. Dewey's favored term was "experimentalism" or "instrumental experimentalism." What he meant is much closer to what Ian Hacking means by "intervention"—stressing the imaginative active engagement which is integral to our cognitive and practical encounters with the world.

In the early 1920s Dewey gave a narrative account of pragmatism in his article "The Development of American Pragmatism." He was aware, of course, of James's "original" narrative as well as James's popular lectures on pragmatism. He was also acquainted with Peirce's 1878 articles discussed by James and with Peirce's sharp defense of pragmaticism in his 1905 *Monist* articles.

Dewey begins by reviewing this material stressing how Peirce's statements "are quite conclusive with respect to two errors which are commonly committed in regard to the ideas of the founder of pragmatism." The first error is that pragmatism "subordinates thought and rational activity to particular ends of interest and profit."[4] Both Peirce and Dewey thought this was not only an error but also a malicious slander. Peirce emphatically declared that "if pragmaticism really made Doing to be the Be-all and end-all of life, that would be its death."[5] As Dewey emphasized, "The rule of action is that of an intermediary" whereby one attributes meaning to concepts. Dewey also stressed that Peirce's theory "is still more strongly opposed to the idea that reason or thought should be reduced to being a servant of any interest which is pecuniary or narrow."[6] Dewey is reacting against the popular charge that has long plagued the pragmatic movement, viz., that pragmatism is little more than an ideological expression of the most vulgar and objectionable aspects of American "materialism." He tells us:

> In considering a system of philosophy in its relation to national factors it is necessary to keep in mind not only the aspects of life which are incorporated in the system, but also the aspects against which the system is a protest. There never was a philosopher who has merited the name for the simple reason that he glorified the tendencies and

characteristics of his social environment; just as it is also true that there never has been a philosopher who has not seized upon certain aspects of the life of his time and idealized them.[7]

Earlier I noted that James's account of Peirce—especially "Peirce's principle"—tells us as much about James as it does about Peirce. So too, the way in which Dewey describes the differences between James and Peirce is revealing about Dewey's understanding of pragmatism and the tendencies that he emphasized in this movement.

Peirce was above all a logician; where James was an educator and humanist and wished to force the general public to realize that certain problems, certain philosophical debates, have a real importance for mankind, because the beliefs which they bring into play lead to very different modes of conduct. If this important distinction is not grasped, it is impossible to understand the majority of the ambiguities and errors which belong to the later period of the pragmatic movement.[8]

In giving his account of the development of pragmatism, Dewey—as he does in other places—assigns special importance to James's *Principles of Psychology*. What Dewey found especially significant in James's *Principles* is "the biological conceptions of the *psyche*."[9] Indirectly, Dewey is bringing forth a dimension of the pragmatic tradition that he always emphasized but that has not always received proper acknowledgment—the robust nonreductive naturalism that seeks to understand human beings as essentially biological beings always engaged in a process of organic interaction with their environments. It is this nonreductive open-ended naturalism that helps to underscore the reconstructive character of human intelligence functioning in a world understood "as being in continuous formation, where there is still a place for indeterminism, for the new, and for a real future" and where "the individual is the corner of creative thought, the author of action, and of its application."[10]

Dewey concludes his narrative of pragmatism in a characteristic manner when he affirms his "own faith in intelligence, as the one and indispensable belief necessary to moral and social life."

The more one appreciates the intrinsic esthetic, immediate value of thought and of science, the more one takes into account what intelligence itself adds to the joy and dignity of life, the more one should feel grieved at a situation in which the exercise and joy of reason are limited to a narrow, closed, and technical social group and the more it is possible to make all men participators in this inestimable wealth.[11]

If I had sufficient space, I would continue in this manner, showing how the pragmatic tradition has always been constituted and reconstituted by "argumentative retellings" of its narrative. I do not think there is any "essence" to pragmatism—or even a set of sharply defined commitments or propositions that all so-called pragmatists share. From the very beginning, pragmatism has been an essentially contested concept. I would go further, for I think that a primary reason for both the richness and diffuseness of the pragmatic tradition is the variety of voices and narratives that constitute it—even when these are strongly dissident. One would also have to do justice to the ways in which George Herbert Mead, Horace Kallen, C. I. Lewis, Sidney Hook, Ernest Nagel, Morton White, Justus Buchler, and many others, tell the story of pragmatism, and situate their own contributions within their narratives.

But I want to come to what some may consider a much more controversial part of my metanarrative. For I want to criticize what is still a widely held belief about the rise and decline of pragmatism. To be deliberately provocative, I will call this the "nostalgic" of "sentimental" story of pragmatism. It goes something like this: Once there was a golden age of American philosophy and American pragmatism. This was the time of such intellectual giants as Peirce, James, Royce, Santayana, Dewey, and Mead. Despite their differences—and even sharp antagonisms—they all shared a largesse, breadth of interest, and speculative audacity. But there has been a significant decline in the creative impulses of American philosophy and American pragmatism. America was invaded by foreign influences—positivism, logical empiricism, ordinary language analysis, which eventually congealed into the ideological smugness of the analytic establishment. By the end of the Second World War, graduate philosophy departments—with very few exceptions—were so transformed that the so-called classical American philosophers were marginalized. Those who still took the pragmatic thinkers seriously found themselves on the defensive. Most of our recent doctoral students have never even studied any of the pragmatic thinkers. There is now a prevalent patronizing attitude toward the "classic" American philosophers. They may have had their hearts in the right place but they lack the rigor, clarity, and logical sophistication that are now demanded for "serious" philosophic work. So even when philosophers who have been shaped by the analytic ethos use the term *pragmatism* favorably, they have emptied it—indeed, eviscerated it—of the rich vital meaning it once had.

Even though the above sketch is something of a caricature, it contains an element of truth. Anyone who has spent time in an academic philosophy department—especially a graduate department—knows all too well how so-called American philosophy has been marginalized and denigrated. Nevertheless I believe that this metanarrative of the rise and fall of pragmatism distorts and obscures what has been happening. It blinds us from appreciating the continuity of pragmatic concerns. What is worse, it tends to reinforce an unpragmatic parochialism and slides into the temptation of demonizing analytic philosophy. Such an attitude violates the very pluralism that pragmatism presumably advocates. Not only do I think that we need to demythologize what is labeled "analytic philosophy," I want to go further. Earlier I indicated that when future historians of philosophy look back on philosophy in America during the twentieth century, they will stress the continuity of concern and controversial debate rather than emphasizing radical breaks. And this future history—these future metanarratives—are beginning to be anticipated *now*.

Here I want to acknowledge the importance of the work of Richard Rorty. I know that there are many philosophers interested in American philosophy and especially pragmatism who are extremely hostile toward Rorty. He is sometimes viewed as the real kidnapper of pragmatism. For when Rorty speaks of "pragmatism" or "we pragmatists," his meaning is so idiosyncratic that one can barely recognize any resemblance between what he says and any of the classical pragmatists. So rather than viewing Rorty as a hero who has helped make pragmatism intellectually respectable, his critics view him as the villain in the story—who betrays the tradition he is always invoking. It is a matter of public record that over the years I have had my sharp disagreements with Rorty—and even over the issue of whether he is being "true to" what is best and most important in the pragmatic tradition.[12] But I do think that Rorty—perhaps more effectively than anyone else—has shown that there is a way of reading such thinkers as Quine,

Sellars, Davidson, and Putnam—sometimes even against their own self-understanding—as contributing to the ongoing refinement of pragmatic themes.

It is well known that Quine himself spoke of pragmatism in his classic article "Two Dogmas of Empiricism." What is less well known is that Quine's critique of the analytic-synthetic distinction was itself part of a much broader pragmatic critique of what Morton White called an "untenable dualism"—a critique shared by Quine, White, Nelson Goodman, and the young Hilary Putnam. Morton White self-consciously related this critique to Dewey's attacks on the epistemological dualisms so characteristic of modern philosophy.[13] Sellars's famous claim in "Empiricism and the Philosophy of Mind" that "empirical knowledge, like its sophisticated extension science, is rational, not because it has a foundation, but because it is a self-correcting enterprise which can put any claim in jeopardy, though not *all* at once" might almost serve as a cardinal principle which all the pragmatists would endorse.[14] Although Rorty's interpretation of Davidson is as "original" as his readings of Quine and Sellars, I do think he has effectively shown how Davidson's own version of holism, and his demythologizing of "truth" can be related to, and integrated into a continuous (albeit contested) pragmatic legacy.[15] Now this reinterpretation of the continuity—if even in subterranean ways—of the pragmatic legacy is not unique in Rorty. There are now a number of us who see it this way. Hilary Putnam, who increasingly understands his own philosophic work as fitting in with and continuing in the pragmatic tradition, declares in the preface to his *Realism with a Human Face:*

> All of these ideas—that the fact/value dichotomy is untenable, that the fact/convention dichotomy is also untenable, that truth and justification of ideas are closely connected, that the alternative to metaphysical realism is not any form of skepticism, that philosophy is an attempt to achieve the good—are ideas that have been long associated with the American pragmatist tradition. Realizing this has led me (sometimes with assistance of Ruth Anna Putnam) to make the effort to better understand that tradition from Peirce right up to Quine and Goodman.[16]

I also think that Cornel West's "genealogy of pragmatism" and some of my own writings have helped contribute to this revised understanding of the continuity and vitality of pragmatism.[17] Of course Rorty, Putnam, West, and I disagree about how to tell this metanarrative.[18] We all think that our differences have pragmatically significant consequences. But if we take Alasdair MacIntyre's statement seriously—that a tradition "is only recovered by an argumentative retelling of that narrative which will itself be in conflict with other argumentative retellings" then this conflict of contested metanarratives is precisely what one would expect in a philosophically vital tradition. And this—as I have tried to indicate—has been characteristic throughout the history of the pragmatic tradition, even from its "origins."

Still it will be objected that, even if one grants that there has been some continuity, this is rather superficial. And this "continuity" has been at the expense of a considerable narrowing of scope. For the contemporary "neopragmatism" simply lacks the scope, the breadth, the speculative audacity of the classic pragmatic thinkers. In one sense this is undeniable although it is also misleading. For if we look at the resurgence of pragmatism, not just in the academic discipline of philosophy but in the range of social and cultural disciplines, then we can detect many signs of a new breadth. Here let me restrict myself to one aspect of this resurgence which I believe is vitally important.

Recently a number of scholars of Dewey and Mead have helped to retrieve the radical impulses of the democratic ethos that was integral to their understanding of pragmatism and their participation in social reform. I am thinking of the excellent scholarship on Mead by Mitchell Aboulafia, Hans Joas, and Dmitri Shalin, the magnificent study of John Dewey by Robert Westbrook, and the forthcoming book on Dewey by Alan Ryan.[19] It is certainly true that the pragmatic themes that one finds in Quine, Sellars, Davidson, the early Putnam, and Rorty barely deal with social and political issues of a democratic community. During the past two decades even this has begun to change. Since the publication of *Philosophy and the Mirror of Nature*, Rorty himself has turned his attention to the role of politics in our everyday lives. He has chided left-wing American intellectuals for giving up on what he calls "real politics"—the politics of everyday life where the rich and strong exploit the poor and the weak. He scorns those "postmodern radical" intellectuals who have become so obsessed with "cultural politics" of the academy that they ignore the disintegration of the black underclass of our cities who find that the only "viable" economic option open to them is a life of crime. In his autobiographical sketch, "Trotsky and the Wild Orchids," Rorty clearly identifies himself with the progressivist side of democratic politics. He speaks of the cultural war that is now taking place which will decide

> whether our country continues along the trajectory defined by the Bill of Rights, the Reconstruction Amendments, the building of the land grant colleges, female suffrage, the New Deal, Brown vs. the Board of Education, the building of the community colleges, Martin Luther King's civil rights movement, the feminist, and the gay rights movement. Following this trajectory would mean America will continue to set examples of increasing tolerance and equality.[20]

When Rorty writes in this vein he is carrying on the tradition of John Dewey.[21] Hilary Putnam has also turned his attention to the ethical and political consequences of pragmatism. He not only agrees with the classical pragmatists that we cannot make a sharp distinction between fact and value, he also wants to retrieve the idea that philosophy is concerned with practical wisdom and leading a good life. More specifically, he wants to show the consequences of a pragmatic orientation for democratic practices.[22]

But the thinker who has most dramatically sought to retrieve, appropriate, and extend the radical democratic ethos of American pragmatism has been Cornel West. And more than that: West by "his own power, provocation and personality" has attempted to revitalize the Deweyan tradition of the public intellectual—the responsible engaged intellectual who addresses a wider public which is not restricted to university communities. Sometimes I am skeptical about the substantive content of West's "prophetic pragmatism," which is so rhetorical and programmatic. When one asks hard pragmatic questions about what precisely West is advocating, the answers are not always clear.[23] But we should not forget that a similar type of objection was frequently raised against Dewey. What is impressive about West's pragmatic orientation is the way in which he is able to address contemporary issues of racism, sexism, religious bigotry, and the growing nihilism of black urban ghetto life without succumbing to the various types of extremism and fanaticism that are so prevalent in our time.

In emphasizing the retrieval and continuity of the radical participatory democratic ethos of the classical pragmatists—especially Dewey and Mead—my intention has been to illustrate what is now happening. For what I think is most exciting and promising about the recent resurgence of pragmatism is its scope, breadth, and depth. It is certainly not limited to "technical" issues concerning "meaning" and "truth." There are many signs of an increasing concern with what Dewey called "the problems of men"—the problems of human beings—and not merely "the problems of philosophers."[24]

Let me conclude by tying together some of the threads. I have argued that the pragmatic movement has always been characterized by a conflict of narratives and metanarratives. "Pragmatism" has always been an essentially contested concept. We should not smooth out the sharp differences of temperament, doctrine, and concern of the pragmatic thinkers. One of the best, most pithy characterizations of a community that I know of is "a group of individuals locked in argument." From its beginnings the pragmatic movement has been an ongoing argument—one in which the participants have raised dissonant voices, and at times have spoken at cross-purposes. The great danger for those of us who have been concerned to keep alive the pragmatic tradition is the danger of nostalgia and sentimentality—a refusal to recognize what needs to be clarified, revised, or even abandoned. We may continue to draw inspiration from the classic pragmatic thinkers, but I cannot think of a more unpragmatic attitude than focusing exclusively on the past rather than on the present and the future. We must also take seriously our commitment to pluralism—even a pluralism in what is appropriated from the pragmatic legacy. Such a pluralism is not to be confused with what I once called "flabby" pluralism—where one falsely assumes that one story or narrative is just as good as another. This is just what I am denying. The pluralism that I take to be characteristic of a vital pragmatism is an engaged pragmatism where we continue the ongoing process of being locked in argument. The contours of pragmatism have always been fuzzy. This is at once a source of its vitality and a frustration for those trying to define it.

Still, it may be objected that even if the contours of pragmatism are vague, there are some characteristics that distinguish pragmatism from other philosophic orientations. I do not want to deny this, but I think similarities and differences are best characterized as family resemblances. Unfortunately the term "family resemblances" has itself been abused and weakened. We should remember that when Wittgenstein spoke of family resemblances, the expression had strong somatic resonances. Not all similarities and differences are to be classified as family resemblances. If we think of how we concretely speak of family resemblances, then we should recognize that although there may be striking resemblances among members of a family, nevertheless individuals within a family (like individual pragmatists) may be strikingly different in their appearance.

I am *not* suggesting that it is inappropriate to try to specify—as James, Peirce, Dewey, Rorty, Putnam, and even I have done—what one takes to be the primary characteristics of a pragmatic orientation. This is essential for our "argumentative retellings." Rather I am calling for a more *self-reflective* attitude about this endeavor—an awareness that in doing so "we" are making a claim about what "we" think is (or ought to be) *taken* as most central and important in pragmatism. We should be wary of anyone who claims that there are *fixed* criteria by which we can decide who is and who is not a pragmatist. Such boundary setting is not only unpragmatic, it is frequently used as a power play to legitimize unexamined prejudices. And those of us who identify ourselves with the pragmatic tradition should be especially alert to the abuse of such boundary fixing—for it has been used to marginalize pragmatism. Slightly parodying the concluding remarks of Rorty's *Philosophy and the Mirror of Nature*, I would say: the only point on which we should insist is that the pragmatist's concern should be with continuing the argument—to continue our argumentative retellings of the pragmatic legacy which will be in conflict with other argumentative retellings. This is the way in which we honor the imperative Do not block the road of inquiry!

RESPONSE TO RICHARD BERNSTEIN

I enthusiastically agree with almost everything Richard Bernstein says in his paper, which is why I have less to say about it than about other papers in this volume. Bernstein seems to me absolutely and importantly right in saying that "pragmatism" is constituted by narratives and in suggesting that there is always room to expand such narratives into longer ones, incorporating additional figures. I wholeheartedly agree with the remark he quotes from Alasdair MacIntyre: that a tradition "is only recovered by an argumentative reading of the narrative which will be in conflict with other argumentative readings."

I also agree with Daniel Dennett's description of selves as "centers of narrative gravity," so I do not think that pragmatism has a True Self, any more than America does. Competing narratives about America are competing proposals for what America should become, and the same goes for competing narratives about pragmatism. The various competing descriptions of pragmatism that are scattered through this volume are abbreviations for rival narratives. The reader's job is to pick out useful strands from each and therewith weave a new, improved narrative. Only if these narratives continue on beyond Dewey's death, however, will it be possible to think of pragmatism as a living philosophical movement. That is why I think Bernstein makes an important point when he protests against nostalgic and sentimental accounts of "the Golden Age of American Philosophy."

Handy terms like "German idealism" or "American pragmatism" or "international postmodernism" could not have gained currency if historians of philosophy looked only for community of doctrine—for propositions agreed to by all the figures grouped under such rubrics. Rather, these isms are created by saying: Here were a bunch of thinkers who shared a spatio-temporal site, some influences, many enemies, some problems, and maybe even some doctrines. Saying that, and writing a narrative about these philosophers that creates the kind of self we call an "ism", is a useful thing to do. It is useful even if the philosophers who find themselves (or their shades) sorted out in this way feel uncomfortable with those with whom they are urged to associate.[1] To create such isms you have to temporarily ignore, for example, Hegel's sarcasm about Schelling, Peirce's sardonic remarks about James, and Derrida's and Foucault's sneers at one another.

When I use the phrase to which Bernstein refers, and to which my critics object—"we pragmatists"—I am implicitly saying: try, for the nonce, ignoring the differences between Putnam and Peirce, Nietzsche and James, Davidson and Dewey, Sellars and Wittgenstein. Focus on the following similarities, and then other similarities may leap out at you. To grasp my nonce, idiosyncratic sense of "pragmatist," forget Sellars on picturing, Dewey on scientific method, Wittgenstein on nonsense, and Nietzsche on big strong warriors. Bracket these and other doctrines that strike me as wrong, or parochial, or tangential, and repackage what is left. The sort of repackaging job which such nonce usages permit seems to be an important element in the construction of narratives.

I think it important to construct a narrative that links the three "classical" pragmatists to Quine, Putnam, and Davidson because I agree with Bernstein that the neglect of the former in American philosophy departments is a mistake, and that the mistake will only be corrected if such a narrative is available. Such a narrative has to get across the point that the linguistic turn was neither a world-historical event, in the course of which philosophers gained a kind of clarity hitherto unknown, nor a lapse into the world-weary frivolity characteristic of what Lavine calls "the troops of the disenchanted, the generation of the college-educated in America, for whom the 1960s fervor has long since burned out" (48)—the people among whom, she believes, I find my readers.

The enthusiasm for the linguistic turn which changed the character of American philosophy departments was due in large part to exasperation with the interminable debates that went on in the 1920s and 1930s between Dewey and Lovejoy, Dewey and Arthur Murphy, Dewey and Russell, Dewey and C. I. Lewis—the sorts of debates one finds in the Schilpp volume on Dewey. A lot of first-rate philosophers, in the 1940s and

1950s, were saying that they could never figure out which side of a given issue Dewey wanted to be on. A consensus had grown up that Dewey's terminology fudged, rather than clarifying, the realism-idealism issue as well as the issues between utilitarians and their critics.

One may think (though I do not) that that consensus was ignorant, or hasty, or wrong-headed. But it was nevertheless real. Along about 1945, American philosophers were, for better or worse, *bored* with Dewey, and thus with pragmatism. They were sick of being told that pragmatism was the philosophy of American democracy, that Dewey was the great American intellectual figure of their century, and the like. They wanted something new, something they could get their philosophical teeth into. What showed up, thanks to Hitler and various other historical contingencies, was logical empiricism, an early version of what we now call "analytic philosophy."

The incursion of this kind of philosophy was neither a triumph of light over darkness and of intelligence over obscurantism nor a debacle, in which the great tradition of American philosophy was mindlessly discarded in favor of unsavory foreign imports. It was, like all such incursions, a mixed blessing. In my judgment it represented a temporarily fruitful confusion of a *very* good idea (that language was a more fruitful topic for philosophical reflection than experience) with a couple of rather bad ones (that there was something worth preserving in empiricism; that deep philosophical significance could be found in the first-order functional calculus). The narrative I have tried to construct in my books tells how the bad ideas gradually, in the course of the 1950s and 1960s, got filtered out and thus made it possible for pragmatism to get a new lease on life by undergoing linguistification.[2]

As I argue in "Dewey between Hegel and Darwin," the linguistic turn was essential if Darwin was to be taken seriously by philosophers. As I say in "Philosophy and the Future," we are still engaged in coming to terms with Darwin—still trying to rework old, Greek ways of speaking about human beings, ways that are dualistic (in the pejorative sense that Dewey gave to that term) through and through. We are still trying to make these ways of speaking chime with Darwin's account of human beings as complicated animals, containing no special extra ingredient. This is the sort of job that can hardly be done in less than a couple of centuries. My hunch is that, just as we see philosophy from 1630 to 1800 ("Descartes to Kant") as an attempt to come to terms with corpuscularian mechanics, future historians will see philosophy from 1860 to (at least) 2060 as an attempt to come to terms with "the biological conceptions of the psyche" that Dewey found in James, and which James developed in response to Huxley and Darwin.[3]

Whereas Bernstein's narratives about pragmatism usually put Dewey's social thought, and its contribution to the self-consciousness of American democracy, at the center of the story, mine tend to center around James's version (or, at least, certain selected versions out of the many that James casually tossed off) of the pragmatic theory of truth. I view the development of the modern democracies as one among many symptoms of a more general change in our self-image, a change as visible in literature as in politics. Darwin's importance lies, ultimately, in having helped make this change occur faster and more smoothly.

One way to describe this change in self-image is to say that human beings (in the richer and more powerful parts of the world) have shown an increasing ability to put aside the question What is the meaning of human life? and to substitute the question What meaning shall *we* give to *our* lives? Men and women in the last two hundred years have become increasingly able to get along without the thought that there must be a deep truth about themselves, a truth that it is their job to discover. This has produced an increased ability to brush aside the suspicion that we are under the authority of something not ourselves: that there is a narrator (roughly, God or Nature) of our lives other than ourselves, a narrator whose description of us must necessarily be superior to any that we dream up on our own (because it describes our True Self).

To escape this latter thought is to think of human beings, either individually or in groups, as self-creators. So my preferred narrative is a story of human beings as having recently gotten out from under the thought of, and the need for, *authority*. I see James's suggestion that we carry utilitarianism over from morals into epistemology as crucial to this anti-authoritarian movement of the spirit. For James shows us how to see Truth not as something we have to respect, but as a pointless nominalization of the useful adjective we apply to beliefs that are getting us what we want. Ceasing to see Truth as the name of an authority and coming to see the search for stable and useful beliefs as simply one more part of the pursuit of happiness are essential if we are to have the experimental attitude toward social existence that Dewey commended and the experimental attitude toward individual existence that Romanticism commended.

5

WHAT IS THE LEGACY

OF INSTRUMENTALISM?

RORTY'S INTERPRETATION OF DEWEY

James Gouinlock

The inheritance from John Dewey has been diverse, and the course of history will likely produce a number of different philosophies claiming direct lineage from his ideas. Such developments will testify to the fecundity of his thought. My intent in this paper is not to speculate about such possibilities, however, but to correct serious misunderstandings of Dewey by Richard Rorty. Rorty continues to call himself a pragmatist and, more specifically, a Deweyan.[1] Insofar as he succeeds in appropriating Dewey's legacy, he will reject what was surely dearest to Dewey himself.

A number of scholars have already written incisively on various aspects of Rorty's *sui distant* pragmatism. They include Brodsky, Edel, Sleeper, Campbell, Alexander, and Boisvert.[2] Sleeper, Campbell, and Alexander have been especially concerned with the moral implications of Rorty's treatment of Dewey, and it is this theme that particularly interests me. My point will be to address issues to which they advert but do not examine in detail. I do not build upon their respective arguments, but start from the beginning. Accordingly, I offer just the barest statement of the views of each.

Rorty, as we know, has distinguished the "good" from the "bad," or "backsliding," Dewey.[3] The good Dewey is antirealist, antimethod, and antimetaphysics, among other things. His principal metaphysical work, *Experience and Nature*, is an epiphany of the "bad" Dewey, and it were better that *Logic: The Theory of Inquiry* had never been written at all.[4] Sleeper attacks these claims frontally, arguing that the *Logic*, more than any other work, culminates Dewey's philosophy, and the *Logic* is predicated on the naturalistic metaphysics of *Experience and Nature*. Sleeper articulates and defends what he calls Dewey's "transactional realism," and he stresses that the great end and function of this realism is to support "the theory of intelligent behavior."[5] In my judgment, Sleeper is correct in this, but he stops short of telling us much about just what this theory of intelligent behavior is. Much in the same vein, Campbell urges that Rorty neglects Dewey's uppermost concern and guiding aim as a philosopher: the commitment to a *methodic* social reconstruction.[6] In other words, Rorty fails to recognize the central importance to Dewey of working out a view of the organically inseparable relation of theory and practice. The gravamen of Alexander's polemic is much the same.[7] It is not part of their respective discussions, however, to contend with Rorty specifically in respect to the role of scientific thinking in moral conduct. For his part, Rorty is not unaware of Dewey's moral commitments, but they are pronounced to be no more than "ungrounded social hope."[8]

I

Rorty's main thesis, which he finds conspicuous in pragmatism, is that objective knowledge is impossible. We are mistaken in supposing that we can use reality to test ideas; we are mistaken in supposing that ideas are in any direct sense about real existences. Propositions do not correspond to, represent, or picture an objective world. The world is "well lost."[9] We do not compare a description to an object, but only to another description, and there is no neutral criterion for saying one description is better than another. Accordingly, we cannot make distinctions regarding cognitive validity between science, philosophy, poetry, religion, theology, and scriptural faith. All, Rorty insists, are literary genres. Hence also, we cannot distinguish between methods of inquiry as being better or worse, and we cannot speak of progress in knowledge, even in science.

At first glance, what seems to be primarily at work here is the famous thesis of the incommensurability of translation, owing principally to Quine and Kuhn. According to this theory, the meaning of observation statements in any alleged body of knowledge is determined by a theory, and any theory is incommensurable with any other. Translations between theories proceed by assumptions and principles within the theory in which a translation is constructed. Hence scientists and philosophers of science will hope in vain that observation statements will provide a way of comparing or commensurating alternative theories. Rorty accepts this conclusion, but he does not accept the premise of incommensurability, which he acknowledges is self-refuting.[10] Indeed, he believes he rids himself of the baggage of both incommensurability and relativism, observing that both conceptions presuppose that competing claims are relative or incommensurate according to some criterion.[11] Inasmuch as criteria belong to epistemology, incommensurability and relativism perish with epistemology.

What is at work is the contingency of language.[12] Language, and all systems of thought, are nothing but literalized metaphors. Metaphors, as such, are meaningless, for to have a meaning is to have a role in a language game.[13] Hence language, or a vocabulary, is the child of the sheer contingency of metaphor. This conclusion does not mean that there are no constraints on language and inquiry. The constraints are sociological, historical, or conversational. Due to the sociological constraints imposed by any community or subculture, its members converse in the given vocabulary, and there are no theory-neutral criteria for selecting one vocabulary in preference to others. Rorty says of the supposed achievements of modern science that they are no more than the triumph of a certain rhetoric.[14]

These are conclusions imputed to pragmatists and, above all, to Dewey. Dewey is to be honored, Rorty says, for "overcoming the tradition." The tradition that Rorty has in mind is the hoary philosophic enterprise of establishing a theory of being, a theory of knowledge, or a theory of language that will provide a rationally incontrovertible criterion in terms of which we can distinguish objectively true knowledge claims. This is the foundationalist's enterprise, and Dewey is said to have devastated it.

What shall we say of this interpretation of Dewey's philosophy? It seems so obviously mistaken that a scholar could refute it in a few paragraphs, as we shall see. Rorty, however, can always impute inconvenient evidence to the "bad" Dewey. This stratagem implies that there are in fact two Deweys. If there are, where is the "good" Dewey? Where does Rorty find the sort of evidence that makes Dewey resemble a deconstructionist? Admittedly, Dewey never won any prizes for clarity. There are many obscure, ill-expressed, and confusing passages in his works, and a scholar might understand them in various ways. One can only guess how Rorty would take a given passage, however, for he rarely cites specific texts. His references to pragmatism are typically offhand, rather than carefully documented.[15]

From several possible sources of misunderstanding, I shall select five that might seem particularly to lend themselves to his interpretation. The most important, which will be the last that I attend to, is Dewey's relation to the classic tradition, and it is here that Dewey's metaphysics is especially relevant. First, however, something must be said about the "bad" Dewey, for this, I believe, is the only Dewey, and it is here that we must eventually look for what is precious in his heritage.

II

Pre-Rortian students of Dewey's thought will be astonished to learn that Dewey was "beyond method," and their astonishment is justified. Starting at least with *Studies in Logical Theory* in 1903, and consummating in *Logic: The Theory of Inquiry* in 1938, he was persistently concerned with the nature of scientific method and its applicability to all types of human predicaments. On various occasions he characterized the method in detail. He does so in *The Quest for Certainty*, for example, and in that volume he declares: "the value of any cognitive conclusion depends on the *method* by which it is reached, so that the perfecting of method, the perfecting of intelligence, is the thing of supreme value."[16] He says things are "*known* in as far as their constituents and their forms are the result of science."[17] There follows a chapter entitled "The Supremacy of Method."

Anyone who makes even a preliminary foray into Dewey's educational writings, moreover, learns that the acquisition of experimental habits of inquiry is one of the foremost aims of education—perhaps the paramount aim. Dewey's objection to religions was not primarily in their specific dogmas, but in the habits of thought that they generate and utilize: "What is not realized . . . is that the issue does not concern this and that piecemeal *item* of belief, but centers in the method by which any and every item of intellectual belief is to be arrived at and justified. . . . The fundamental question, I repeat, is not of this and that article of . . . belief but of intellectual habit, method and criterion. "[18]

The virtue of the method is not that it attains final truth, but that it is self-corrective, progressive, just as Peirce had characterized it in his epochal article, "The Fixation of Belief." Some of its further virtues will be noted later, but for the moment we need only note that there is textual evidence beyond the point of satiety that Dewey was convinced there is a scientific method and convinced that its universalization might well be the salvation of the human race.

> [T]he outstanding problem of our civilization is set by the fact that common sense in its content, its "world" and methods, is a house divided against itself. It consists in part, and that part the most vital, of regulative meanings and procedures that antedate the rise of experimental science in its conclusions and methods. In another part, it is what it is because of the application of science. This cleavage marks every phase and aspect of modern life. . . .
>
> It is for this reason that it is here affirmed that the basic problem of present culture and associated living is that of effecting integration where division now exists. The problem cannot be solved apart from a unified method of attack and procedure.[19]

And again: "The demand for reform of logic is the demand for a unified theory of inquiry through which the authentic pattern of experimental and operational inquiry of science shall become available for regulation of the habitual methods by which inquiries in the field of common sense are carried on."[20]

No doubt Dewey is premature in speaking of *the* scientific method (he was sometimes more cautious), but it is clear all the same that he did not think of himself as "beyond method." The important functions of method will be brought out in the following inquiry into how Rorty tries to make the author of such statements into a "good" pragmatist.

III

Attention to method will be the first of the five themes that might be construed in a manner favorable to Rorty's interpretation. Rorty quotes with approval from a discussion in Dewey's *Human Nature and Conduct*: "The elaborate systems of science are not born of reason but of impulses at first sight flickering; impulses to handle, to move about, to hunt, to uncover, to mix things separated and divide things combined, to talk and to listen. Method is their effectual organization into continuous dispositions of inquiry, development, and testing. . . . Reason, the rational attitude, is the resulting disposition."[21] Rorty characterizes these statements as a move "beyond method," and a couple of pages later he quotes from the same page, where Dewey speaks of rationality as "a working harmony among diverse desires."[22]

Recognition of the context of Dewey's discussion suggests a different interpretation. His general subject matter is "The Place of Intelligence in Conduct," and he argues that intelligence, or reason, is not an original faculty of human nature, but is a function of behavior. The immediate context is a discussion of rationality *as a trait of character*: what is also called reasonableness, or in Dewey's own terms here, "the rational *attitude*" or "*disposition*."[23] Rationality, Dewey insists, is not an inherent faculty, contradistinguished from the faculty of desire. It is a particular organization of desires, or—more properly—habits, which incorporate desire. It is not disembodied reason, but these habits—such as handling, mixing, moving about—that generate science. When desires function as a certain complex of habits, they are methodical, or rational. Dewey at this point says nothing about the formal properties of method, he writes at length about the dispositions that unite to make us reasonable. There is no justification for treating these passages as a treatise against scientific method or as a reduction of method to a balancing of desires. Dewey is here concerned with psychology, not logic.

Given Rorty's interpretation, however, it is no surprise to find him saying, typically, "Dewey wants the distinctions between art, science and philosophy to be rubbed out."[24] If method is a myth, then, of course, there is equal cognitive worth (or worthlessness) to art and science and, presumably, to reading tea leaves as well; but Rorty has again missed the point. Dewey frequently attacked the assumption that art and science are utterly different. They share, in fact, a fundamentally important trait: they are both forms of practice—the reconstruction of materials of ordinary experience into a new order, in which the reordering is directed by a more or less explicit plan. Artistic creativity is not conceived as the exclusive work of a subjective and private faculty, and science is not conceived as addressing a realm of reality transcending events of ordinary experience. The artist, of course, aims at a reconstruction to be judged by aesthetic criteria, while the scientist intends to discover the relations of dependence between experienced phenomena under controlled conditions.[25] Dewey's claim that art, science, and practical activity have significant subject matter and procedures in common is an instance of the position already documented: the perplexities of modern life require unified method. This is not the eradication of method, but its extension to all problems of conduct. It is not a denial of disciplined intelligence, but a demand for it.

The second confusion stems from Dewey's repudiation of the correspondence theory of truth, to which Rorty adverts on several occasions. Perhaps here there is ground for concluding that Dewey believed that objects do not constrain truth claims. He repeatedly says that ideas do not correspond to, represent, refer to, or picture antecedent reality. But in the qualifier "antecedent," we find the drastic difference between Dewey's view and that of Rorty. Dewey's objections to traditional realisms consisted above all in their assumption that a full-fledged object of knowledge exists prior to inquiry. Inquiry, he says, is initiated just because the situation is problematic in some crucial way. Prior to inquiry, the status of relevant events in the environment is somehow puzzling or uncertain; otherwise, inquiry would not occur. The very process of inquiry is inseparable from manipulating and organizing overt events, and its intent is to *produce* the full-fledged object. Clearly, it is not reducible to conversation.

Dewey's reflections on this issue are not confined to procedures of inquiry; they have to do with the psychology of perception as well. Starting with "The Reflex Arc Concept in Psychology" and continuing through several writings, he argued that a perception is not a virgin image, appearing in systematic articulation to the passive spectator. It is an outcome of complex interactions of the organism and the environment.[26] In order to produce objects of perception (as of knowledge) suitable to the peculiarities of a problematic situation, some sort of intentional reorientation toward the troubling conditions must be undertaken. Rorty (like many of Dewey's critics) has missed this crucial and remarkably innovative constituent of Dewey's theory of knowledge.

Following Peirce and James, Dewey says that ideas are neither summaries of what has already occurred nor intuitions of essences. Ideas are anticipations of the future. Expressed in propositions, they are hypotheses or predictions. If this is a mushroom, for example, it will display certain qualities, including its culinary and nutritive uses. If it is a toadstool, it will show some similar, but some crucially different, traits under test. Inasmuch as ideas are predictors of events, they are validated by what they entail, rather than by their antecedents or by comparison to an archetype. Neither are they validated by comparing a subjective image to an external object. To tell the difference between mushrooms and toadstools, we need no recourse to Platonic forms; we just see which ones make us violently ill. Dewey called this view the true correspondence theory.27

So much is familiar to students of Dewey's instrumentalism. What is equally familiar is the notion that the meaning of ideas is intrinsically related to action *with an environment.* Of necessity, as the respective properties of objects vary, our behavior with them must vary. Due to the differences between mushrooms and toadstools, our conceivable interactions with the former must differ in some ways from our conceivable interactions with the latter. Hence the full idea of the object denoted by *mushroom* is the sum of the conceivable behaviors that can be taken with that fungus, including all manner of experimental tests that might be conducted.

Dewey, accordingly, frequently refers to ideas as plans of action. This notion will be clearer if we speak of hypotheses rather than ideas. In a perfectly straightforward sense, hypotheses direct conduct. They specify that if certain conditions are introduced, certain consequences will follow, and the hypothesis is tested by undertaking just the actions prescribed. If you consume this little gray fungus, it will nauseate you; if you make certain observations with prescribed instruments at a prescribed place and time on a prescribed date, you will observe an eclipse of the moon. We deliberately institute certain conditions and manage them in definite ways—as prescribed by the hypothesis—in order to attain an outcome consequent upon the process, as predicted by the hypothesis. If the hypothesis is incorrect, there will be failure in activity; the objects turn out to be such that interactions with them do not occur as projected. Nature has its way in the end.

One would normally feel apologetic about reciting such routine features of instrumentalism, but Rorty's influence might be such as to convince many scholars that there is no need to study Dewey's writings at first hand, much less to investigate their implications for the conduct of life. Accordingly, I will introduce an additional feature of Dewey's philosophy that bears on his particular realism and devastates Rorty's imputation of antirealism.

I have in mind Dewey's notion of habit, as articulated especially in *Human Nature and Conduct.* Nothing is more fundamental in his analysis than the notion that human nature is constituted of habits. Habits are forms of action, and they are a function of the behavior of the individual and the environment together. A child manipulates objects, acts on them in various ways—beats on them, chews them, squeezes and shakes them—and the features of the resultant behavior are as much a product of the properties of the object as of the impulsive activities of the child. Hence the child learns to treat fire differently from water, cats differently from rubber balls, and so. Thus an appropriate repertoire of habits develops. In Dewey's terms, to have a habit, then, is to possess the meaning of an object, to be able to act toward it appropriately. In an awkward but telling remark, he says "objects represent habits turned inside out."[28] Habit formation, of course, is not just the work of children; growth is lifelong. Moreover, as indicated previously, Dewey regards experimental inquiry as a methodic, directed refinement of the same impulses that initiate habit formation.

It is hard to imagine a theory of ideas more rigorously controlled by the nature of objects than this one. A Platonic or Cartesian essence, by contrast, gives us not the first clue as to how natural events might deliberately be seized and redirected to desired outcomes. Likewise, an idea conceived as an image or a composite of sensations is equally impotent in conduct. An image, as such, has no implications. Knowledge as Dewey conceived it, is of the meanings of natural events. It is constrained by these events, and life depends on its accuracy. "The exacting conditions imposed by nature, that have to be observed in order that work be carried through to success, are the source of all noting and recording of nature's doings. They supply the discipline that chastens exuberant fancy into respect for the operation of events, and that effects subjection of thought to a pertinent order of space and time."[29]

A third and closely allied issue is Dewey's philosophy of science, and in this connection he has made many statements that might well have caught Rorty's attention and convinced him that Dewey is a "good" philosopher. Dewey likes to make such statements as the following: "Scientific conceptions are not a revelation of prior and independent reality. They are a system of hypotheses, worked out under conditions of definite test, by means of which our intellectual and practical traffic with nature is rendered freer, more secure and more significant."[30] Remarks of this sort might be taken to be an allusion to what Rorty, rather darkly, calls coping—we use our ideas to "cope," but we could not claim, presumably, that our ideas refer to an extralinguistic reality. Dewey, indeed, convinced more than one critic by such statements that he was a crypto-idealist.[31]

An interpretation of the passage just quoted would have to draw on the particular nature of Dewey's correspondence theory, as outlined above, but still more should be added. What we know, in the sciences and elsewhere, are nature's potentialities *under definite conditions.* The object of knowledge is the correlation between distinguishable processes of change—as pressure, for example, varies with temperature in an enclosed volume of gas. These specific changes are deliberately introduced and controlled by the inquirer, and the object of knowledge is the correlation between just these variations. Dewey was much taken by this procedure, emphasizing in particular the deliberate introduction of variations. That is, the process of inquiry does not passively observe a static reality; it is concerned with relations of *change.* It *produces* change in order to see what follows from it. This procedure does not imply that "antecedent reality" is utterly plastic. If it were, indeed, then it would be absurd to believe that anything in particular followed from variations in it. As Dewey said:

> Were it not for the teachings of sad experience, it would not be necessary to add that the change in environment made by knowing is not a total or miraculous change. Transformation, readjustment, reconstruction all imply prior existences: existences which have characters and behaviors of their own which must be accepted, consulted, humored, manipulated or made light of, in all kinds of differing ways in the different contexts of different problems. Making a difference in reality does not mean making any more difference than we find *can* be made under the given conditions—even though we may still hope for different fortune another time under other circumstances.[32]

Science may function teleologically. It may introduce change in order to achieve a desired result. It has massively increased our power to introduce deliberate control of natural events, and this is why Dewey was so enamored of it and wanted so much that it be adopted as a constituent part—but *only* a part—of all practical endeavor. It makes the difference between "arts of acceptance and arts of control."[33] It is precisely because the object of knowledge is the correlation between processes of change that we are able to introduce deliberate variations and novelty. We may vary the elements in a process and introduce new conditions and thereby change its outcome in a predictable manner. We could not do so if definite relationships were not discovered. Nature indeed has its "brute structure of things," as Dewey called it.[34] We cannot break the law of gravity; our lungs cannot extract oxygen from water; and we cannot grow vegetables in ice or on the desert.

However, with further knowledge of nature we can introduce new interactions. We can build flying machines and parachutes, submarines and aqualungs, greenhouses and systems of irrigation. Dewey is interminably calling for controlled experiments that will reorder natural processes in behalf of human growth and well-being. It is precisely knowledge of specific extralinguistic relations that would give us the means to convert disease into health, privation into plenty, peril into security, conflict into harmony, frustration into growth, vice into virtue.

A fourth possible source of misunderstanding is Dewey's philosophy of language. Although Rorty offers no systematic study of Dewey's views on this subject, one suspects that this might be a crucial issue. Perhaps something closely akin to Rorty's language-game theory can be found in Dewey's writings. Like Dewey, Rorty speaks of language as a tool, but he assimilates the notion of language as tool to the language-game notion. "The Deweyan notion of language as tool rather than picture is right as far as it goes. But we must be careful *not* to phrase this analogy so as to suggest that one can separate the tool, Language, from its users and inquire as to its 'adequacy' to achieve our purposes. The latter suggestion presupposes that there is some way of breaking out of language in order to compare it with something else."[35] Dewey himself, Rorty believes, did not hold the errant presupposition. He says that if we understood Dewey, "we would be receptive to notions like Derrida's—that language is not a device for representing reality, but a reality in which we live and move."[36]

Dewey says: "Language . . . is the cherishing mother of all significance."[37] Events would be all but meaningless without language, and, in fact, we would be mindless without it, in Dewey's conviction.[38] At the same time, he is fond of reiterating that language is a function of social action and is saturated with cultural bias: the meaning of words for a person in any society is determined by the beliefs and behavior of its members. This seems indistinguishable from Rorty's view that vocabulary reduces to sociology.

The similarity is misleading. Dewey's claim is that language is a function of shared activity, again, *with an environment*. Features of our surroundings—trees, rivers, fish, animals, friends, enemies, the earth, implements of all kinds, and so on, without limit—enter into shared life in a multitude of crucial ways. Language, Dewey argues, is whatever succeeds in creating concerted activity with just such things. The properties of these *things* are conditions of meaningful discourse, depending on how they are incorporated into conduct in a particular culture. A long, cylindrical piece of wood, for example, has various uses. It is a spear, a fishing pole, something to propel a raft with, something to hang your clothes on, a scepter, a quarterstaff, a shepherd's staff, a combustible, and so on. In every case, real properties of the object are registered in language. Were it not so, shared conduct with the object in the expected way could not succeed.

Dewey is surely not flirting with the language-game theory. His view is instrumentalist in the most pregnant sense: it is conceived as inseparable from properties of real existences. Language is a tool, and any tool, Dewey says, "is a thing in which a connection, a sequential bond with nature is embodied. It possesses an objective relation as its own defining property. . . . A tool denotes a perception and acknowledgment of sequential bonds in nature."[39] That is, language is a bond with nature, not an intervening obstacle. Its function attests to real connections. It connects, at any rate, if the tool is not defective; but frequently it is. The meanings of language are typically localized and limited, and they are often mistaken: *scepter* means "possessing divine power"; *black cat* means "ill fortune"; *woman* means "can't do anything but clean house and bear children"; *chicken soup* means "will heal just about anything"; and so on. We identify these meanings as deficient when their implied consequences do not in fact occur, and we remedy deficient meanings with responsible inquiry. Endorsing the cognitive primacy of scientific discourse, Dewey says it pursues a certain ideal: "the maximum convertibility of every object of thought into any and every other."[40] There are many similar remarks, and he has repeated praise for scientific abstractions, for they avoid the parochial and culture-laden biases of ordinary language, and they allow us to state the correlations of change between phenomena that are qualitatively diverse.

Even after inquiry, our experience is mediated by language, but mediation is not distortion, much less is it concealment—at least not necessarily so. To be sure, the hunter experiences the shaft as a spear, as a meaning acquired by communication and shared activity in his community. But this mediation is not distortion; it is selectivity. After all, the shaft can be hurled through the air and can penetrate the hide of the prey. The statement "This is a spear" is not tested by comparing the object in question to a prelinguistic thing-in-itself or to the perfect essence of spearhood. Neither is it tested by seeing whether the utterance is consistent with the language in use. No, it is done by using the object denoted *as* a spear—by throwing it. What more objective reality could one want?

The statement "This is a spear" is conspicuously theory laden, meaning laden, but the meaning does not conceal some underlying true being. Quite to the contrary. For experience to be meaning-laden is an indispensable asset. So long as we get them right, meanings help us to function effectively as participants in natural events.

Just as an object is not a tool except in relation to natural processes, a vocal sound cannot be an instrument of conduct except as it testifies to relations between objective events. In the jargon of their collaborative work, *Knowing and the Known*, Dewey and Bentley declare: "We reject the 'no man's land' of words imagined to lie between the organism and its environmental objects . . . and require, instead, definite locations for all naming behaviors as organic-environmental transactions."[41]

Rorty can find little comfort in Dewey's philosophy of language, but perhaps the nerve of the issue regarding the nature of Dewey's pragmatism has to do with the meaning of the classic tradition and what it means to overcome it. This is the fifth and last of my candidates for locating Rorty's "good" Dewey somewhere in Dewey's own writings. Rorty sees the classic tradition as a series of attempts to provide universal commensuration between vocabularies and to provide a vocabulary-neutral criterion of truth. If this is what the tradition is reduced to, and if the tradition is overcome, then of course there is not much for philosophers to do. One must give up on knowledge, method, progress, and intellectual authority. Because Dewey declared himself against the tradition, assaulting it repeatedly and undermining its claims, then it must be true that, in effect, he embraced Rorty's thesis that "nothing grounds our practices, nothing legitimizes them, nothing shows them to be in touch with the way things really are."[42] Thus also, Rorty is puzzled and disappointed by Dewey's recurrent backsliding, by his various forays into a metaphysics of his own, which Rorty describes as an attempt to provide "a permanent neutral matrix for future inquiry."[43]

Dewey had a much more complex appraisal of the tradition than Rorty suspects. He did reject the tradition's quest for certainty; he rejected the notion of philosophy as a superscience and a foundational discipline. Its masquerade as superscience, however, was not the only feature of the tradition that drew Dewey's attention. He was particularly concerned with its *specific* knowledge claims, whose effects he judged to be unwholesome in the extreme. I will review just a few of these claims—even neglecting one of Dewey's favorite targets, Cartesian dualism.

One of the most recurrent ideas in the classic tradition is that the true nature of things is inherently systematic and changeless. Change represents an inferior realm of being—mere appearance or mere subjectivity. According to this scheme, the really real is the object of rational knowledge, in the Platonic or Cartesian sense; so all the traits of things exclusive of such knowledge are somehow unreal, not properties of true being. The traits of ordinary life-experience are expelled from full ontological standing. The absorbing and varying qualities that give value to experience are banished; likewise the contingent, the plural, the ongoing sorts of things on which mortal life depends.

If being is changeless and eternal, the fundamental cognitive act is the direct intellectual intuition of the supremely real. Specific events are known—insofar as they can be known at all—according to their classification in conformity to the antecedent scheme. By this conception, the good is conformity to a static order. One must cognize the antecedently real and simply conform to it. Particular acts are judged by classifying them according to this order. In various guises, this view is found in Plato, theological and natural-law theories, Kant, classical liberalism, and idealism.

If change is an intrinsic trait of all existences, however, the demand for conformity represents simply a requirement to comply at any cost with the biases of a given culture, handily exempted from analysis and criticism. For an experimental logic, the good is and can only be a certain kind of activity, a unifying process of change—what Dewey called growth and elaborated at length and, I think, brilliantly. Likewise, the cognitive act must be the experimental determination of the relationships between changing events, such that situations of disorder and distress might be transformed into unified activity.

The monism of the classic tradition consists in the assumption that all things are systematically interconnected, as in the Absolute of philosophical idealism—a special target for Dewey, as it had been for James. In an obvious and crucial sense, Dewey observes, all things are not interconnected. The birth of a child in Georgia has no bearing on the failure of the rice harvest in China. Humanly significant yet independent events are among the most striking and momentous features of natural existence. Yet no process remains encapsulated. When events intersect, there is disruption, perplexity, failure in ongoing activity. We are always contending with the uncertain, unknown, unexpected, and unmanageable. Droughts, earthquakes, flat tires, uninvited visitors, illness, criminal assaults, train wrecks, and an inheritance from an unknown relative are a sampling of the numberless occasions great and small that we must somehow deal with every day. Yet in a reductively monistic philosophy they are not part of the real order of being. The contingencies of life are dismissed as an inferior level of existence. The remedy for the problems of this lower order is somehow to gain access to the higher order and conform to it, whereupon one will presumably recognize the unreality of one's confusions and torments.

In accordance with Dewey's conception of the nature of things, on the other hand, the generic task of intelligence is to reconstruct and direct processes of change that have been made problematic by the intrusion of the new and unexpected. This view is momentously different from that of the extremes of the classic tradition. The latter had a coherent view of being, the good, and reason; but the view was mistaken, and as such it was a bar to enriched, fulfilling conduct. In redefining the nature and tasks of intelligence, Dewey made a massive contribution to our self-understanding and to our powers of action.

Dewey's metaphysics, found principally in *Experience and Nature*, is the attempt to provide a generic characterization of the human involvement with the nature of things. The characterization of nature must give a full and proper account not only of order, but of change, plurality, the contingent, the qualitative, the values of life-experience, and experimental knowing. Dewey's metaphysics is emphatically not an attempt to provide "a permanent neutral matrix for future inquiry." It is an attempt to articulate a conception of reality such that our actual experience is made intelligible, such that we can identify our resources and limitations, our opportunities and liabilities in a changing precarious world—yet a world that is answerable to inquiry and intelligence, a world that can yield profoundly fulfilling experience. In brief, Dewey's metaphysics is an attempt to characterize the inclusive context of human existence in such a way that we might learn how to function in it as effectively as possible.

My own judgment is that he did so exceedingly well, but in an obvious sense *his* success or failure is immaterial. If knowledge of the salient characteristics and instrumentalities of existence is possible at all, it is eminently worthwhile to strive for it. Yet Rorty says there is nothing of that sort that can be gained, and he apparently feels no loss at our alleged impotence.

Dewey could hardly be sympathetic to Rorty's conclusion. In denying knowledge of nature, it is the sort of philosophy he struggled *against* throughout his career. He had a richly orchestrated vision of human life in its fullest setting. At the heart of that vision was a conception of the intimate and organic continuities of man with the plural, ever-changing processes of nature. The orchestration included a formulation of the powers, constraints, and consummations that these continuities might provide. This vision is unrecognizable in Rorty's rendition, where nature is and must be a meaningless cipher. He seems to believe that our only intelligible engagement with nature is of the sort that would be, to use his own expression, "underwritten" by the foundationalist enterprise. Dewey, by contrast, identified and articulated the many ways, obvious or subtle, that we may enter into finely discriminated relations with the natural world. Unwittingly but inexorably, Rorty threatens to undo Dewey's work, rather than carry it forward.

IV

I remarked earlier that I would attend to the bearing of Rorty's interpretation of pragmatism on Dewey's legacy to our culture. Rorty has at best obscured this legacy, at worst denied it. I will conclude by trying to bring further clarity to Dewey's heritage.

Every commentator but Rorty has observed Dewey's passion for scientific method, and Dewey seemed to be persuaded that its increasing use could work a miracle. I noted in my resumé of Dewey's critique of the classic tradition that an intelligible account of how science can be used in conduct presupposes a new set of assumptions about the nature of nature, which were systematized in Dewey's metaphysics. In providing that alone, Dewey earned his place in history.

When moving from the generic to the particular universe of discourse, Dewey sometimes gives the impression that all one need do in a problematic situation is determine the facts of the case and then contrive a plan of action that will bring about restored and reunified activity. This is using scientific method, to be sure, but it seems simplistic to suppose that such a procedure will reconcile disagreements about what ends ought to be pursued. Taken as it stands, it *is* simplistic, but it is only one element in Dewey's position.

To pursue this issue further, it will be helpful to shift attention to another idea intimately associated with Dewey's name: that of democracy. Dewey always spoke of democracy as a way of life—as a manner of conducting all phases of associated living. Democracy as a way of life, then, is the preferred mode of addressing moral problems. We do not have the democratic life on the one hand and the moral life on the other. Democracy *is* the moral life. Or rather, Dewey urgently recommends it to us as the moral life. He repeatedly elaborates democracy as both moral ideal and moral method.

Are there two distinct methods, then—that of science and that of democracy? No, there is one. Or, more precisely: the norms of science are incorporated into those of democracy. In Dewey's ideal, experimental inquiry and democratic behavior become fused. The nature of their combination can perhaps best be suggested by thinking of them as a union of certain moral and intellectual virtues—with the distinction between moral and intellectual less fixed than it seemed to be for Aristotle. The virtues include a willingness to question, investigate, and learn; a determination to search for clarity in discourse and evidence in argument. There is also a readiness to hear and respect the views of others, to consider alternatives thoroughly and impartially, and to communicate in a like manner in return. One is not irrevocably committed to antecedent convictions but is ready to qualify or change his views as a consequence of inquiry and communication. There is an urgency to persist in shared discourse in the direction of agreement. These virtues embrace novelty, innovation, growth, regard for the concerns of others, and scientific discipline. They reject the blind following of custom, authority, and impulse. They preclude not only dogmatism and absolutism, but deliberately hurtful conduct as well.

These might be viewed as the virtues of the experimental inquirer, but they are also virtues in the process of collective moral deliberation. What makes democratic behavior more than free speech and counting votes is that the participants use scientific intelligence in determining the nature of their situation and in formulating plans of action, and they are not stuck on foregone conclusions. Moreover, the scientific mentality is leavened by a respect for persons and a moral impartiality that would convert adversary situations into a search for cooperative and inclusive solutions. All these virtues are both powers and constraints: powers in being instrumentalities for shared and fulfilling conduct, constraints in being limitations on igno-rant and prejudicial conduct. Knowledge, too, is both power and con-straint. It provides powers by converting brute relationships into consum-mations. It is a constraint in that our intentions for action are always chas-tened by an awareness of nature's real possibilities and limitations.[44]

Dewey does not conceive democracy as a squabble over antecedently fixed goods. In a world intrinsically marked by change, the constant and inevitable task of intelligence is to mediate between past and future, to mediate change by introducing experimental proposals for reconstruction of present disturbances and conflicts in the direction of novel unifications.

Without scientific intelligence, this entire process is disabled. The idea of democratic method and aim as mere conversation was, in effect, vigorously opposed by Dewey in such works as *The Public and Its Problems* and *Liberalism and Social Action*. The classical liberals, he wrote, "did not rec-ognize the place in experiment of comprehensive social ideas as working hypotheses in direction of action."[45] He continues: "The instruments of analysis, of criticism, of dissolution, that were employed were effective for the work of release. But when it came to the problem of organizing the new forces and the new individuals . . . into a coherent social organization, possessed of intellectual and moral directive power, liberalism was well-nigh impotent."[46]

Dewey did not suppose that the experimental democratic method would solve moral problems after the fashion of traditional absolutisms.[47] It would be liberating, self-corrective to an extent, and always challenged. He did not think it would or could bring moral unanimity. But given his understanding of our shared condition, he regarded democratic intelligence as the best method so far conceived for contending with our common and evolving tasks. His extensive writings on education are centered especially on the responsibilities of schools to provide an environment in which scien-tific-democratic virtues will be acquired as an organic part of the learning process.

Are Dewey's democratic commitments no more than "ungrounded social hope"? Dewey himself did not think so. His moral recommendations were not issued from on high, but were a deeply reflective response to what he took to be the pervasively problematic situations of modern life. The philosophy of social intelligence is a response to existent needs—needs to bring order and even abundance to societies plagued by strife and uncertainty. The appropriate test of Dewey's moral philosophy consists only in its capacities to meet the real demands of life experience. But that is test enough.

I have not given a full account of the resources of social intelligence as Dewey elaborated them. It should be clear, nevertheless, that there are far more assets there than Rorty has identified. For his part, of course, Rorty might well dismiss them as products of "bad" philosophy and have done with Dewey. That in itself would be a gain, for scholars might then evaluate Dewey's philosophy in its own terms.

No doubt Dewey failed to canvass all our resources as natural and social beings, but I do not know of any philosopher who has accomplished as much in this regard. It might well be that he expected too much from the utilization of the instruments he recognized or conceived, but that is hardly reason to discard them. They might be the best that we could contrive. In any case, we owe it to ourselves to study them and try to develop them further. They are a precious asset, and they are our principal inheritance from Dewey. It would be a great tragedy if they were obscured. It would be a tragic irony if they were obscured in his name.

RESPONSE TO JAMES GOUINLOCK

I am not sure that Gouinlock and I disagree about as much as he thinks we do. For example, when he says that I am "not unaware of Dewey's moral commitments" but regard them as "no more than 'ungrounded social hope,'" or when he contrasts "democratic method" and "mere conversation," only the terms "no more than" and "mere" seem to divide us.

I think that an ungrounded social hope, the sort that Jefferson, Whitman, and Dewey had for the America of their various days, is the best sort of moral commitment to have. For to regard such hope as "ungrounded" is simply to recognize, as these men did, that nothing is on the side of this hope except the energies and intelligence that those who share it devote to it. I cannot see what further sort of grounding a Deweyan like Gouinlock might think that moral commitments could have.

Sidney Hook seems to me to have been right when, in "Pragmatism and the Tragic Sense of Life," he insisted that pragmatists were as aware as existentialists that our commitments to, for example, democratic practices cannot be grounded in the way the philosophical tradition hoped to ground them. The tradition wanted some sort of guarantee from outside of the human enterprise that that enterprise was moving in the right direction. I think that Plato was right that such a guarantee would be available only if there is something like an Absolute Good. Hook's essay invokes Dewey's doctrine that every evil is a lesser good to make clear why any non-Platonist must live in what Hook calls "a world of inescapable tragedy—a tragedy which flows from the conflict of moral ideals."[1] That is the conflict which

Plato thought would cease to exist once we had reached the top of the divided line.

It may be, however, that Gouinlock is contrasting "ungrounded hope" with "commitment arrived at by the scientific method." So it may be that our only disagreement is about the utility of the notion of "method." I do, indeed, find this notion pretty useless. Thus when Hook says that we can use "the method of critical intelligence" to "make it possible live with the tragic conflict of goods and rights and duties."[2] I do not see what is be lost if we erase "the method of." If we do, we shall be saying what no non-Platonist disputes: that in a tragic world we muddle through as best we can. "Critical intelligence" is as good a name as any for being experimental, nondogmatic, inventive, and imaginative, and for ceasing to expect, or try for, certainty. But nobody should expect to be taught a *methodical* way of being inventive and imaginative.

As I see it, the main reason Dewey constantly attached the term "method of" to "critical intelligence" was to provide a contrast to "the a priori, deductive method"—the method supposedly followed by intellectuals in the bad old days before the New Science came along. But no such method was in fact followed. Nobody who ever actually made a difficult moral or political decision followed the demonstrative procedure sketched in Aristotle's *Posterior Analytics*, a method Aristotle himself held to be inapplicable to such decision making. Critical intelligence has been alive and well since the dawn of history.

The only other reason I can think of why Dewey, early and late, insisted on using the vacuous notion of "method" is that he wanted philosophy to stop offering a body of knowledge, while still offering *something*. "Method" was the name he chose for what he thought it might still provide. But it was not a fortunate choice. It promised more than he could offer—something positive, rather than the merely negative admonition not to get trapped in the past.

If there is an exegetical question at issue between Gouinlock and myself it is whether one can isolate, in Dewey's work, something both wide enough to be "extended to all problems of conduct" and also narrow enough to have "formal properties"—something which is both generic enough to be, as Gouinlock says it is, the method of democracy as well as of science, and yet specific enough to be contrasted with other methods that people have actually employed. I do not think one can. I think that "scientific method" is a name for an unfindable middle ground between a set of virtuous habits (the ones which Gouinlock says make up "rationality") and a set of concrete, teachable techniques.

As I said in my introduction to volume 8 of *The Later Works,* Dewey's description of "reflective thought" as opposed to reliance on "tradition, instruction, imitation" did not seem to mark off anything except the willingness to challenge accepted beliefs.[3] Nobody except some people with whom not even my worst enemies confuse me—Burkean conservatives and religious fundamentalists—doubts the value of challenging such beliefs. But unless we can contrast "scientific method" with something beside what Peirce called the methods of tenacity and authority, then "scientific method" will remain too noncontroversial to make a fuss about.

The third of the methods with which Peirce contrasted "the scientific method" is what he called "the method of finding what is most 'agreeable to reason.'"[4] But the only difference I can see between that method and what Peirce called "the scientific method" is, once again, that the former discourages, and the latter encourages, bold and imaginative speculation. This is the difference between attempting to make everything you presently believe coherent and actively attempting to go out and get some new beliefs (for example, by making new observations or performing new experiments, hunting up anomalies and counterexamples, lending an ear to seemingly outrageous suggestions, or redescribing your data in unfamiliar terms). If you do the latter, you have a constantly enlarging and shifting body of belief to make coherent. But you do not employ a method for making it coherent that is different from the one you would have used if you had stuck with your old beliefs.

Peirce, to be sure, tried to distinguish scientific method from the three alternative methods he listed and rejected by saying that it tests beliefs against "some external permanency . . . something upon which our thinking has no effect," and went on to say that the "fundamental hypothesis" of "the method of science" was that "there are Real things, whose characters are entirely independent of our opinions about them."[5] But *that* way of characterizing scientific method is of no help to Dewey or to Gouinlock, who rightly says that "Dewey's objections to traditional realisms consisted above all in their assumption that a full-fledged object of knowledge exists prior to inquiry," and notes that this led people to think Dewey a "crypto-idealist" (78, 80).

Gouinlock says that Dewey "characterized the [scientific] method in detail in *The Quest for Certainty*," but I confess that I do not find such a detailed characterization in that book. All one gets in the chapter called "The Supremacy of Method" is his standard, endlessly repeated, polemic against epistemological and metaphysical dualisms—dualisms which interrupt the continuity between mind and the object of inquiry, theory and practice, humanity and nature, and so on. The only positive advice we get is to be reflective but determined, open yet disciplined, tolerant but discriminate, bold but not too bold, imaginative yet not wild. Is it really disrespect to Dewey's memory to admit that, when he gets started on method, he sounds a lot like Polonius?

What I meant by saying that Dewey moved "beyond method" was that he gave up on the idea, favored by nineteenth-century positivists and resuscitated by Carnap and Reichenbach, that you could skim off some rules from what natural scientists were doing, and, by applying those rules, transform other areas of culture. Dewey's attitude toward nineteenth-century positivism seems to me epitomized in his puckish remark that "Hegel is the quintessence of the scientific spirit."[6] Nothing to Dewey's purpose came of the later resuscitation of positivism, as can be seen by asking how one could hope to extend the latest contributions to the post-Carnapian literature on the logic of confirmation to "all problems of conduct."[7] So I conclude that when it comes to what Gouinlock calls "rationality as a *trait of character*" we shall never have anything remotely like a set of algorithms, but only some epistemic analogue of Aristotelian *phronesis*. People who want science to be a rule-governed procedure, it seems to me (and, I think, seemed to Dewey), are asking for more precision than the subject matter admits. They ask for rules when only imagination will do.

Granted that Dewey never stopped talking about "scientific method," I submit that he never had anything very useful to say about it. Those who think I am overstating my case here should, I think, tell us what this thing called "method"—which is neither a set of rules nor a character trait nor a collection of techniques—is supposed to be. Unless some reasonably definite third element can be specified, and chapter and verse cited from Dewey showing that this is what he had in mind, I shall stick by my claim that Dewey could have said everything he needed to say if he dropped the term "scientific method." He could have gotten just as much leverage out of saying that we needed, in all areas of conduct, more of the courage and imagination which Bacon and Galileo shared (despite their radically different conceptions of the nature of science), as well as more willingness to toss old ideas that have not panned out.

Still, what about Gouinlock's charges that I am unable to "distinguish between methods of inquiry as being better or worse" or to "speak of progress in knowledge, even in science" (73)? If these charges were correct, then I would indeed be a long way from Dewey. But the second charge, at least, is not. I follow Kuhn in describing the progress of knowledge in science as increased ability to get what we want out of science. One of the things we want—in an addition to the ability to predict and control our environment more efficiently—is an ability to explain why past science got right what it got right and got wrong what it got wrong. This is the sort of ability which we take to the mark of a progressive discipline and which helps us differentiate between microbiology and interior decorating. If Gouinlock would not count what Kuhn calls scientific progress as progress of *knowledge*, then he has to show that what Kuhn means by problem solving is different from what Dewey meant. I do not think he could do that. Kuhn and Dewey seem to me at one in arguing that the positivists' hope of substituting rules for *phronesis* was hopeless.

There is, however, a sense in which Gouinlock's first charge—that I cannot distinguish between "methods of inquiry" as better or worse—is correct. This is because I have trouble finding a principle of individuation for "methods." The term *method* is ambiguous between something as general as Peirce's four "methods of fixing belief" and something as specific as using magnetometers rather than dowsing rods. So I should prefer to drop the term, and to call the sort of thing Peirce described a *social practice* and to call the skilled use of magnetometers a *technique*. The social practices which determined what it took to count as "rational" and "irrational" were different in primitive tribes, medieval schoolrooms, and nineteenth-century scientific laboratories. But none of these three practices is reducible to rules, and none of them seems happily described as a "method."

If we count Peirce's "methods of tenacity and authority" as "methods of inquiry," then I shall condemn them on the same pragmatic grounds as everybody else—namely, that in the ages when these social practices were more prevalent, life was not as good as it has become since our society adopted different practices and, therefore, a different notion of what counts as being rational. But if we forget about these methods of straw—constructed by Peirce to serve as butts—then we have to ask what the criterion of individuation of a "method" is. I doubt that we shall find any such criterion before we get down to the level of specific techniques. Choosing between dowsing rods and magnetometers is not, however, a matter on which philosophers have much to say.

Many contemporary philosophers of science—Philip Kitcher, for example—continue to speak of choosing among "methods" in order to discover which have had most success in producing true beliefs. But, in addition to my holist doubts about whether we can use "true belief" as an independent check on practice, I do not think Kitcher and his colleagues have done nearly enough to explain what counts as a break between one method and another.[8] I can see how to individuate, roughly but sufficiently, *techniques* (magnetometers versus dowsing rods, asking the populace versus asking the Pope, computerized stylometry versus *Sprachgefuehl*, and the like) but *methods?* Assessment of how well techniques have worked, like devising new ones, is the province of the scientist in the trenches, not of the philosopher of science or the historian of inquiry.

To sum up: the reason I think that Feyerabend was justified in being "against method," and in suspecting that philosophy of science may be a subject "with a great past," is not that I think that Feyerabend was right about voodoo, but that I think he was right that there is nothing more philosophically profound or interesting to be said against voodoo (or astrology, or asking the Pope) than that these techniques do not seem to get us what we hoped for. After we have drawn the rather thin analogy between abandoning astrology for astronomy and abandoning feudalism for democracy, I do not think we can make further use of the suggestion that we look more closely at what scientists do in order to figure out what the rest of culture should do.

I turn now from the topic of method to the question of whether I have "missed" what Gouinlock calls "a crucial and remarkably innovative constituent of Dewey's theory of knowledge"—namely, that "in order to produce objects of perception (as of knowledge) suitable to the peculiarities of a problematic situation, some sort of intentional reorientation toward the troubling conditions must be undertaken" (78). I agree with Allen Hance that Dewey got this point from Hegel's *Phenomenology*, and that the point was restated nicely (with appropriate acknowledgments to both Hegel and

Dewey) in Sellars's polemic against "the Myth of the Given." Sellars's target was the idea that a perception is, to use Gouinlock's words, "a virgin image, appearing in systematic articulation to the passive spectator" (78). But since I have been borrowing heavily from this essay of Sellars's since I started publishing, I cannot believe that I have missed the point.

In various papers (including "Dewey between Hegel and Darwin," chapter 1 of this volume) I have tried to enlarge on Sellars's criticism of empiricism by arguing that if you understand the causal relations between the acquisition of beliefs and the environment of the believer you do not also need to ask about representational relations. It seems to me that a causal, nonrepresentational account of intentional states—an account along Davidsonian lines—gives you every reason in the world to say that "real properties of the object are *registered* in language" (83; Gouinlock's words; my italics), even after you have denied that they are *represented* in language. They are registered in the sense that if the objects did not have those properties you would probably not be saying what you say, or believing what you believe.

Yet Gouinlock doubts that I am able to join him in saying this. It is true that I do not think that *intrinsic* properties of the object are so registered, but that is because of doubts about the notion of intrinsicality.[9] It is true that I do not think that we should interpret "register" as "represent," but that is because I share Dewey's contempt for the Cartesian skeptic who asks "Why do you think that success in solving your problems means that you have accurate representations of the real?" I think that the most efficient way to dismiss such questions is to interpret "registration of real properties of the object" as "caused by real properties of the object, and capable of causing changes in those properties"—thereby exchanging a representational account of belief for a causal one. I should say of Davidson what Gouinlock says of Dewey: "It is hard to imagine a theory of ideas more rigorously controlled by the nature of objects than this one" (80). But, thanks to the substitution of linguistic behavior for "experience," Davidson's theory seems to me superior to Dewey's in being able to provide "definite locations for all naming behaviors as organic-environmental transactions."[10]

One reason I think that Davidson's way of doing things is superior to Dewey's is that it makes it unnecessary to worry about whether "a full-fledged object of knowledge exists prior to inquiry." I can accept Gouinlock's claim that Dewey's denial that such an object exists was central to his objection to traditional realism, but that seems to me just the reason why his objection was found so baffling, so hard to understand, so reminiscent of idealism. As I said in "Dewey's Metaphysics", Dewey's way of splitting the difference between realism and idealism just didn't work—in the sense that his philosophical colleagues found it impossible to figure out what he meant by saying that objects of knowledge change in the course of inquiry.[11] Sometimes Dewey seemed to mean, uncontroversially, that the beliefs which inquirers invoke to explain what they are talking about change—that the intentional object changed. But at other times he seemed to mean more than that. The moral to be drawn from Dewey's ill success, it seems to me, is that we should drop the notion of "object of inquiry."

This is facilitated by taking the linguistic turn and talking semantics rather than metaphysics. But I take it Gouinlock would condemn this move, for he is suspicious of what he calls "the language-game theory." His description of this theory, however, gives me pause. He says it is a theory which denies that "language is a function of shared activity, again, with an environment" (82).[12] I cannot think of any philosopher of language who has ever denied this. Does Gouinlock really think that Wittgenstein, the philosopher who put the term "language-game" in circulation, believed that a person could speak an *un*shared language, or speak one *without* interacting with an environment?

Perhaps, however, we can pass over what Gouinlock says about language-games in favor of his discussion of whether truth is correspondence—for this topic suggests a clearer opposition between what each of us gets out of Dewey. Gouinlock interprets me as "concluding that Dewey believed that objects do not constrain truth claims" (78). I would not dream of denying that. What I want to deny is that truth claims do not represent objects, and are not "made true" by objects. These denials amount to making the holist point that there is no way to pair off sentences or beliefs with things in the world in order to answer questions like Which objects make that sentence true? or Which objects does that sentence accurately represent? This is because there is no way to divide language from world in such a way as to resolve the question at issue between correspondentists and coherentists: is it the world itself, or other beliefs, which is the truth-maker? Nor is there any way to answer the question Is it the object in itself, or the object under a description, which is represented? Davidsonians, who reject the scheme-content distinction, reject both questions, and the notions of "making true" and "representing" along with them.

Dewey's sometimes rejected questions and terminology, and I wish he had done so more often. Unfortunately, he often employed the alternative technique of giving new, puzzling, senses to words like *object, experience, nature,* and *correspond.* A sentence which Gouinlock quotes approvingly from Dewey—"I hold that my *type* of theory [one that analogizes the relation between true belief and object to that between key and lock] is the only one entitled to be called a correspondence theory of truth" (216–17, note 27)—seems to me a perfect example of Dewey at his word-twisting worst. He unfortunately forewent the chance to say "Just *forget* about 'correspondence'" in order to say "Here is something you *could* mean by correspondence, even though it has nothing to do with the meaning used by those who worry about whether truth consists in correspondence."

As I said in response to Thelma Lavine, I think that the letter of Dewey's teachings often became a stumbling block to a grasp of their spirit. Gouinlock thinks that we can preserve most of the letter, and that doing so will save us from having to distinguish between a good Dewey and, if not a bad Dewey, a less good Dewey. I think that the reception of Dewey's attempts to clear up the idealism-realism dichotomy, and their present obsolescence, shows that those attempts failed. Dewey, after all, was perfectly conscious of being part of an ongoing process of experimentation. I doubt that he would be terribly upset to learn that some of his experiments did not pan out, and that his students had had to try some new ones.

6

PRAGMATISM AS NATURALIZED HEGELIANISM: OVERCOMING TRANSCENDENTAL PHILOSOPHY?

Allen Hance

From its inception pragmatism has displayed an ambivalent relation to Hegelianism. John Dewey conceived his experimentalism as a more modest alternative to Hegel's system of absolute idealism, which he deemed "too grand for present tastes."[1] At the same time, pragmatists from James and Dewey to Quine and Rorty have all assimilated important Hegelian motifs. These include, most importantly, a deep suspicion of modern representationalist epistemology, in both its rationalist and empiricist versions; a conception of intelligence as a form of practice, best conceived in terms of making, doing, and acting; and a commitment to a nonreductionist, holistic appreciation of our beliefs about the world (one which induces a general distrust of dualistic thinking). To this list Rorty adds an appreciation of Hegel's conception of the philosophical enterprise as *Nachdenken,* as a kind of edifying recollective summary.

Rorty has also provided what is perhaps the most concise formula for expressing at once pragmatism's debt to and criticism of Hegel: pragmatism is a form of "naturalized Hegelianism."[2] In this paper I wish to examine what it means to naturalize Hegel and whether this really is such a good thing to do. Naturalism can mean many different things, but I am interested primarily in naturalism as a theoretical critique of transcendental philosophy. For Rorty, naturalizing is synonymous with a process he calls "detranscendentalization." My question can thusnaturalized Hegelianism and if naturalism is a critique of transcendental philosophy, then in what, specifically, does the detranscendentalization of Hegel consist? I will argue that Rorty does not provide a satisfactory answer to this question. Since few if any of the charges Rorty levels against Hegel withstand careful scrutiny, and, indeed, seem to have been articulated in one form or another by Hegel himself, we are left to wonder not only what nonnaturalized Hegelianism really is, but also how it stacks up against contemporary pragmatism. Pursuing these issues can show us that Rorty is mistaken in his claim that "holism takes the curse off of naturalism."[3] I will argue, to the contrary, that Hegel's holistic idealism exemplifies a form of philosophical theory superior to naturalism insofar as it saves the phenomena more comprehensively than the reductive explanatory strategies of naturalism.

To this end I want to examine how Rorty sets up Kant as the paradigmatic transcendental philosopher and then uses his critique of Kant to advocate a wholesale rejection of the transcendental project. My claim is that because Rorty's understanding of transcendental philosophy is filtered almost entirely through a reading of Kant, his understanding of Hegel (as well as others within the transcendental tradition, including Husserl, Heidegger, and Derrida) is for the most part reductive and off target. The point is not merely that in Hegel himself we find many of the same objections to representationalist epistemology that Rorty supposes originate with linguistic philosophy, though this is true and deserves careful scrutiny. Equally important is that fact that through his construction of a straw man called "transcendental philosophy" Rorty suppresses a philosophical voice distinct not just from contemporary Anglo-American philosophy but from the empiricist and rationalist traditions of modern philosophy in general. That Rorty is unable to distinguish this voice from the chorus of modern philosophy is in part due to the fact that this voice's lexicon derives largely from Descartes and Hume rather than from Plato and Aristotle, with whom it perhaps shares more in common. Ultimately, however, this inability has to do with the very proximity of Rorty's own thought to the epistemological tradition whose founding arguments and guiding metaphors he has so trenchantly criticized.

I

Rorty has claimed that Hegelianism consists principally in having a historical sense. To have a historical sense is to believe "that nothing, including an a priori concept, is immune from cultural development."[4] This healthy historical sense is exemplified, presumably, in Hegel's view that different peoples constitute loci for different forms of spirit. The idea of fluid discursive webs suggested by this notion of spirit might alone have served as the basis for a critique of Kant's theory of a priori categories. It might have opened the door to the central argument of Rorty's pragmatism, which is that the rationality of assertions is a function not of correspondence with some extralinguistic ground but rather of "what society lets you say."[5] Instead, however, of developing a historically informed sociology of knowledge, Hegel made the mistake of engaging Kant on epistemological matters, criticizing, for example, the intelligibility of the thing-in-itself. The upshot of this critique of Kantian epistemology was not the rejection of a priori conceptual schemes in general, but rather the development of the grandiose alternative categorial framework found in the *Science of Logic*. As Rorty puts it: "Hegel . . . kept [Kant's] epistemology, but tried to drop the thing-in-itself, thus making himself, and idealism generally, a patsy for realistic reaction."[6]

Later I will contest Rorty's claim that Hegel's critique of the thing-in-itself commits him to some form of phenomenalism. For the moment I wish to emphasize that, for Rorty, the underlying problem with Hegel is that despite his pointed anti-Kantian rhetoric he never really breaks with Kantian epistemology. This argument is unsound and derives, I would like to suggest, from Rorty's chronic conflation of the transcendental with the epistemological. Because Rorty conceives of transcendental philosophy in general as a species of epistemology, he is left no option, after registering the fact that Hegel worked within the tradition of transcendental philosophy, but to claim that Hegel also drank deeply from the chalice of modern epistemology. What Rorty chooses not to investigate closely is the extent to which post-Kantian transcendental philosophy from Hegel to Husserl and Heidegger has itself constituted a prolonged attack on the representational theory of mind developed jointly by modern empiricism and rationalism. The only way Rorty can make his general critique of transcendental philosophy stick is by reductively identifying transcendental philosophy with Kant's critical philosophy, with the one version of transcendental philosophy least free from the trappings of modern representationalist epistemology.

Rorty's guiding assumption about transcendental philosophy is that it carries to a higher level of abstraction the "battle"—as Dewey characterizes it in his 1948 introduction to *Reconstruction in Philosophy*—between science and religion, between the real and the ideal. This battle was initiated by Plato's discovery of mathematics and his subsequent attempt to define philosophy as that which parses the intelligible, actual, transcendent, and sacred from the sensory, apparent, immanent, and profane. It was Descartes and Kant, however, who gave form to the distinctly modern variant of this project. More rigorously conceived, transcendental philosophy consists in a cluster of theses about the distinctive character of philosophical, in contrast to everyday, knowledge. The most important of these theses, according to Rorty, are (1) the view that philosophy is an apodictic science modeled on logic and mathematics and made up of nonempirical, a priori knowledge-claims; (2) the view that a nonempirical practice of introspection or inference discloses this region of philosophical knowledge; (3) the view that this philosophical knowledge serves as a canon for judging the legitimacy of empirical claims forwarded by extraphilosophical disciplines.[7] This model of philosophy was carried into the late nineteenth century by the neo-Kantians and by British and American idealists, and received new impetus from the critiques of psychologism developed by Frege and Husserl. These gave birth, in turn, to the major variants of transcendental philosophy in the twentieth century: in the analytic tradition, the logico-mathematical and linguistic theories of Russell, Carnap, and the early Wittgenstein (as well as neo Fregean formalist semantics); and, in the continental tradition, the phenomenology of Husserl, the philosophical hermeneutics of the early Heidegger and Gadamer, and the transcendental pragmatics of Apel and Habermas.

The particular brand of naturalism that Rorty employs to challenge transcendental philosophy (so defined) is linguistic behaviorism. For all his dissatisfaction with various practitioners of analytic philosophy and for all his gestural appropriations of continental philosophy, Rorty's philosophic outlook was shaped primarily by certain foundational arguments of the analytic tradition. These include Frege's claim that the sentence is the minimal unit of meaning, Wittgenstein's notion that meanings are rules for the use of words, Ryle's assertion that introspection is a learned behavior rather than a privileged mode of access, Quine's argument that the analytic-synthetic distinction is untenable, Sellars's critique of the notion of givenness, and Davidson's demonstration that the idea of a conceptual scheme is but one more dogma of empiricism. Taken together, these arguments constitute the interpretative grid through which Rorty receives the philosophical tradition and in terms of which he narrates its fateful twists and turns. They also define the self-interrogative process through which, in Rorty's opinion, recent (post-) analytic philosophy has detranscendentalized itself and the wider tradition from which it stems.

Rorty's essay, "Strawson's Objectivity Argument," clearly exemplifies the critique of transcendental philosophy enabled by linguistic behaviorism.[8] This critique centers on the fact that Kant's transcendental arguments attempt to isolate two sorts of privileged representations: meanings or concepts, and sensory data or intuitions. Arguments that Kant phrases using the representationalist language of concepts and intuitions, Rorty contends, can be restated in terms of the way we use certain kinds of words. Thus, for example, Kant's argument that the sensory manifolds presented through the forms of intuition do not of themselves constitute experience, but must be synthesized conceptually by the a priori category of substance, can be understood as the semantic claim that the use of adjectival terms such as *red* or *hard* (sensory quality words) makes no sense in isolation from the substantives or indexicals that form the nominal cores of complete sentences. We are dealing, in other words, not with the inner workings of the mind but with the logic of particular language games. To understand this logic we have no need for the mysterious first-person practice of introspection or for equally obscure transcendental deductions. We need only see whether speakers of the given language, as a matter of publicly verifiable fact, deviate from this pattern and still make sense.

Rorty does, however, credit Kant with beginning the move away from the Cartesian-style philosophy of consciousness that would culminate eventually in the behaviorist's complete repudiation of transcendental philosophy. Kant's argument that neither unsynthesized intuitions nor a priori categories are able to be experienced directly challenges the Cartesian view of subjective mental states as incorrigible, immediate, and self-evident. But here, unfortunately, Kant stopped. Rather than abandon the representational model of mind altogether, Kant instead outlined what he believed to be a radically new way of doing philosophy. For Kant, Rorty writes, "The study of the relations between these two sorts of unapperceivable entities becomes the pseudo-subject of a pseudo-discipline, transcendental philosophy."[9]

Rorty promises a nonmentalistic account of the functions Kant attaches to his two species of mental entities. A concept is not a representation, "it is a skill, a skill at linguistic behavior—the ability to use a word."[10] Intuition is not a nonconceptual representation or an unsynthesized mental content or a nondiscursive presentation of an object. It is, rather, the disposition toward certain definite speech acts of a linguistic animal standing in a causal relation to an object. Accordingly, the epistemological problem of reconstructing necessary relations between different species of mental contents gives way to an investigation of the causal ordering of linguistic behaviors: "With both concepts and intuitions thus analyzed into dispositions to linguistic behavior, the notion of 'representation' itself seems to be left without work to do. The notion of *Vorstellung*—something in the mind which stands in place of the object to be known—thus vanishes, and with it the notion of epistemology as the discipline which investigates the internal relations between *Vorstellungen*."[11]

Rorty's arguments in "The World Well Lost" and later essays complement and extend the arguments from this earlier piece. Here we see again that Rorty's critique of transcendental philosophy consists in revealing the various dogmas of empiricism still latent in Kantian epistemology. As Rorty sees it, doubts raised by Sellars and others about the intelligibility of an uninterpreted given, and by Quine about the tenability of a hard and fast distinction between the necessary and the contingent, give rise to Davidson's more global questioning of the meaningfulness of conceptual schemes in general. If all acts of perception are theory-laden, then there are no intuitions (if by intuition we mean that which is purely received). In the absence of an idea of raw data yet to be categorized, however, the postulate of a spontaneously imposed interpretative scheme ceases to be necessary. Rorty thus argues that when the receptivity-spontaneity distinction falls by the wayside, so too does the distinction between the merely given and the now categorized, the unschematized and the schematized. Furthermore, if with Quine we understand a priori concepts simply as concepts that, pragmatically speaking, we find it exceedingly difficult to do without in most of our scientific and nonscientific pursuits, then talk of the conditions of possible experience in general is better understood in fallibilistic terms as the absence of plausible alternatives. To say this is not to return to the contrastive notion of "the world as we happen to conceive it with our conceptual scheme" versus "the world as it is in itself." The very contrast between the "in itself" and the "for us" depends on a scheme-relative concept of world. The world is not something "out there," not an independent evidential ground that verifies our conjectures, not a noumenal realm forever beyond our phenomenal knowledge. These concepts of world are all generated by the confrontational picture of knowledge: concepts and a picture well lost.

II

Rorty's argument that Hegel shares something of Kant's epistemology is premised on the true assertion that Hegel develops a theory of categories and the false assertion that he utilizes some kind of scheme-content distinction. The "Hegelian picture," as Rorty characterizes it, is one which leads "to the notion of conceptual thought as 'shaping' and thus to the notion of the World-Spirit moving from one set of a priori concepts to the next."[12] Hegel, on this view, rejects the rigidity and arbitrariness (the "finitude") of Kant's table of categories and develops in its stead a truly comprehensive system of categories, one sufficient to embrace the whole of being. Though he questions the adequacy of Kant's distinction between sensibility and understanding, Hegel does not break decisively with the notion of a conceptual scheme which organizes a given experiential field.

Those familiar with Hegel cannot help but be struck by a sense of déjà vu. Was it not Hegel who claimed to "overcome" Kantian epistemology precisely through a critique of the residual empiricism of critical idealism? In my view, Rorty does not sufficiently appreciate Hegel's critique of empiricism and representational thinking and, as a consequence, is unable to recognize the nonepistemological and, for that matter, nonmetaphysical character of Hegel's kind of transcendental philosophy.[13] Hegel calls into question traditional philosophical ways of conceiving the "relationship" between world and the categories of thought. At the same time, he argues that an overcoming of the impasses to philosophical thinking can result only from a radicalization of the transcendental project begun by Kant. The problem with Kant is not that he is a transcendental philosopher, but that his transcendental philosophy remains too deeply rooted in modern representational epistemology. For Hegel, the problem of how thought or language (subjectivity) hooks up with the world (objectivity) is a philosophical canard introduced by presuppositions about mind shared in large measure by both Cartesian rationalists and Lockean empiricists. These presuppositions together constitute what Hegel calls picture-thinking.

The issue we must pursue, then, is whether Hegel's critique of picture-thinking addresses the same complex of problems which Rorty articulates in his critique of empiricism and representationalist epistemology. If so, then obviously Rorty's suggestion that we extend these criticisms to Hegel and to post-Kantian idealism and transcendental philosophy in general will prove seriously misleading. This raises further questions, first about what really distinguishes the naturalist critique of representationalist epistemology from the transcendental critique, and second about whether Rorty himself succeeds in extricating his pragmatism from picture-thinking.

A clarification is in order here. I do not deny that Rorty has argued persuasively that "the mental," as described by post-Cartesian epistemological theories, is a construction generated by certain misleading metaphors and unsatisfactory pictures of cognitive achievements. I am claiming that transcendental philosophy, having itself dispensed with the epistemological project through its critique of naturalism (through the critique of the notion of mind as a substance or a bit of the world), does not think about thought, meanings, and categories in terms of subjective mental processes. At least in this respect it shares with Frege's philosophy a deeply antipsychologistic conception of meaning. Clearly, however, the very intelligibility of transcendental explanations becomes problematic if one calls into question the intelligibility of meanings; and Rorty suggests that we have good reasons to do so. He arrives at these reasons, however, through the erroneous equation of transcendental theories of categories and meanings with epistemological ones. In Rorty's view, what transcendental philosophers refer to as categories and meanings are simply surrogate names for the mental entities that epistemologists call concepts, representations, and ideas. The entire epistemological project is an attempt to isolate some set of privileged representations and to claim for them a governing position with respect to other representations. For Rorty, all such mental entities are fictitious, the imaginary progeny of a pseudo-discipline. In spite of all its innovations, transcendental philosophy—whether Kantian, Hegelian, or Husserlian—remains bewitched by the notion of a mental realm independent of or prior to the physical realm. Accordingly, as soon as a transcendental philosopher refers to his or her project as an explanation of the possibility of thinking and experience, Rorty sees the Mirror of Nature rearing its ugly head.

This perception is the result, I would submit, of Rorty's failure to comprehend the extent to which the transcendental turn, initiated (but not completed) by Kant, itself constitutes a radical attack on the modern epistemological conception of mind as a secondary or derivative subjective sphere set over against a primary objective realm. With Hegel, the transcendental turn does not result in insouciant pragmatism with its conception of truth as what society lets us say. It results, rather, in the elaboration of a phenomenological ontology. This becomes possible when, according to Hegel, philosophy is once again *able* to take "thinking" (*das Denken*) seriously. To recover this ability is the aim of Hegel's critique of picture-thinking.

III

So what is Hegel's conception of "thinking," and how does it diverge from Kantian philosophy while remaining within the transcendental tradition? A satisfactory response to these two questions requires that we become more conscious of the embedded presuppositions that guide many contemporary interpretations of Hegel. Among Anglo-American readers of Hegel there has until quite recently been almost universal agreement about "what is living and what is dead of the philosophy of Hegel." Concurring for the most part with Croce's judgment in the famous 1907 monograph of that title, commentators on Hegel have deemed it a matter of intellectual respectability and common sense to pronounce Hegel's speculative logic and philosophy of nature dead, while treating his philosophical anthropology and diverse reflections on cultural and historical forms (minus his distracting thesis about an "end to history") as the living core of his thought. This view is nicely summarized by Allen Wood in his study of Hegel's practical philosophy: "The living traditions that derive from Hegel's thought— the traditions of Marxist social theory and existential philosophy—are distinctly antimetaphysical in their orientation. The Hegel who still lives and speaks to us is not a speculative logician and idealist metaphysician but a philosophical historian, a political and social theorist, a philosopher of our ethical concerns and cultural identity crises."[14]

While Hegel's thought surely spawned the still-living traditions of Marxism and existentialism, it is likewise true that those traditions, in their turn, have shaped our contemporary approach to the study of Hegel. Indeed, Karl Löwith has suggested that the interpretative horizon that governs most contemporary approaches to Hegel has an even earlier and more specific origin: it was Schelling's widely attended Berlin lectures, he argues, that set in motion both the Marxist and the existentialist reactions. The assumption that these lectures installed in the minds of Kierkegaard, Engels, Bakunin, Burckhardt, and others in attendance, and which had been resurrected by successive generations of existentialist, hermeneutic, Marxist, pragmatist, naturalist, historicist, deconstructive, and postmodernist interpreters is that Hegel's philosophy of the Absolute, insofar as it is based on his speculative logic, neglects "real being" and "positive existence."[15] In an important sense the appeals to existence, facticity, and materiality in all these influential forms of post-Hegelian philosophy represent an attempt to revitalize the theory of intuition on which Kant bases his critique of rationalist metaphysics. Most of Hegel's critics share the conclusion that his rejection of Kant's theory of intuition causes him to backslide into some form of pre-Critical metaphysics. An increasing number of Hegel scholars are now arguing that this is a seriously mistaken interpretation.[16] It is mistaken because the transcendental critique of metaphysics does not rest necessarily on a Kantian-style theory of sensuous intuition. Hence, although Hegel clears the way for his own conception of speculative thinking through a critique of the Kantian theory of intuition, this critique does not, of itself, necessitate a renewal of substance metaphysics. For internally connected reasons, the second key part of Hegel's critique of Kant—his rejection of the thing-in-itself—does not lead to phenomenalism.

Contra Rorty, the Hegelian conception of thinking is itself based on a critique of representational epistemology and scheme-content theories of cognition. Hegel rejects the notion that categories are a priori rules of synthesis that bind together pregiven manifolds into objective appearances. He likewise rejects the argument internal to Kant's transcendental psychology that space and time are a priori forms of intuition that prediscursively order the contents of sensibility. He rejects these views because both are premised on a picture of the subject's relation to things-in-themselves and, following from this picture, on a theory of the faculties the subject must possess if we are to make sense of (what for Kant constituted) indisputable universal and necessary knowledge claims.

This picture, according to Hegel, distorts our capacity as philosophers to examine the contents of thought. Hegel conceives philosophy in general as the inquiry into mind (*Geist*), where by mind is meant the system of the contents of thought. As understood by speculative philosophy, thought is not a possession or predicate of a subject, psyche, or mental faculty; and the contents of thought are not contained somehow in intramental representations of the external world. Indeed, the project of the *Phenomenology of Spirit* is in large measure to disabuse us of these mistaken assumptions of modern epistemology, assumptions which, in Hegel's view, give rise both to modern skepticism and to realist reactions against skepticism. At least on the surface, then, Hegel's attempt to overcome the impasse between skepticism and realism through a critique of epistemology shares much in common with Rorty's attempt.

The trouble with representational epistemology is that it puts forward a theory of mind that reduces the determinations of thought—public, linguistically mediated meaning-contents—to subjective states. In this deficient theory "the self is a represented subject (*ein vorgestelltes Subjekt*) to which the content is related as an accident and predicate."[17] Still caught up in an externally pictured and hence substantialized conception of mind, such theories proceed surreptitiously to assign things-in-themselves a being-status apart from what is, so to speak, "brought to mind" in and through thought-determinations. Representational epistemology does so, and believes it does so legitimately, because it interprets thought as a function of the subject and hence as a complex of psychological events. If our knowledge consists merely in representations caused by external things impinging on sense organs, then we have no reason to suppose that our particular view of things is the best, most accurate, or really real, one. Our view is thoroughly conditioned by the particular array of sense organs we, as human beings, just happen to possess. It could have been otherwise for us and it might well be otherwise for other intelligent beings.

Once these assumptions are made, however, it becomes necessary to posit the thing-in-itself in order to prevent the slide into subjective idealism. According to Hegel, however, Kant's retention of the thing-in-itself is precisely what blocks the development of a thoroughgoing idealism and the comprehensive thinking through of the dogmas of representational epistemology. Both it and the causal theory of perception Kant inherits from Hume are residues of a naive form of realism which persists when the critique of epistemology begun by the transcendental turn is not completed. Phenomenalism, moreover, is the dialectical partner which comes to haunt the naive realist during his or her skeptical moments.

For Hegel, the realist postulate of a thing-in-itself is "contradictory" and dogmatic because it constitutes a theoretical posit for which Kantian and empiricist philosophers cannot themselves account. Identification of the thing-in-itself, in other words, presupposes a relation of subject to object that is itself inaccessible to the thinking self (that is, to the thinking self as described by representational epistemology). Representational epistemologists seem to claim that the subject has direct access only to its own intramental contents. Presumably representational epistemologists, when they themselves are engaged in the reflective philosophical activity of developing theories of mind, are not exempt from this universal rule of cognition. If that is so, however, we are well on the way to proving that it makes no sense at all to call that which is experienced by the subject its own "representations" or "mental contents." For if the subject knows only via its own representations, we must conclude that that same subject (in its role as an epistemologist) could not attain a position external to its own representations in such a way as to identify them *as* representations. This same argument extends to the thing-in-itself. The subject has no experiential access through representations to that which it sets up as the causal basis of its represented experiences. The representational epistemologist's model of mind is thus a fiction founded on the picture of consciousness somehow standing outside itself just long enough to identify the field of "real things" that might, the skeptical argument goes, be represented differently by other consciousnesses. To make this assumption, however, is to postulate for consciousness a relation to itself and its other that it does not and cannot possess.

Hegel concludes that the Kantian thing-in-itself cannot be meaningfully understood as a limit to thought because it itself is a posit of thought. But this means, of course, that the thing-in-itself is not other to thought at all. Indeed, by this chain of argument we are led to the absolute idealist's assertion that only thought itself (nonrepresentationally conceived) deserves the title of the thing-in-itself. When the ego comes home to itself in this way we are left with what Hegel calls thinking (*das Denken*): we have moved from the *Ding an sich* as a limit to thought, to thought as the *Ding an sich*, or better, to thought as *die Sache selbst*. More prosaically put, Hegel's absolute idealism radicalizes the turn to the subject initiated by Descartes and Hume by recognizing the fallacious character of epistemological questions concerning the relation of subject to object and by attending exclusively to the determinations of thought. Thought, as Hegel puts it, must be conceived as infinite rather than as something limited by something other to itself (intuition or the thing-in-itself).[18] Only when we have gotten away from oppositional or confrontational models of subjectivity and objectivity can we articulate the nature of pure thought (*reines Denken*) and its categorial determinations.

Hegel's category theory does not, in Kantian fashion, generate a scheme-relative conception of the world (the phenomenal world of nature). In general terms, Hegel—much like Davidson—argues that the question "Relative to what are these categories valid?" proves meaningless once we abandon an epistemological orientation to philosophy of mind. More specifically, however, Hegel attempts to dissolve the problem of scheme-relativity through a critique of Kant's theory of sensuous intuition. As with all other proposed limits to thought, Hegel's strategy is to show that intuition is not an originally given, self-evident, or incorrigible element in immediate consciousness, but is itself a mediated content or determination of thought. Thought itself, in Hegel's view, ultimately provides no warrant for its division into the component parts of concept and intuition. The latter is an abstraction. Space and time are not, as Kant argues, irreducible media that provide the subject with the nondiscursive matter to be taken up and shaped by categories into objective experience. Here again, the problem is that Kant annexes space and time to the subject rather than treating them as determinations of thought. Conceived absolutely, space and time are categorical determinations specific to particular fields of inquiry. We should not treat space and time as subjectively given epistemological coordinates of empirical thought but as moments internal to the categorially determined system of thought as such.

In summary, then, Hegel speaks of his categorial system as absolute because he claims to have overcome an epistemological problematic, with its misleading assumptions about the genesis, reference, and adequacy of representations. Because his philosophy of mind is founded on the premise that categories as modes of presentation are not functions of the empirical subject, Hegel can claim at once that objectivity is wholly a matter of thought, and that his theory, though idealist, is not phenomenalist.[19] Indeed, to make this charge is to remain committed, in however sublimated a form, to a misleading realist conception of thought and its relation to the "world."

IV

I have tried to indicate how a number of the positions Rorty imputes to Hegel, and which in his view need to be naturalized in order to yield an acceptable form of historicized holistic pragmatism, are not, in fact, held by Hegel. As it turns out, they are positions more appropriately referred to Kant or to the pre-Critical tradition of representationalist epistemology. Moreover, they represent positions which Hegel himself cogently criticizes. It would appear that, in the end, Hegel's critique of Kant results in something very similar to what issues from Rorty's linguistic-behaviorist deconstruction of Kant. Rorty has argued in Wittgensteinian fashion that "all that transcendental arguments—a priori arguments about what sort of experience is possible—can show is that if you have certain concepts you must have certain other concepts" (or, more precisely, that to use certain words you need to know how to use certain other words).[20] For Hegel too, webs of concepts replace intuitions and the doctrine of synthetic a priori knowledge. So what is it in the final analysis that separates Hegel from Rorty? Both Rorty and Hegel seem to be left with an internalist account of how our beliefs hang together and why we take them to be true, for the most part. Perhaps we have just shown that Rorty is much more Hegelian than he supposes because, in point of fact, Hegel himself was more of a pragmatist than is ordinarily granted. Or perhaps we have shown that Hegel was always already detranscendentalized, that Hegel was a naturalized Hegelian *avant la lettre*.

In this last section I would like to clarify just how much distance in point of fact continues to separate Rorty and Hegel. The best way to do this is to raise two internally related questions. First, in what sense does Hegel, despite his profound differences with Kant, remain a transcendental philosopher; and, second, how does the holism that issues from this species of transcendental philosophy differ from that of Rorty's naturalist pragmatism?

Hegel's speculative idealism remains a form of transcendental philosophy because it does continue Kant's project of articulating a transcendental logic. Kant distinguishes transcendental logic from formal logic in that it is a theory of objective possibilities rather than pure logical possibilities. Thus the Kantian categories, as applied to the pure forms of intuition, carve out the a priori nexus for possible objects of experience. The doubts we have seen Hegel express about Kant's theory of pure intuition also impel him to question the narrow conception of objectivity found in Kant's transcendental logic. These doubts do not, however, prompt him to abandon the effort to expound a logic of "actual possibility." Whereas Kant, in other words, restricts actual possibility to the categorially determined spatio-temporal field of nature, Hegel seeks a richer and more comprehensive account of actual possibility, one that extends from his speculative logic through the entire real philosophy (the philosophies of nature and spirit).

With his speculative logic, however, Hegel is not constructing a transcendental doctrine of method.[21] He offers neither a canon nor an organon, neither an accounting of the principles for the correct employment of understanding or reason nor an instrument for acquiring empirical knowledge. Both these notions are forward looking, whereas Hegel's speculative logic is resolutely backward looking. Hegel's statements on this issue are strong and unequivocal. The image of the owl of Minerva in the preface of the *Philosophy of Right* testifies to Hegel's general disdain for the conception of philosophy as an applied or applicable science; his reminder in that same passage that philosophy comes on the scene too late to be of any practical use indicates his belief that philosophy's orientation is essentially retrospective. Once these claims are taken into account it no longer makes sense to charge Hegel with attempting to constrain empirical inquiry. To assert that it is possible to reconstruct the most basic norms or categories operative in different domains of experience is not to claim that no further judgments can be made or actions taken within those domains, that everything has been thought and done, or that we stand at the end of history. Nor does Hegel's insistence that speculative reconstruction be systematic commit him to a closed and unrevisable theory of categories. It does, however, commit him to the holistic endeavor of establishing a reflective equilibrium between past and present accounts and between contradictory present accounts by demonstrating that incommensurabilities posited in or between rival philosophical accounts are not aspects of actuality but are products of category mistakes, reductive ontologies, or faulty models of mind. This process of philosophical adjudication is pursued through a method of progressive recontextualization through which categorial schemes that offer seemingly contradictory accounts of the nature of being, mind, or society are shown to be compatible within a larger explanatory frame. Hegel refers to this activity of thought itself attempting to come to terms with the limitations of its own accounts as dialectic. As Hegel writes,

> The forms of thought must be studied in their essential nature and complete development: they are at once the object of research and the action of that object. Hence they examine themselves: in their own action they must determine their limits, and point out their defects. This is that action of thought, which will hereafter be specially considered under the name of *Dialectic*, and regarding which we need only at the outset observe that, instead of being brought to bear upon the categories from without, it is immanent in their own action.[22]

From the standpoint of his dialectically developed system (in which the forms of thought have, as it were, thought themselves through), Hegel claims to be able to offer a critique of those philosophical theories that operate with deficient, though not necessarily defective, categorial schemes. For example, various forms of naturalism propose to be able to describe all phenomena, including human thought and action, as natural events. Natural events are those explicable in terms of the fundamental category of efficient causality. Hegel argues that this proposition inevitably (and literally) proves self-defeating. In understanding explanation as the tracing of effects back to causes, naturalism reduces what explains (thinking) to the level of what is explained. But if, in the final analysis, it is thought that does the explaining, then the supposition that this explaining itself is caused by something other than itself (that such explaining is not spontaneous) undercuts the possibility of explanation; for if thinking is itself caused by another, then (as Fichte argues) it could not know this about itself. The defect of naturalism is thus that it utilizes categories appropriate to natural objects to account for activities of subjects, activities which cannot be properly understood as mere causal events. The point here is not to reject causal analysis but to demand of thinking that it do justice to the phenomenon in question. Logic must, accordingly, be able to account for how thinking is able to think itself.

We are now in a better position to address the frequently voiced objection that Hegel's speculative philosophy is an ill-conceived exercise in foundationalist metaphysics with absurd pretensions to exhaustive ("absolute") knowledge. Both the charge of foundationalism and the interpretation of what Hegel means by absolute knowledge are largely mistaken. The system that Hegel's dialectic seeks to elucidate is not "founded" on anything external to itself. Unlike Descartes, Hegel offers no axiomatic first principle from which he attempts to deduce his system. For Hegel there are no absolute beginnings; there is no indubitable ground or rudimentary set of principles from which the science of philosophy can proceed; there is not even a minimal premise, such as Davidson's principle of charity, to which everyone will consent. Indeed, Hegel maintains that the foundationalist enterprise is precisely what his speculative system successfully avoids, while at the same time fulfilling the traditional philosophical task of articulating a presuppositionless science of sciences. It is of course far beyond the scope of this paper to assess Hegel's notion of science, especially the strictness of its claim to necessity. What we are interested in is Hegel's account of philosophical beginning, which holds that we begin inevitably with premises that arc taken for granted, with *doxa*. The mistake is to suppose that we can secure these starting points prior to the activity of philosophical investigation, that we might somehow learn to swim before getting into the water. The initial assumptions lodged in our opening gambit are discharged only through the development of an internally coherent system of thought; only the end product of speculation, the science of the whole, confirms the validity of one's starting points. This argumentative strategy forms the basis of what Tom Rockmore has aptly referred to as Hegel's "circular epistemology."[23]

Absolute knowing has two basic senses for Hegel, neither of which has anything to do with divine omniscience. It refers in the first place to a theoretical standpoint achieved once thinking frees itself from the forms of dogmatism and skepticism generated by representational epistemology. This standpoint marks the conclusion of the *Phenomenology of Spirit* and the beginning of the *Science of Logic*. It is from this standpoint that thought, trusting its contents, dialectically investigates the limits and internal inconsistencies of its own categorical determinations. Second, absolute knowing refers to the outcome of dialectical investigation insofar as this investigation is a developmental process that produces a system of categorial determinations. In this sense the absolute notion, as Hegel writes in the *Encyclopaedia Logic*, "is what contains all the earlier categories of thought merged in it."[24]

A comparison with a widespread modern conviction about knowing and what it yields clarifies further the distinctiveness of the Hegelian conception of absolute knowing. Unlike a long line of philosophers beginning with Frege and including Davidson and Rorty (who remain, in this measure, tacitly influenced by the modern epistemological tradition), Hegel does not sever the notion of "taking to be true" (appearance) from that of "being-true" (reality). Frege supposed that logical analysis of the accomplishments of thinking collapses into mere psychology if we link our account of reference to the thinking subject's intuitive registration of what is the case. He saw the failure to separate subjective states from the specification of truth-conditions as leading inevitably to a psychologistic account of truth. As a consequence, he argued that what is the case must be accounted for exclusively with reference to a noncontingent, nonpsychological realm of "thoughts" (the ontological status of which, as has often been remarked, is never sufficiently clarified).25

Hegel, too, was acutely aware of the problem of psychologism and, as his trenchant criticisms of Jakob Fries indicate, was seriously concerned to combat it. His attempt to circumvent psychologism proceeds not by detaching appearance from truth but by detaching his account of thinking from the subjective activities of a determinate consciousness and by conceiving of thinking "absolutely" rather than as the synthetical or associative activity of an ego. Categories are not forms that we impose on the world. They are the ways the world presents itself to thought. When Hegel states that the categories of speculative logic are absolute he means that they make being present in and for itself. These forms of thought are not representations of an epistemological subject but are rather the ways that being manifests itself or becomes seen and known under descriptions given in everyday talk, as well as in the theoretical accounts of particular sciences. Hegel's category theory is not a contribution to epistemology or to anthropology, but is the basis of a phenomenological ontology.

Here, again, for Hegel the work of dialectic is retrospective and interpretative rather than introspective and postulative. To be reconstructed are the most basic categorial schemes that govern our thinking about being. These historically developed and inherited ways of thinking about experience, nature, politics, and history together comprise the appearances (*Scheine*) of truth. Dialectical reconstruction aims at saving these appearances: it moves from appearance to truth by revealing that deficiencies within these schemes lie in the scope and richness of the categories brought into play in particular descriptive or explanatory projects. The truth of appearances thus lies in the systematic reconstruction of the increasingly more concrete whole internal to which each of these varied accounts assumes a determinate place.

In contrast to Hegel, Rorty proposes to overcome representational epistemology and psychologism through behaviorist semantics. Dissatisfied with Frege's mysterious appeal to "thoughts" and yet still suspicious of appeals to intuition (how things appear to the subject), behaviorist semantics hangs its account of truth-conditions on contingent but still nonpsychologistic (because overt and publicly observable) behaviors of linguistic organisms. Rorty's more sociologically minded version of linguistic behaviorism thus refers the truth-conditions of assertions to "what society lets us say." Though it, too, then is founded on the recognition that modern epistemology falsely reduces the criteria for knowledge-claims to subjective representations, Rorty's linguistic behaviorism neither recovers the kind of trust in thinking that Hegel's speculative philosophy does nor elaborates a theory of interpretation that frees it decisively from the foundationalist enterprise of modern epistemology.

Rorty is unable to embrace a fuller conception of Hegelianism because his thinking remains fundamentally constrained by naturalism and nominalism, which together form what might be termed the two dogmas of neopragmatism. There is a strange way in which Rorty's linguistic behaviorism, shaped by these dogmas, effects only a partial paradigm shift, one that succeeds only in turning both representationalist epistemology and modern scientific theories of mind and society inside out, but does not succeed in thinking them through. Ultimately, Rorty's attempt to think holistically works through explanatory reductionism rather than through the dialectical engendering of richer and more inclusive systems of explanation.

Of course, Rorty takes great pains to distance himself from objectivistic and scientistic theories of knowledge, so there is a prima facie implausibility to my claim that his pragmatist project itself uncritically extends presuppositions of the New Science, and that it itself is underwritten by the foundationalist and representationalist epistemological tradition he seeks to undermine. In the essay "Pragmatism without Method," for example, Rorty identifies two fundamental strands of thought in the pragmatist tradition: one that uses modern science and experimental technique as a model for rationality in general, and another that brings science down off its high horse by appealing to the "softer" disciplines of history, literature, and religion, as well as the local knowledge and know-how of common sense.[26] Sidney Hook and others are singled out for criticism because they exhibit a latent positivistic urge to measure all belief, knowledge, and intelligence in terms of their adequacy to an ideal postulated by scientific method. Rorty recommends instead that we develop the "holistic and syncretic"[27] side of pragmatism, which, having given up the residual objectivism that drives the search for a unified method, contents itself with the more modest task of reweaving webs of belief, learning and translating foreign discourses, and litigating, where possible, between differing parties.

Through it all, however, Rorty retains faith in a kind of pragmatism that is "naturalistic without being scientific," one that "wants to hold on to the materialistic world-view that typically forms the background of contemporary liberal self-consciousness, while refraining from the claim that this view has been 'established' by a *method*."[28] While Rorty's embrace of this materialist world-view does not necessarily commit him to the philosophical dream of a *mathesis universalis*, it does betray his uncritical acceptance of the interpretation of being that the experimental sciences introduced into modern European philosophy—an interpretation whose phenomenological genesis remains unexplored in his work. This failure of self-reflection is, as we have already seen, the upshot of thoroughgoing naturalism. Naturalism is a habit of thought that forgets that physical nature, as understood by the natural sciences, is not the primary datum of consciousness; it forgets that the world intended in the scientific attitude cannot be inhabited, but only focused on temporarily. Or, to use Hegel's categorial language rather than the language of phenomenology, naturalism is a kind of explanation that forgets that the categories it employs in the explanation of natural being cannot account for the thinking that uncovers natural being.

Because Rorty's accounts of language and interpretation are tacitly structured by the ontological commitments of his naturalism, his pragmatic nominalism is not the theoretically neutral position he would have us believe it is. As a pragmatist, Rorty asks us to adopt a picture of "people in whose minds new vocabularies developed, thereby equipping them with tools for doing things which could not even have been envisaged before these tools were available."[29] As a nominalist, Rorty recommends that we see "language as just human beings using marks and noises to get what they want."[30] According to Rorty, there are many different and at times overlapping uses to which we put language in pursuit of food, sex, science, and beauty, but there is no reason at all "to lump these uses together into something big called 'Language,' and then to look for its 'conditions of possibility.'"31

Now while Rorty claims to resist identifying some common denominator of our multiple language uses, he nonetheless asserts something quite determinate about the nature of language in identifying his position as nominalistic. This identification strikes me as very odd, because if any philosophical doctrine is the direct result of the subjectivizing, representational turn taken by modern epistemology (the turn criticized, of course, in *Philosophy and the Mirror of Nature*), it is the nominalist thesis that the world consists only in particulars and that so-called natural kinds or species are in fact reifications of language use. In my view, it is precisely this nominalist outlook that blocks a sufficiently radical account of the constitutive character of language. Rorty's account of language as a contingent and shifting web of vocabularies issues from a curious subterfuge wherein this internally related system of vocabularies is identified as such "from outside," by someone detached from a first-order involvement in language. His nominalism rests unselfconsciously on the assumption of a prelinguistic disclosure of the world as an infinite manifold of discrete particulars, and of language as an arbitrary system of signs. His pragmatism is thus structured by an antecedent (and illegitimate) viewing of us and our webs, one that places these webs within a reductive ontological frame. Ultimately, language is, for Rorty, simply one part of nature that human beings (another part of nature) utilize to cope with the rest of nature.

It is the naturalistic and nominalistic presuppositions of Rorty's account of language that separate his frankly ethnocentric, conventionalist theory of belief from Hegel's conception of speculative thought, as well as from contemporary hermeneutic theories of language and meaning derived from Hegel's philosophy of spirit. Rorty argues that knowledge and belief cannot be explained epistemologically but only "sociologically": they are functions of what our society lets us say. In this idea of what our society lets us say Rorty would no doubt have us hear a less ghostly version of what Hegel calls spirit. Society is a complex natural entity comprised of persons engaged in multiple practices structured by shifting webs of discourse. By naturalizing the background conditions of meaningfulness or of what we are able to think and say, however, Rorty has simply begged the question.

To identify society as the pregiven or already constituted empirical totality internal to which our thoughts and sayings hang together is to assume, for the sake of the theory that explains those thoughts and sayings, a standpoint external to them. Thus Rorty has called upon something which is revealed through thought and language—nature—to serve as the explanatory ground of thought and language themselves.

What Hegel calls spirit is precisely that which is beyond nature, not because it excludes nature, but because it comprehends—in the double sense of the term—the principles of nature within itself. Spirit takes up the principles of nature within itself and it knows itself as having taken them up. Nature, on the other hand, is not in possession of itself (knowingly or otherwise); it is not self-related but is constituted through external causal relations. As such its essence lies outside its being. Nature is comprehended and has significance only because there is an entity whose essence it is to understand nature and itself as at once belonging to and existing beyond nature. Spirit's activity, whether described in terms of thought or language, cannot therefore be "naturalized" without committing the most egregious of category mistakes. To naturalize spirit is in effect to eliminate precisely those explanatory principles that enable both spirit's account of itself and its account of nature. In the final analysis, then, Rorty's naturalized Hegelianism is inadequate to Hegel because it is inadequate to our consciousness of ourselves as spirit. Spirit cannot be naturalized because nature cannot account for who we are. The reason that nature cannot account for who we are is simple: nature cannot account.

By naturalizing or detranscendentalizing Hegel, Rorty supposes he can eliminate the bogus metaphysical and epistemological presuppositions of Hegel's philosophy of spirit while bolstering its holistic, historicist, and antifoundationalist tendencies. I have demonstrated here that Rorty's naturalizing zeal also leads him, quite consistently, to eliminate that most basic transcendental principle that Hegel takes over from Kant: the principle of self-consciousness. Rorty, to put things mildly, has yet to own up to the serious consequences that his attempt to naturalize self-consciousness and spirit present for his thinking; for in assuming the stance of the thoroughgoing naturalist, Rorty undercuts the possibility of accounting for himself and his own activity of giving account. The problem with being a consistent naturalist is that you ultimately argue away the condition of possibility of your own argument: yourself (your self's own consciousness of itself).

RESPONSE TO ALLEN HANCE

I am grateful to Allen Hance for having read widely in my writings and for giving a very accurate account of my view of the history of modern philosophy. In writing about that history, I have never been happy with what I have said about Hegel. Much of Hegel remains mysterious to me. In particular, I cannot read *The Science of Logic* with interest, or pleasure, or understanding, or to the end. I envy people like Klaus Hartmann, Robert Pippin, Terry Pinkard, and Allen Hance who can. Yet I am almost as baffled by their account of what that book is supposed to be good for as I am by the book itself. I suspect that they see something important in Hegel—specifically, a new possibility that Hegel opened up for philosophical thought—which I do not. But I have great trouble pinning down what this possibility could amount to. I should rather like to achieve—if only as a momentary, experimental *frisson*—the sort of "trust in thinking" which Hance says Hegel recovered, but I cannot seem to manage it.[1]

As I say in "The Future of Philosophy" (chapter 9), I think that the opportunities open to philosophical thought are typically created by events outside of philosophy—events like the New Science, the theory of evolution, psychoanalysis, the American and French Revolutions, and the rise of industrial capitalism. These events are hard to deal with in old vocabularies—vocabularies created to deal with a different world, one in which these events had not yet erupted and changed the landscape. The people we call "great philosophers" seem to me the people who have found ways of marrying the new ways of speaking—and, more generally, the new social practices—suggested by these events with older ways of speaking and acting.

If that is philosophy's assignment, however—the assignment which Hegel summed up as "holding its time in thought"—then it is hard to see how the same discipline might be expected to produce a "phenomenological ontology" that would exhibit what Hance calls "the system of the contents of thought" (109). Coming from the historicist side of Hegel—the side which is most prominent at the end of the introduction to the *Philosophy of Right*—I have trouble seeing how "thought" can have a system of contents, as opposed to a series of reactions to problems. I entirely agree with Hance that Hegel *thought* he had gotten beyond such merely reactive and reflective philosophy to an autonomous, self-generating, speculative kind of philosophy. But I agree with Kierkegaard that it was precisely that mistaken notion that made Hegel fall on his face.[2]

This point can be restated by glossing Hance's remark that "Ultimately, language is, for Rorty, simply one part of nature that human beings (another part of nature) utilize to cope with the rest of nature" (120). As with Alexander's and Gouinlock's uses of "mere," I have trouble with Hance's use of "simply" in this sentence. I would also add the phrase "and to create new identities for themselves" at the end of the sentence. Despite these caveats, however, the basic thrust of Hance's sentence is quite right. The reason this description of language seems wrong to Hance and right to me is that he contrasts both *nature* and *language* with *thought*, whereas I cannot see that *thought* means anything more than *language* does. Because I cannot, I cannot achieve the "trust in thinking" which Hance, like Heidegger, gained from Hegel. There is no such thing, I take it, as "trust in language," as opposed to trust in one or another vocabulary to do a certain job. So, because I cannot think of thinking as something different from using language, I cannot contrast *nature* and *thought*.

Hance says at the end of his chapter that people like me, who try to be "consistent naturalist[s] . . . argue away the condition of possibility of [their] own argument" (121). One of my reasons for thinking that Hegel (as Hance puts it) "drank deeply from the chalice of modern epistemology" (102) is that I think nobody would take the notion of "condition of possibility" seriously who did not lust after the sort of certainty that Descartes wanted and that Dewey scorned. If What is the condition of possibility of *X*? is a good question, there must be a noncausal relation between *X* and something else. Inquiries into merely causal relations are, for the usual

Humean reasons, unlikely to produce certainty.

As I see it, the *only* function of the idea of a condition of possibility, as opposed to a causal condition of actuality, is to provide the illusion of a domain of inquiry that can produce certainty. Where Hance thinks that Hegel discovered a domain of inquiry, I think he invented a domain of fantasy. He did so, I suspect, because he found the possibility that philosophy might be *just* its time held in thought—or, more exactly, the thought that one's time might *not* be a clue to something ahistorical—too depressing. What Hance sees as a triumphant insight I see as a failure of nerve—the same sort of failure that made Descartes thirst for more than what Bacon and Hobbes had found sufficient (and Socrates thirst for more than what Sophocles had found sufficient).

This mention of Hobbes, however, should not be taken as an endorsement of Hance's claim that, as Hobbes may have done, I believe that "the world consists only in particulars" (120). I do not think that the world consists only of anything, because I do not think that there is a Way the World Is. But Hance is right that I think that "so-called natural kinds or species are, in fact, reifications of language use" (120). (This goes, in particular, for the natural kind called "particulars.") There is no point in trying to figure out whether a given term signifies a natural or an unnatural kind, but a lot of point in figuring out whether it is a relatively useful term or a relatively useless one.

That is why I cannot take seriously the idea that we should reconstitute the Greek appearance-reality distinction (as Hegel and Hance do) as that between less concrete and more concrete wholes. I cannot see a use for the notion of "concrete whole" any more than for that of "natural kind." The only use I can find for it is in enlarging on the fantasy of finding the whole "system of the contents of thought." From my point of view, notions like "conditions of possibility," "contents of thought," "concrete whole," *Denken*, "thing in itself,"[3] and "essence lying outside of being" are all parts of the same set of interdefinable notions. I see these notions as fitting together to form a tool that is necessary if one is to produce something like *The Science of Logic*. But because I cannot find a use for the product, I have no use for the tool.

Hance sees it as a tool that is forced upon us once we realize that naturalism is self-refuting. But naturalism is self-refuting only if one thinks that *What are the conditions of possibility for my self's consciousness of itself?* is a good question. One will not think that unless one has already picked up the very tool that I think should have been discarded. As I see it, there will always be an unbreakable standoff between *Denken* and naturalism. Neither can claim neutrality with respect to the other. (I do not, *pace* Hance, regard pragmatic nominalism as a theoretically neutral position, any more than I regard Hance as occupying such a position.) Naturalists have no use for *Denken*, and nobody would be interested in *Denken* unless they had first become dissatisfied with naturalism.

I do not think that my nominalism—my view that there is no point to the question of Natural or unnatural kind?—"rests unselfconsciously on the assumption of a prelinguistic disclosure of the world as an infinite manifold of discrete particulars" (120).[4] Nor do I think that language is "an arbitrary system of signs," any more than that the constellations are *arbitrary* arrangements of stars. Given the conditions we live in, they are among the arrangements of stars that it is useful for us to talk about. More generally, given the conditions we live in, the language we use is the obvious way for us to talk. There may be better ways, but they will not be discovered by analyzing the "conditions of possibility" of present ways, or by "the dialectical engendering of richer and more inclusive systems of explanation" (118). They will be discovered by somebody proposing a new idiom, its being tried out, and its being found to work better than its predecessor.

In order to continue my argument with Hance, Pinkard, Pippin, and other fans of *The Science of Logic*, I would have to have a better idea of the phenomena which my critics think need to be saved, and which they think naturalism does not save. Apparently they see, as I do not, a way of putting forward a philosophically neutral problematic—a set of problems about how to save phenomena, problems that confront us prior to the choice between Hegel and Dewey, and that Hegel was better at solving than Dewey was. In particular, they see the possibility of thought as such a problem. I see it as what Hance (referring to "the problem of how thought or language hooks up with the world") calls a "philosophical canard" (106).

7

VULGAR PRAGMATISM:

AN UNEDIFYING PROSPECT

Susan Haack

SHE: For the last time, do you love me or don't you?
HE: I DON'T!
SHE: Quit stalling, I want a direct answer.
—Jane Russell and Fred Astaire, "carrying on the conversation"[1]

The main target of this paper is Richard Rorty, since the publication of *Philosophy and the Mirror of Nature*[2] probably the most influential critic of the epistemological enterprise in contemporary English-speaking philosophy. The secondary target is Stich, who has of late shifted his allegiance from the scientistic to the "pragmatist" camp.

There are significant differences between Rorty's and Stich's arguments, and in the conclusions they reach. But they have in common at least this: both repudiate the idea that criteria of justification should be judged by their truth-indicativeness. Rorty thinks the idea makes no sense; Stich, that it is narrow-minded and parochial.

Referring to Rorty and Stich as "vulgar pragmatists" is intended as an implicit challenge to their claim to be the philosophical descendants of the classical pragmatists, a challenge that will be made explicit in the closing paragraphs of this paper. But the main goals here are epistemological rather than historical. The major theme is that neither Rorty nor Stich has any good arguments that the familiar epistemological projects are misconceived. A secondary theme will be that both Rorty and Stich fail to grasp that to believe that p is to accept p as true; with the result that the "edifying" philosophy into which Rorty wants the ex-epistemologist to put his energies masks a cynicism which would undermine not only epistemology, not only "systematic" philosophy, but inquiry generally; and that the liberated post-analytic epistemology which Stich envisages turns out to consist in a search for more efficient techniques of self-deception. As my title says: not an edifying prospect.

Still, the hope is, by revealing the poverty of the revolutionaries' post-epistemological utopias I can begin to articulate why, in my view, epistemology is indispensable—and to sketch some of the contours of the problem of ratification, of the relation of justification and truth.

I

Rorty wants, he says, to replace *confrontation* with *conversation*. This sounds like a plea to stop the bombing and get around the conference table. But it means something more like: we should abandon the conception of philosophy as centered in epistemology, as seeking "foundations" for knowledge in "privileged representations," and accept that there is nothing more to the justification of beliefs than local and parochial convention, our practices of objection, response, concession. This bears on its face the characteristic stamp of Rorty's This-or-Nothingism: *either* we accept this particular composite, a certain conception of the role of philosophy within culture, of the role of epistemology within philosophy, of the role of "foundations" within the structure of knowledge, this "neo-Kantian consensus," *or* we jettison the whole lot and take "carrying on the conversation" as our highest aspiration.

According to Rorty, the idea that there is such a discipline as epistemology, as a distinctively philosophical theory of knowledge which is to inquire into the foundations of science, and *a fortiori* the idea of philosophy as centered in epistemology, is quite a recent one. It could arise only in the context of a perceived distinction between science and philosophy, an idea implicit in the work of Descartes and Hobbes, which came to seem obvious only since Kant. Locke, learning from Descartes to look inward, conceived of the theory of knowledge as the science of the mind; then Kant's Copernican revolution made this "science of the mind" distinctively philosophical by raising it to the a priori level (131–64).

The philosophical theory of knowledge has developed, furthermore, under the influence of a variety of perceptual or ocular metaphors, an analogy of knowing with seeing, which encourages a confusion of knowledge that p with knowledge of x, of justification with causation, and of which the idea of "foundations" of knowledge is a product. This conception of epistemology and its role in philosophy, and this set of metaphors, are "optional" (146, 159, 162–63).

That this "foundationalism" is fundamentally misconceived has been revealed, Rorty argues, as the epistemological tradition has worked itself out in analytic philosophy, by the combination of Quine's and Sellars's critical arguments. Between them, Sellars's critique of the notion of the given, and Quine's of the notion of the analytic (and hence, by implication, of the a priori) combine to undermine the whole conception of epistemology as foundational. Sellars's critique unmasks the confusion of justification with causation; Quine's reveals the hopelessness of seeking foundations of an a priori character (169ff.).

Neither Quine nor Sellars, Rorty thinks, fully appreciates the revolutionary impact of their combined work, but he is convinced that it makes the conclusion inescapable that justification is nothing more than a matter of social practice. To say that A knows that p is to say "something about the way human beings interact" (175). For a belief to be justified is for it to be defensible against "conversational objections." "[W]e understand knowledge when we understand the social justification of belief," Rorty writes, "and thus have no need to view it as accuracy of representation" (170).

The last clause is an indication of just how radical Rorty's position is. The differing criteria of different times or cultures or communities, he holds, are "incommensurable"; no agreement can be expected about which standards of defending beliefs are correct. And neither does it make sense to seek to ratify these or those criteria of justification by arguing that beliefs which satisfy them are likely to be true; for this requires the idea of truth as correspondence, as faithful picturing—another legacy of the ocular metaphor, and covertly unintelligible. Justification is not only a social, but also an entirely conventional, matter: it makes no sense to suppose that our practices of criticizing and defending beliefs could be grounded in anything external to those practices (178).

Rorty urges the repudiation of the idea that the abandonment of epistemology leaves any gap that needs to be filled. Still, he thinks there remains a role for the ex-epistemologist; but it is to be "hermeneutic" rather than epistemological, "edifying" rather than systematic, rather poetic than philosophical in the traditional sense, a matter of "carrying on the conversation," of seeking new vocabularies instead of persisting in a hopeless attempt to commensurate incommensurable discourses (315ff.).

Well, no, certainly one wouldn't want to waste one's time doing *that!* But while pondering the futility of trying to commensurate incommensurable discourses may have convinced some to abandon epistemology, it leads me to suspect that the tautological is being transmuted into the tendentious: e.g., that we judge by the standards by which we judge, into, it makes no sense to ask what the basis of our standards might be; or: that we can't describe anything except in language, into, there is nothing outside language for our descriptions to represent accurately or inaccurately.

But I digress. The question at issue is: does Rorty have any arguments that establish that it makes no sense to suppose that criteria of justification need, or could have, objective grounding?

Fortunately, it is not necessary to engage in detailed discussion of Rorty's claims about the history of epistemology. (This *is* fortunate, because there are significant difficulties in determining just what Rorty's historical story is. Is the enterprise he repudiates supposed to have begun with Descartes? with Locke? with Kant? Does he gloss over the relevance to Descartes' project of the then recently-rediscovered writings of the ancient skeptics because to acknowledge its importance might lead us to perceive the disputed conception as much older, much less "recent," than he would have us suppose? And so on.) The point on which I want to insist is simple: it is of course true that what we now perceive to be the problems and projects of epistemology have evolved during a long and complicated historical process, a process involving multi-layered and overlapping shifts and refinements in the ways problems were conceptualized and tackled; but this has not the slightest tendency to show that "epistemology" is just a term for a bunch of pseudo-problems. It is, surely, a fact familiar from the history of the sciences as well as from the history of philosophy that reformulating, refining and refocusing problems is one way of making progress. I would go so far as to say that a discipline in which problems had ceased to evolve *would* be dead.

Nor is it necessary to engage in detailed consideration of Rorty's claims about the influence of ocular metaphors. (This is doubly fortunate, because there are significant difficulties here, both in reconciling Rorty's stress on the importance of a style of metaphor which was at least as predominant in

Plato as in Descartes or Locke or Kant with his claim that the disputed conception of the philosophical theory of knowledge is recent, and in reconciling it with the resolutely non-cognitivist theory of metaphor he elsewhere defends.) For, once again, the point on which I want to insist is simple. I don't deny the epistemological importance of metaphors—how could I, given my concern to replace the model of the mathematical proof by an analogy with a crossword puzzle as better representing the structure of justification? But it has yet to be shown that ocular metaphors have led to a preoccupation with problems which, cleared of their metaphorical accretions, would be seen to be misconceived.[3]

The arguments considered thus far amount to little more than an inference from "optional" to "misconceived," obviously a non sequitur.

The focus must be on Rorty's arguments that "foundationalism" is not just optional, but misconceived. It is impossible to assess these arguments, however, without disambiguating "foundationalism" and "epistemology as foundational." Sometimes Rorty uses these expressions to refer to experientialist versions of the foundationalist style of theory of justification;[4] sometimes to refer to the idea that epistemology is an a priori enterprise the goal of which is to legitimize the claim of the sciences to give us knowledge; sometimes to what might less confusingly be called "epistemic objectivism," the thesis that criteria of justification require objective grounding. The required distinctions may be marked as follows:

> (experientialist) foundationalism: theory of justification distinguishing basic beliefs, held to be justified, independently of the support of any other beliefs, by experience, and derived beliefs, held to be justified by the support of basic beliefs [i.e., which postulates basic beliefs justified by experience as the foundations of knowledge];
>
> *foundationalism*: conception of epistemology as an a priori discipline; of the explication of criteria of justification as an analytic enterprise, of their ratification as requiring a priori proof of their truth-indicativeness [i.e., which regards a priori epistemology as founding the sciences];
>
> FOUNDATIONALISM: thesis that criteria of justification are not purely conventional but stand in need of objective grounding, being satisfactory only if truth-indicative [i.e., which takes criteria of justification to be founded by their relation to truth].

FOUNDATIONALISM does not imply *foundationalism,* nor *foundationalism* foundationalism. It could be that though criteria of justification stand in need of ratification (as FOUNDATIONALISM holds), ratification is not to be achieved a priori (as *foundationalism* holds) but within, or with the help of, empirical knowledge. Or it could be that the way to ratify criteria of justification is (as *foundationalism* holds) a priori, but that the correct criteria are not foundationalist, but coherentist or foundherentist.

The allegation of a confusion of justification with causation, like the appeal to Sellars's critique of the given, is relevant to foundationalism; the appeal to Quine's critique of analyticity, to *foundationalism*; and only Rorty's remarks about the unintelligibility of truth-as-mirroring to FOUNDATIONALISM. So I shall comment only briefly on the first two lines of argument, since clearly it is on FOUNDATIONALISM, not *foundationalism* or foundationalism, that the legitimacy of epistemology depends.

Sellars's critique of the idea of the given does damage the experientialist foundationalist style of theory of justification—though strong more than weak versions.[5] And Rorty is right, experientialist foundationalism is not defensible, even in its weaker forms. The allegation of a confusion of justification with causation, however, can be answered, indeed, has been answered in my account of the interaction of the causal and the evaluative aspects of justification. This is important because, like experientialist foundationalism, foundherentism insists on the relevance of the subject's experience to the justification of his empirical beliefs, and thus acknowledges a causal element.

This last observation throws another point into sharp relief: that experientialist foundationalism fails is quite insufficient to oblige one to accept anything like Rorty's conversationalist alternative. One might, like Davidson (who agrees with Rorty that experientialist foundationalism rests on a confusion of justification with causation), opt for some form of coherentism; or, like myself (disagreeing with Rorty and Davidson on this issue), for foundherentism.[6]

Rorty is right, also, in thinking that *foundationalism* is not defensible. But the appeal to Quine's critique of analyticity is neither necessary nor sufficient to establish this.[7] Not sufficient: because even if there are no analytic truths it follows that there is no a priori knowledge only on the assumption that only analytic truths can be known a priori; more importantly, not necessary: because, given that the ratification of criteria of empirical justification will require synthetic assumptions (assumptions about human cognitive capacities), that *foundationalism* is false would follow from the repudiation of the synthetic a priori alone.

Rorty is also rightly critical of Quine's attempt to turn epistemology into psychology. Given the significance he attaches to the fact that the distinction between science and philosophy is relatively recent, it seems likely that he has in mind some such further argument as this: once the idea is abandoned that philosophy deals with the sphere of the a priori, science with the a posteriori, the idea of a distinctively philosophical theory of knowledge is seen to be untenable. But if this is what he is thinking, it misses a significant subtlety: giving up the idea that philosophy is distinguished by its a priori character encourages a picture of philosophy as continuous with the sciences, as part of empirical inquiry; but this does not oblige one to deny that there is a difference of degree between the sciences and philosophy. So it by no means follows that all legitimate questions about knowledge must be answerable by the sciences; nor, therefore, that (as Rorty may be thinking) any question about knowledge not answerable by the sciences is not legitimate.

So the whole weight of Rorty's case against epistemology, to repeat, rests on the repudiation of FOUNDATIONALISM, which depends on considerations about truth. And here one finds less argument than assertion. (Also a rather neat piece of strategy: though section 5 of chapter VI of *Philosophy and the Mirror of Nature* is entitled "Truth Without Mirrors," and section 6 "Truth, Goodness and Relativism," *there is no entry under "truth" in the index!* Rorty is, I take it, letting us know the importance he attaches to the concept.) A key passage is this one, from one of the sections with unlisted telephone numbers:

> [T] here are . . . two senses apiece of "true" and "real" and "correct representation of reality," and . . . most of the perplexities in epistemology come from vacillation between them . . . [C]onsider the homely use of "true" to mean "what you can defend against all comers." . . . It is [this] homely and shopworn sense of "true" which Tarski and Davidson are attending to. . . . The skeptic and Putnam switch to the specifically "philosophical" sense of . . . "true" which, like the Ideas of Pure Reason, [is] designed precisely to stand for the Unconditioned. . . . (308)

This is (especially coming from a philosopher who likes to align himself with Dewey) a stunningly untenable dualism. We seem to be offered a choice between identifying truth with what is defensible against conversational objections, and taking it to be—well, something else, something not specified but hinted at in the allusion to Kant and to Putnam's distinction of metaphysical versus internal realism; something, anyway, rather pretentious, something aspired to despite, or even because of, its inaccessibility.

To deal with this false dichotomy I need, first, a more discriminating and less confusing classification of concepts of truth. At the strongly irrealist end, there is (i) Rorty's proposed identification of "true" with "what you can defend against all comers." Between this irrealist conception and anything that would appropriately be called "realist" is (ii) Peirce's conception of truth as the hypothetical ideal theory, the "ultimate opinion" that would survive all experiential evidence and full logical scrutiny. If realism with respect to truth is taken, as seems appropriate here, as requiring a conception which is non-epistemic, i.e., which allows that even a hypothetical ideal theory might be false or incomplete, then the realist category would include (iii) Ramsey's redundancy theory, according to which "it is true that p" is just an elaborate way of saying that p; (iv) Tarski's semantic theory, which makes truth a relation between closed formulae and infinite sequences of objects; (v) Wittgenstein's and Russell's Logical Atomist correspondence theories, which make truth a structural isomorphism of proposition to fact, and Austin's correspondence theory, which makes truth a relation of conventions linking statements to states of affairs; and (vi) a conception of truth as copying or mirroring Things-in-Themselves. I will sometimes refer to (i) as "irrealist"; (ii) as "pragmatist"; (iii) and (iv) as "minimally realist"; (v) as "strongly realist"; and (vi) as "grandly transcendental."

Simple as it is, this classification enables us to struggle free of the wool Rorty is trying to pull over our eyes. Rorty hopes we will choose his first option as obviously more palatable than his second. But, to repeat, the dichotomy is false—grossly false, in fact. It is not just that we are being maneuvered into a choice between extremes (the irrealist versus the grandly transcendental), but also that the maneuvering consists in part of tendentious reclassification of the intermediate positions. We can, and most certainly should, decline to choose either of the options Rorty offers us. It cannot be said too plainly that there is *no* sense of "true," homely or otherwise, in which it means "what you can defend against all comers"; neither does Tarski, or Davidson,[8] think there is. Declining the irrealist option does not oblige us to go grandly transcendental. We may opt, instead, for a Peircean pragmatism, for a minimal, or for a stronger realism.

Nor should we allow Rorty's grossly false dichotomy to disguise the fact that he is relying on our being repelled by the grandly transcendental instead of supplying arguments against pragmatist (for reasons to be explained below, I am strongly disinclined to give Rorty the word), or minimally realist, or strongly realist, conceptions of truth. Indeed, he hasn't really any *arguments* even against the grandly transcendental.

The present goal, remember, is to show that Rorty has no good arguments against the legitimacy of epistemology. Since only his repudiation of FOUNDATIONALISM is relevant to the legitimacy of epistemology, the issue is whether he has any good arguments against FOUNDATIONAL-ISM. And since his repudiation of FOUNDATIONALISM depends on his views about truth, I conclude that, since he has no arguments against pragmatist, minimally realist, strongly realist, or even grandly transcendental views of truth, he has, *a fortiori*, no good arguments against them, nor, therefore, against FOUNDATIONALISM, nor, therefore, against epistemology.

This is not, of itself, sufficient to establish the legitimacy of epistemology. But I think that a closer look at the post-epistemological future Rorty envisages, and the conception of justification that motivates it, will begin to make it apparent that abandoning epistemology is not an appealing prospect.

Rorty's conversationalist conception of justification takes justifying a belief to be a matter of social practice or convention, variable both within and between cultures, and nothing more. A natural interpretation, and one which comports with Rorty's frequent admiring references to the later Wittgenstein, would take conversationalism as a conjunction of two theses: contextualism at the level of explication, conventionalism at the level of ratification.

Contextualism is a style of theory of justification; it contrasts with foundationalism, coherentism, foundherentism. Its characteristic thesis is that "A is justified in believing that p" is to be analyzed along the lines of "with respect to the belief that p, A satisfies the epistemic standards of the epistemic community to which A belongs."

Conventionalism is a meta-epistemological thesis, a thesis about criteria of justification; it contrasts with epistemic objectivism, i.e., FOUNDA-TIONALISM. Its characteristic thesis is that epistemic standards are entirely conventional, that it makes no sense to ask which criteria of justification (those of this or that epistemic community) are correct, which are really indicative of the likely truth of a belief.

Though contextualists sometimes make observations about the structure of justification which have a vaguely foundationalist air ("contextually basic beliefs are those which stand in no need of justification within the epistemic community; all other justified beliefs are justified by reference to these contextually basic beliefs") contextualism is distinct from foundationalism, for (i) it insists on the addendum "in the epistemic community to which A belongs," and (ii) it does not posit beliefs justified otherwise than by the support of further beliefs. And though contextualists maintain, as coherentists do, that justification is a matter of relations among beliefs, contextualism is distinct from coherentism too, for (i) it insists on the addendum "in the epistemic community to which A belongs," and (ii) it does not make relations of coherence sufficient for justification.

So contextualism has sometimes been welcomed as a third alternative to the traditionally rival theories—and some readers may have been wondering why I didn't consider it more carefully before proposing my "third alternative." The reason can now be made clear. Contextualism may appear a harmless, even attractive, option with respect to the problem of explication, but it leads to a radical, indeed revolutionary, attitude to the project of ratification—to conventionalism, the second element in Rorty's conversationalism.

Contextualism is pointless unless (a) different epistemic communities have different epistemic standards and (b) there is no distinguished epistemic community, C*, such that the standards of C* are, while those of other communities are not, truth-indicative. For if (a) were false the characteristic contextualist addendum would be vacuous; and if (b) were false the status of the epistemic standards of C* would be so distinguished relative to the standards of other communities as to oblige one to concede that for A to be *really and truly* justified, he should meet the standards of C*. Rorty is a little coy about what exactly the "incommensurability" to which he appeals amounts to (though he is quite concerned to distinguish it from the meaning-variance thesis with which, in Kuhn's work, it is associated); but the likeliest interpretation seems to be: that there is no higher court of appeal in which agreement could be reached among the different epistemic standards of different communities—i.e., that it is an amalgam of theses (a) and (b).

Since contextualism contrasts with foundationalism (as well as coherentism and foundherentism) and conventionalism with FOUNDATIONALISM, this makes it even less surprising that Rorty, *qua* conversationalist, should fail to distinguish foundationalism and FOUNDATIONALISM. But doesn't it suggest that Rorty has a reply to one of the arguments used earlier, that a refutation of foundationalism is irrelevant to the standing of FOUNDATIONALISM? No: because, although contextualism indeed provides strong motivation for conventionalism, the falsity of foundationalism does not provide strong motivation for contextualism; the options of coherentism and foundherentism remain.

Rorty perhaps fails to appreciate this because (naturally enough, he does not consider the foundherentist option, and) he shows the occasional tendency to describe his position as "coherentist" (178). But he does that for no better reason than that his position is opposed to "foundationalism"— thus compounding his indiscriminate use of "foundationalism" with a correspondingly undiscriminating use of "coherentism."

Conversationalism, on the present interpretation (= contextualism + conventionalism), is quite a tightly-knit conception, since contextualism, as we saw, provides strong motivation for conventionalism. It is, however, both relativist and cynical.

It is relativist, because contextualism makes justification depend on the epistemic community to which the subject belongs, and, since conventionalism precludes the possibility of any higher-minded conception of really-truth-indicative justification* (justification by the standards of C*), it must treat the epistemic standards of any and every epistemic community as on a par.

And it is cynical, because if one really believed that criteria of justification are purely conventional, wholly without objective grounding, then, though one might conform to the justificatory practices of one's own epistemic community, one would be obliged to adopt an attitude of cynicism towards them, to think of justification always in covert scare quotes. The problem is not that, in general, one cannot engage in a practice one regards as wholly conventional. It is that, in particular, one cannot coherently engage fully—non-cynically—in a practice *of justifying beliefs* that one regards as wholly conventional. For *to believe that p is to accept p as true.*

(This is not a sophisticated remark about truth, but a truism about belief.) And, since to believe that p is to accept p as true, for one who denies that it even makes sense to suppose that there is any connection between a belief's being justified according to our practices, and its being true, it is impossible to see why a belief's being justified, conforming to those practices, should be thought to have any bearing on whether one should hold it.

From time to time, however, Rorty protests against the accusations— which, you will gather, I am not the first to make—that he is "relativist" or "cynical." His defensive remarks have more than a little of the flavor of Berkeley's protests that he is not denying the reality of physical objects. ("I'm not a relativist, I believe in objectivity—you just have to realize that objectivity is a matter of social agreement, not correspondence to some supposed 'reality'"). But the real reason he thinks the accusation of relativism can be brushed off is to be found elsewhere. Even in the *Mirror*, there is evidence against, as well as evidence for, the interpretation of Rorty's conversationalism as combining conventionalism with contextualism. Sometimes, at least, Rorty sounds less contextualist than, as I shall say, tribalist; for example, "The Quine-Sellars approach [i.e., the Rorty approach] to epistemology . . . say[s] that truth and knowledge can only be judged by the standards of inquirers of our own day" (178). This suggests not contextualism but tribalism: "A is justified in believing that p iff A satisfies the criteria of *our* epistemic community." And by the time of *Objectivity, Relativism and Truth* (1991) Rorty's commitment to tribalism ("solidarity"), rather than relativism, seems clear.

This enables Rorty to answer the criticism that he is relativist, but does not get him off the hook; on the contrary, it reveals just how deep his difficulties are. Tribalism is entirely arbitrary and unmotivated unless one thinks that the criteria of one's own epistemic community are better than those of other communities; that is, it pulls *against* conventionalism, to which, however, Rorty is unambiguously committed. Hence conversationalism is either (first interpretation, = contextualism + conventionalism) both relativist and cynical, or (second interpretation, = tribalism + conventionalism), no longer relativist, but still cynical, and incoherent to boot.

This begins to explain why Rorty's own *modus operandi* seems so odd, and why his accounts of the post-epistemological philosophy he envisages are so puzzling.

We have ("as a matter of social practice," Rorty would say) criteria for what counts as good reasons, as flimsy evidence, as jumping to conclusions, and so forth. And Rorty apparently aspires to conform to those criteria when he tries to persuade us that those criteria are wholly without objective grounding, entirely conventional. If he really believes that those criteria are entirely conventional, however, he can't be fully engaged in this enterprise; he must, rather, be abiding by those standards only as a ploy to persuade others less enlightened than himself by playing the game by their rules. He must be a cynic.

In the introduction to *Philosophy and the Mirror of Nature*, no doubt as a preemptive strike against the charge of cynicism, Rorty tells the reader that he will be not so much arguing against more traditional conceptions as suggesting an alternative vision of what philosophy might better be. But in fact much of the body of the book is taken up with arguments against "foundationalism" (though, as I have said, it is hard to find arguments, as opposed to rhetoric, against FOUNDATIONALISM). By the time of *Contingency, Irony and Solidarity*, Rorty has a different defensive strategy: he describes those who, like himself, have grasped the "contingency" of language, the conventionality of justification, as "ironists." Ironists, he tells us, use the "final vocabulary" they find themselves with, but, realizing there are no objective grounds for choice between vocabularies, are "never quite able to take themselves seriously."[9] I shall not pause to protest the skillful insinuation that non-ironists are humorless prigs;[10] nor to press the point that acknowledgment of the possibility and the importance of linguist innovation is most certainly not the exclusive privilege of Rorty's ironists. The important point for now is to see that this re-description does not mitigate, though it does quite cleverly disguise, the cynicism on which I have been dwelling. The cleverness lies in suggesting that the ironist is simply more aware than the rest of us of the possibility that our criteria of justification may turn out to be in need of revision, and hence is less dogmatically committed to them. But this suggestion is thoroughly misleading; Rorty's ironist is no fallibilist, he is a cynic hiding behind a euphemism. He engages in "our" practices of justifying beliefs only at arms' length not because he thinks they might need revising, but because he thinks it makes no sense to ask whether they are or aren't really indicative of truth.

This reinforces the diagnosis suggested earlier, that construed—as Rorty's earlier work allows, and his later work encourages us to construe it—as combining conventionalism and tribalism, Rorty's conversationalism is incoherent. Tribalism requires "solidarity" with "our epistemic practices"; "irony" reveals that Rorty's supposed solidarity is no more than *pro forma*, cynical conformity with those practices.

It also reinforces the impression one gets from the *Mirror*, that Rorty's conception of the tasks to which the newly enlightened ex-epistemologist is to turn his energies is less edifying than baffling. (One is entitled to wonder, in any case, why, if the problems of epistemology really are misconceived, one should expect there to *be* any work conveniently awaiting the ex-epistemologist.) The edifying philosopher, one is told, will compare and contrast the incommensurable discourses which, as epistemologist, he confusedly hoped to commensurate (343); what does this mean, one asks oneself, if not that he is to turn sociologist of knowledge? One is told that he will study "abnormal" discourse (320); what could an abnormal discourse be, one asks oneself? If an attempted conversation between participants from incommensurable discourses, what more illuminating conclusion could the ex-epistemologist hope to reach than that there is irresoluble disagreement? And one is told that he will "carry on the conversation" of Western culture (377–78); but what, one asks oneself, if the various discourses which constitute Western culture really are incommensurable, could this be but participation in what he already knows must inevitably be mutual incomprehension?

There could be no honest intellectual work in Rorty's post-epistemological utopia. Unless there is such a thing as better and worse evidence for accepting this or that proposition as true—objectively better or worse evidence, that is—there can be no real inquiry of any kind: epistemological . . . or scientific, forensic, historical, mathematical. Since not even Rorty himself accepts this conclusion, and since his argument for abandoning epistemology rests, at bottom, on nothing more than a manifestly false dichotomy of extreme realism versus extreme irrealism about truth, the legitimacy of epistemology seems pretty secure.

II

Or *seemed* pretty secure; but now, with *The Fragmentation of Reason*[11] we have Stich's new critique to deal with.

Stich doesn't deny that it makes sense to ask whether these or those epistemic standards are truth-indicative, he only insists that it is parochial and narrow-minded, a kind of "epistemic chauvinism," to *care* whether one's beliefs are true; and he doesn't want to abandon epistemology altogether, but to revolutionize it, to shift its focus away from these narrow-minded concerns and onto the really important questions: how to improve cognitive processing so as better to achieve the things people really value—such as survival, fame, fortune, power, etc., etc. Stich is also unlike Rorty in welcoming, rather than resisting, the description "relativist." (But in the shifting kaleidoscope of Rorty's contribution to the conversation one finds this description of "the tradition in Western culture" from which he would have us turn away: "[t]he idea of Truth as something to be pursued for its own sake, not because it will be good for oneself, or for one's real or imaginary community . . .." [12] The sentiment, though not the prose, could be Stich's.)

To avoid any confusion, it should be said that now Stich admits that people do, after all, have beliefs. It should also be said that he now conceives of beliefs along the lines of "sentences in the head" (109ff.). This may be partly responsible for some of the difficulties I shall diagnose. At any rate, someone who thinks it illuminating to imagine the subject's head equipped with two boxes of sentences, one labeled "beliefs" and the other "desires," [13] runs the risk of failing to notice that *assent, acknowledgment of truth*, is part of the concept of belief.

It should also be noted that Stich's critique is informed by certain preconceptions about what epistemology does, specifically, by Goldman's conception of theories of justification as giving criteria of rightness of systems of rules of belief-formation, and his framework of deontological versus consequentialist theories, and, within the consequentialist, category of reliabilist versus explanationist versus pragmatist accounts. This may also be partly responsible for some of the difficulties I shall diagnose. At any rate, someone focused exclusively on processes of belief-formation runs some risk of losing sight of the connection of justification and evidence, and someone assuming that justification must be tied to truth either as directly as reliabilism ties it or not at all runs the risk of choosing the latter option for no better reason than the implausibility of the former.

Stich presents himself as arguing against "analytic epistemology," which he means "any epistemological project that takes the choice between competing justificational rules or competing criteria of rightness [note the use of Goldman's terminology] to turn on conceptual or linguistic analysis" (91). This Stich describes as parochial, chauvinistic: epistemic standards, he argues, are culturally acquired and vary from culture to culture, and so do the evaluative epistemic concepts embedded in everyday thought and language. And "[u]nless one is inclined towards chauvinism or xenophobia in matters epistemic, it is hard to see why one would care much that a cognitive process . . . accords with the set of evaluative notions that prevail in the society into which one happened to be born" (94). Unlike Rorty, Stich is rather repelled than attracted by tribalism.

But what if it could be shown that satisfaction of these or those epistemic criteria is an indication that one's belief is true? This, according to Stich, is still parochial; it assumes that having true beliefs is something to be valued. And this, he maintains, is "for most people . . . very dubious indeed" (98). In fact, according to Stich truth is neither an intrinsically nor an instrumentally valuable property for a belief to have.

A belief, according to the 1990 time-slice of Stich, is a brain state mapped by an interpretation function onto a proposition which has a truth-value, and which is true just in case the proposition onto which it is mapped is true. Stich proposes a "causal/functional account of our commonsense interpretation function," i.e., of the function mapping brain states on to propositions. He then points out that there are many possible alternatives to this function. The "standard" function, Stich continues, maps the belief he would express by "There is no water on the sun" onto the proposition that there is no H_2O on the sun, but an alternative function might map it onto the proposition that there is no H_2O or XYZ on the sun. He describes the standard function and the possible alternatives as generating different notions of reference (reference, REFERENCE*, REFERENCE** . . . etc., and truth (truth, TRUTH*, TRUTH** . . . etc.). Truth, he concludes, is just one among many possible truth-like values a belief might have (110ff.).

Once one grasps this, Stich thinks, one will come to doubt that truth is intrinsically valuable, realizing that valuing truth for its own sake is "a profoundly conservative thing to do" (118).

And, he continues, one will also realize that it is no less questionable whether truth is instrumentally valuable. Consider, for example, poor Harry: he believed that his flight left at 7:45 A.M., and this belief was true; unfortunately, the plane crashed, and Harry died. An alternative interpretation function would map the belief Harry would express by "my flight leaves at 7:45 A.M." onto the proposition that Harry's flight leaves at 8:45

A.M., and so make Harry's belief TRUE**** (though not, of course, true). Harry would have been better off with this TRUE**** belief than the true one he had. And this kind of argument, Stich continues, generalizes to lots of other goals that people take to be valuable. So "[t]rue beliefs are not always optimal in the pursuit of happiness or pleasure or desire satisfaction . . . [or] peace or power or love." Hence, "the instrumental value of true beliefs is far from obvious" (123, 124).

Urging, therefore, that we break out of the old, parochial, conservative, truth-oriented mould, Stich offers a "pragmatic" account of cognitive evaluation. Cognitive processes are to be evaluated as tools for achieving whatever it is that the subject actually values. The formula would presumably be something like: P is a good cognitive process, for A, iff P produces beliefs which conduce to whatever A values. This account is, as Stich notes, both relativistic and pluralistic: "in general it will not make sense to ask whether one system is better than another (full stop) . . . [I]t may well turn out that one system is best for one person or group, while another system is better for another person or group" (135–36).

It is open to question whether, in the relevant sense, epistemic standards really are local, parochial, culturally variable. Yes, there are scientific and pre-scientific cultures, there are cultures where the authority of a sacred text is respected and cultures where it is not; and yes, there may be, even within one culture, a great variety of *theories* of evidence or justification professed. But I am not sure that there is, or has been, a culture in which the fit of a proposition into an explanatory net of propositions anchored in sense and introspection (that is, explanatory integration and experiential anchoring) is not grounds for thinking it true. And I notice that the evidence Stich offers of cultural diversity is astonishingly thin: he refers to *one* piece of work, which he reports as claiming—contrary to the usual English-Yoruba translations—that Yoruba does not distinguish knowledge and true belief as we do, but the first- from the second-hand.[14] Interesting as it is, if true, that Yoruba speakers are equipped with something like Russell's 1912 distinction of knowledge versus probable opinion,[15] this is inconclusive, to put it mildly, with respect to the claim that our epistemic standards are simply idiosyncratic and parochial.

It would be unwise, however, to put much weight on this point here, because the relevance of cultural diversity to Stich's main thesis is marginal. For one thing, he is careful to hedge his bets, as: "other languages and other cultures *certainly could and probably do* evoke conceptions of cognitive evaluation that are significantly different from our own" (94, my italics). But, more important, that our epistemic standards are, or could be, culturally local, features as premiss only in a relatively minor, softening-up phase of Stich's argument. The main phase acknowledges the possibility that our standards (local or not) might be demonstrably truth-indicative, and maintains that, *even so*, a preference for those standards would be "chauvinistic," depending on a "profoundly conservative" preference for truth over TRUTH*, TRUTH**, TRUTH***, . . . etc.

One can see why Stich thought the reader might need to be softened up before the main phase of the argument, though, because what he offers next is remarkably feeble. What he would need to do is to show that truth is valuable only if either intrinsically or instrumentally valuable, and that it is neither; what he offers is little more than mere assertion that it is "not obvious" that truth is either. Stich admits that his arguments are "not knockdown" (120). His strategy is dismayingly familiar from his earlier work: he hints that he has arguments for a startling thesis, offers considerations which go nowhere near establishing it, disarms the reader by conceding that his arguments are inconclusive, and then, urging that it is *possible* that his startling thesis is true, thrusts the burden of proof on the opposition.

Just to keep the record straight: all Stich offers to persuade us that truth is not intrinsically valuable is the observation that truth is just one of a whole range of semantic properties a belief might have (truth, TRUTH*, TRUTH**, . . . etc.), the one which happens to be picked out in our culture. Frankly, I have no idea even what it might mean to say that another culture picked out, say, TRUTH* instead of truth; and I would protest the suggestion that TRUTH*, TRUTH**, etc., are *truth*-values.[16] But in any case, that truth is one of a range of semantic properties of beliefs simply has no bearing on whether it is or isn't intrinsically valuable. And all that Stich offers to persuade us that truth is not instrumentally valuable is the observation that in some circumstances, Harry's for example, a true belief may lead to one's death while a TRUE**** belief would have saved one's life. This shows—what I don't deny—that an isolated true belief may not be *optimally* instrumentally valuable. But it simply has no bearing on whether truth is or isn't instrumentally valuable, period.

This establishes, I hope, that Stich has no good arguments why, because of their orientation to truth, the familiar epistemological projects are misconceived. It is tempting to leave it at that—by way of parting shot, perhaps, noting that what Stich purports to do is not to show that accepting his startling thesis would conduce to whatever the reader values, not to show that it is TRUE*, TRUE** . . . or whatever, but to give reasons for thinking it true. But, as so often, there is a better view from the steeper path; or maybe I should say, benefit to be gained from the exercise of shouldering, for a while, the burden of proof Stich thrusts at those of us who value truth.

The first part of my argument will be that truth is *epistemically* valuable, in this sense: that each of the concepts of inquiry, justification and belief is internally connected with the concept of truth.

I speak of inquiry, in the way characteristic of philosophers, in the most general sense: inquiry-into-how-things-are, so to speak. What is the goal of inquiry, thus broadly construed? Something like: to get as much interesting and important truth about the world as possible. But the suggestion of uniqueness is misleading, since "the" goal decomposes into two elements: truth, on the one hand, and interest or importance on the other. Obviously there is potential for tension between the two components, since it is a lot easier to get truths if one doesn't mind the truths one gets being trivial. There are plenty of unimportant or uninteresting truths.

But truth is, though not *the* goal, *an aspect of the goal* of inquiry. If you aren't trying to find out how things are, to get truth, you aren't really inquiring. (There is, however, a lot of pseudo inquiry about; that is why, when the government institutes an Official Inquiry into this or that, some of us reach for our scare quotes.)

Because inquiry has this double goal, appraisal of a person's success in inquiry has two dimensions, which might be roughly characterized as depth and security, the former being importance- and the latter truth-oriented. (Correspondingly, appraisal of a person *qua* inquirer has two dimensions, roughly characterizable as creativity and carefulness.)

When one focuses on questions of justification, however, one is *ipso facto* restricting oneself to the second of the two dimensions. Truth-indicativeness is the characteristic virtue of criteria of justification. (Goldman is quite right to insist on a connection of justification and truth—the very point on which Stich parts company with him; where he goes wrong is in making the connection too direct, attributive instead of referential.)

And to believe that p is to accept p as true.

That truth is epistemically valuable is entirely compatible with the fact that in some circumstances one may be better off not inquiring, or better off having an unjustified belief, or better off having a false belief; and with the fact that some truths are trivial, boring, or unimportant.

Stich would no doubt regard all this as no more than a quaint elaboration of my "profound conservatism." "So," he might say, "the concepts on which epistemology has traditionally focused are internally connected to the concept of truth—but why, except for a culturally-inherited bias towards truth-orientation, should we be interested in *them*?"

Part of the answer is that truth *is* instrumentally valuable. Knowledge of how things are enables us to bring about desired ends and to avoid undesired ones. Not always, of course; but when (as in Harry's case) a true belief serves us worse than a false belief would have done, more complete true beliefs could have served us better (if Harry had believed, truly, that his plane was due to leave at 7:45, and that it would crash, he could have saved not only his own life, but others' too).

The other part is harder to articulate. The best way I can put it is this: beliefs are what we have—so, since the concepts of belief and truth are internally connected, it is no cultural bias to value truth. Compared with other animals, human beings are not especially fast or strong; what we do have is a capacity to figure things out. This capacity is very imperfect, and it isn't an unmixed blessing, but who could seriously doubt that it is of instrumental value to us? The present point, though, is that it is the fact that we are animals who have beliefs and act intentionally that makes the epistemic value of truth something much deeper than a cultural quirk.

That this is right is confirmed by reflection on what Stich's post-revolutionary epistemology would do. Its task, we are told, is improvement of our cognitive processing; the goal, beliefs, whether true or false, such that his accepting them as true would conduce to what the subject values. That it must be *beliefs* which are produced is clear from the case of Harry; what would leave him better off is his *accepting as true*, i.e., believing, a proposition which is not true but TRUE****. 'TRUE****' is of course a magnificently misleading piece of typographical sleight of hand, as is apparent when one translates the last clause into English: Harry would be better off believing a different proposition which is not true but his believing which conduces to something he values.

There would not be much honest intellectual work in Stich's post-revolution-

ary epistemology, either. The explicative task is trivial: "good cognitive processing is processing which produces beliefs such that the subject's holding them conduces to what he values" is all there is to it. This lack of substance, by the way, is only to be expected; it is the mirror-image of the insubstantial character of Goldman's reliabilist explication. What of the regulative task, the "improvement of our cognitive processing" that Stich aspires to undertake? The "improvement," as we know, is to consist in our accepting as true, propositions, whether true or false, such that our believing them is advantageous. How is this to be achieved? If not by magic (though Stich's references to a helpful Genie suggest he may be hoping for magical assistance),[17] how else than by *better techniques of self-deception?*

Since Stich might reply that this is just profoundly conservative moralizing, I had better say that, though self-deception is, by my lights, always an epistemic failing, it is not always or necessarily a moral failing. The moral qualms one rightly feels about the project of helping the fence to believe that the surprisingly cheap goods he buys are not, after all, stolen, his believing which conduces to something he values, namely being on the right side of the law, do not extend to the project of helping the cancer victim to believe that he will recover, his believing which conduces to something he values, namely, surviving.

Stich might reply that this answers the charge of moralizing, but not the charge of profound conservatism. ("Why should I care that self-deception is an *epistemic* failing?—that's just a cultural quirk.") Tempting as it is to reply that this reveals that Stich's post-revolutionary "epistemology" would no longer be recognizably epistemology, it is more important to stress that it prompts, also, the realization that Stich's post-revolutionary epistemology, or "epistemology," could not displace the more traditional projects.

Why not? Because any non-trivial specification of what would constitute "cognitive improvement" (in Stich's peculiar sense) would require detailed knowledge of the circumstances in which true beliefs will conduce to what the subject values, and the circumstances in which false beliefs will do so. This "detailed knowledge" would have to be just that, detailed *knowledge*; false beliefs that conduced to something Stich values wouldn't do. And so the familiar, truth-oriented epistemological questions would still arise.

It is a fine irony that this last point was made, nearly a century ago. by C. S. Peirce, the founder of pragmatism. The context is a review of Pearson's book, *The Grammar of Science*; Peirce is objecting to Pearson's thesis that the goal of science is to forward the interests of society:

> I must confess that I belong to that class of scallawags who purpose, with God's help, to look the truth in the face, whether doing so be conducive to the interests of society or not. Moreover, if I should ever tackle that excessively difficult problem, "What is for the true interest of society?" I should feel that I stood in need of a great deal of help from the science of legitimate inference . . .[18]

So, having carried the epistemological burden thus far, I hope I may be permitted to put it down long enough to make some brief historical comments.

The passage just quoted is absolutely characteristic of Peirce, who insists on the importance of what he calls "the scientific attitude," of "a craving to know how things really [are]," "a great desire to learn the truth"; and that the truth "is SO . . . whether you, or I, or anybody thinks it is or not."[19] This could hardly be further removed from what Rorty or Stich calls "pragmatism."

Still, the philosophical tendencies known as "pragmatism" are formidably diverse; and it would be foolish to deny that there are some elements in some pragmatist writers that might seem to suggest what I have called the "vulgar pragmatisms" of Rorty and Stich. For example, in James's urging that philosophers pay more attention to concrete truths and curb their obsession with abstract Truth,[20] one might hear something akin to Rorty's impatience with anything supposedly grounding what is presently defensible. But this would be to forget that James maintains that the notion of concrete truth depends on the notion of abstract Truth, and could not stand alone. Again, in James's defense of the "will to believe," of the propriety of believing without evidence if belief will enable one to live one's life better, one might hear something akin to Stich's identification of "justified belief" with "belief that conduces to what one values." But this would be to forget that James also says, not only that this doctrine applies only to propositions, e.g., of a religious character, in principle incapable of settlement by evidence, but also that it is distinct from, and independent of, pragmatism.[21] It would also be to forget that, when he says that "the true is only the good in the way of belief," James is stressing—exaggerating—the instrumental value of true beliefs. James used to complain about critics who put "the silliest possible interpretation" on his words;[22] now, it seems, the "friends" of pragmatism are doing the same.[23]

RESPONSE TO SUSAN HAACK

Susan Haack is right that my view "precludes the possibility of any higher-minded conception of really-truth-indicative justification . . ." (136). Indeed, it precludes the idea that we can, or need to, worry about whether our practices of justification are "really-truth-indicative." But I am not sure why she thinks that this view is "cynical"—why she goes on to say that "one cannot coherently engage fully—non-cynically—in a practice *of justifying beliefs* that one regards as wholly conventional. For *to believe that* p *is to accept* p *as true*" (136). I agree with the second italicized phrase, but I do not see why Haack thinks that this fact supports the claim she makes about cynicism. I miss the force of "For."

Haack seems to think that if I really understood what I was doing when I accepted a belief as true, I would realize that I *do* take my way of justifying that belief to be really-truth-indicative. For the "For" in the passage I have cited suggests that once one realizes that "to believe that *p* is to accept *p* is true" one could not avoid taking one's justificatory activities as indicative of truth. But everything turns on whether there are criteria for truth *distinct from* criteria for justification to the best, most critical, and most informed audience that I can imagine. If there are not, then to say that I take the latter criteria to be truth-indicative adds nothing to saying that I use them in justifying my beliefs. Unless we can provide a criterion for achieving truth different from our criterion for achieving justification, there will be no way to answer, and thus no point in posing, the question Am I using the right standards?

Haack calls the view that there is no room for this question "conventionalism." She defines this as the view that "it makes no sense to ask which criteria of justification (those of this or that epistemic community) are correct, which are really indicative of the likely truth of a belief" (135). If one alters "it makes no sense to ask" to "you will not get anywhere by asking,"[1] then I am, indeed, a conventionalist in her sense. The reason I think you will not get anywhere is the same as the one Haack brings to bear in arguing against reliabilism in chapter 7 of *Evidence and Inquiry.* She says there:

> Our criteria of justification are, indeed, what *we take to be* indications of the truth, or likely truth, of a belief. Reliabilism, however, identifies the criteria of justification with whatever *is in fact* truth-indicative, whether or not we take it to be. The effect is to trivialize the question, whether our criteria of justification are really truth-indicative: the solution of the problem of ratification is already trivially contained in the reliabilist response to the problem of explication.

It seems to me that any epistemologist has to make this reliabilist-style move sooner or later, or else be out of a job. The only way to avoid becoming a reliabilist would be to find a way of picking out true beliefs by some other means than applying our best present criteria for justification. But, once again, I do not see that epistemologists could possibly find any such way.

I take it that Haack finds an ambiguity in the notion of "accepting as true" between an endorsing use of true—one which makes "to believe is to accept as true" as empty as "to approve is to accept as good"—and a "substantive" and "realistic" use of true, in which when you accept *p* as true you do something *more* than accept it as justified. But granted that *true* and *justified* are not interdefinable, any more than *approved of* and *good* are interdefinable, this ambiguity does not in itself show that there is anything substantive to be said about truth or goodness once we have finished talking about justification. Indeed, it seems to guarantee the opposite. For, as Putnam has pointed out in his "naturalistic fallacy" argument, it always makes sense to say "_____, but maybe not true," just as it does to say "_____, but maybe not good," no matter what you put in the blank. The gap between either truth or goodness on the one hand, and justification on the other, is forever unbridgeable, but this unbridgeability is not a result of the fact the former notions have criteria of application distinct from the criteria of application of the latter. On the contrary, it is a result of the fact that we have no independent criteria of application for the former.

Nor do we need such criteria in order to use *true* and *good* in their cautionary senses, as when we say "unquestionably approved of by all, but maybe not good" or "justified to the hilt, but maybe not true." I take this cautionary use suggest that maybe somebody will come along with a better idea, a better epistemic community, a better form of life—thus reminding us that inquiry is not over yet, and, indeed, that we cannot imagine what it would be like for it to be over.[2] But many people would say that the cautionary use of "true" has a further function: that of suggesting that maybe even a splendidly justified belief may not accurately represent the intrinsic nature of reality. I read (or, as Haack, Lavine, Gouinlock, and others would claim, misread) James and Dewey as arguing that these notions of "accurate representation" and "intrinsic nature" have been more trouble than they are worth, and that we should see how things go if we discard them.

In addition to the endorsing and cautionary uses of *true*, there are of course its disquotational use, its use to signify the property preserved in valid inferences, and perhaps still other uses. But none of them seems to me to offer a handle for the epistemologist who wants to judge the truth-indicativeness of our contemporary practices. My critics seem to find something more in the notion of truth than I do—if not the idea of accurate representation of intrinsic nature, then that of "referentiality" or "transcendence" or *something*—but I cannot get straight what this more is supposed to be. Whatever it is, spotting it makes them anxious to defend what they call our "realistic intuitions." So perhaps the simplest thing to do is to label what they see in the notion of truth and I do not *E* for "extra." *E* is what many people think Davidson misses when he disdains the notions of "correspondence" and "representation."[3] It is what Farrell, who thinks it important to defend "realism," believes that Davidson sees, but that I miss.[4]

To grasp *E*, I take it, would be to see that epistemology is not only legitimate, but something all of us automatically and instinctively engage in—at least to the extent of being reasonably confident that our justificatory practices are truth-indicative. Because I do not grasp *E*, I find the question of whether they are truth-indicative to be pointless, and the "For" in my initial quotation from Haack, unclear.

Despairing of shedding further light on the nature of *E*, and thus on the apparent divergence between Haack's and my understanding of "accepting as true," I turn now to an ambiguity in the notion of "justificatory practices." In chapter 10 of Haack's *Evidence and Inquiry*, she distinguishes "background beliefs" that determine what we take as relevant to the justification of a belief from "standards of evidence."[5] Epistemology, she says, concerns only the latter. In respect to standards of evidence, she continues, there is little divergence between periods and cultures.[6] They all have the same epistemology. For once we put background beliefs and a sense of relevance to one side, there is not much divergence in what "counts" as evidence; in appraising the security of a belief, prescientific as well as scientific peoples, and converts to the new paradigm as well as defenders of the old, may be assessing its fit to their experience and their other beliefs. I entirely agree with this point, and am happy to grant that if epistemology says only that everybody should always assess a belief by "assessing its fit to their experience and their other beliefs," then it says something incontrovertible.[7]

The trouble is that saying this seems pointless, for nobody knows how to *stop* assessing the fit of novel data and hypotheses to their experience and their other beliefs. Commending this process is like commending the autonomic nervous system. Haack seems to think that she has looked into the concept of truth and found *E*, and *E* has told her that this is how we *should* assess belief-candidates in order to attain what she calls "the goal of inquiry . . . substantial, significant, illuminating truth."[8] Unable to spot *E*, I can only ask, "But how *else* would you assess a belief than by assessing its fit to experience and other beliefs? How could we *help* doing that?"

Because I do not know what it would be like to stop assessing this fit, I see no need to discuss truth-indicativeness, nor to say, with Haack, that truth is a goal of inquiry.[9] I think inquiry—fitting whatever comes down the pike into our previous experience and beliefs as best we can—is something nobody can help doing. We do not need a goal called truth to lure us into this automatic, involuntary process of adjustment to the environment. (Further, it seems to me misleading to use the word *goal* to refer to something we could not recognize when we had found it, and from which we shall never be able to measure our distance.) Whereas Haack thinks it helpful to answer the question "*Why* should I try to get my beliefs to fit in with experience and with each other? by saying "Doing so is conducive to acquiring true beliefs," I cannot imagine anybody asking that question. It strikes me as analogous to "Why should I breathe?" or "Why should I eat?"[10] We do not, as far as I can see, have any choice about how to form beliefs. We do sometimes, under fortunate cultural circumstances, have a certain amount of choice about which epistemic community to belong to, whose background beliefs and sense of relevance to share.

Insofar as there is a choice to be made among Peirce's four methods, it is not a choice among what Haack calls "standards of evidence." It is, rather, a choice between considerations to be taken as relevant. To say that somebody adheres to Peirce's "method of tenacity" is to say that she thinks the fact that everybody has always believed *p* more relevant to the credibility of *p* than the rest of us. To say that somebody adheres to the method of authority is to say, for example, that he is more inclined to take it as relevant that the Pope has proclaimed *p* a dogma than are the rest of us. *All* the interesting questions which people have hoped that epistemologists would help them with turn out, it seems to me, to be questions about what they should and should not take as relevant. None of them have to do with what Haack calls "standards of evidence."

By setting questions of relevance to one side, Haack legitimizes epistemology by trivializing it. For relevance is where the action is. Standards of evidence would be of interest only if there were somebody around who told us to *stop* fitting our beliefs in with our experience and our other beliefs. But nobody does that, and anybody who tried would be unable to respond to requests for an alternative. Epistemology got a new lease on life when the New Science began to make new suggestions about what sorts of beliefs were and were not relevant to justifying belief about, for example, the movements of the heavens. These were admirable suggestions if one wanted increased predictive power, but not if one prized the Christian faith above such power. Fans of the New Science hoped to back their own choice by reference to truth-indicativeness, considered as something distinct from these various costs and benefits.[11] But the history of epistemology seems to me to show that these hopes were vain.

I agree with Haack that the difference between scientific and prescientific cultures is "a matter of greater willingness to submit beliefs to criticism, a greater awareness of alternatives."[12] But I demur when she adds "and hence more openness to questions of justification."[13] As I have remarked elsewhere, it is hard to see Duns Scotus as more or less open to questions of justification than Darwin, even though his views about what beliefs were relevant to what other beliefs were quite different.[14] I think that Haack here runs together openness to justification *ueberhaupt* with interest in the justificatory considerations which *we* find relevant.

Let me conclude by coming back to *E*, the extra element in the notion of truth which I cannot seem to grasp. I am not sure whether this failure is the cause, or rather an effect, of what Haack thinks of as the vulgarity of my views. But whichever it is, it certainly blinds me to the possibility of "any higher-minded conception of really-truth-indicative justification." Does it also, as Haack goes on to say, force me to "treat the epistemic standards of any and every epistemic community as on a par" (136)? Yes, if "epistemic standards" means what she calls "standards as evidence." But that is harmless, because I agree with her that no two communities have ever differed on the topic of such standards. No, if "epistemic standards" includes differences in background beliefs. I prize communities which share more background beliefs with me above those which share fewer.

I cannot see the difference Haack sees between prizing these communities for their greater like-mindedness and prizing them for their greater truth-indicativeness (any more than I see the difference between praising myself for having achieved a really tight fit between all my beliefs and experiences and praising myself for being a good truth-indicator). The two compliments seem to me not to differ in their pragmatic implications, except that the latter gives the epistemological skeptic (the person who asks, "How do you *know* they are truth indicative?") an opening that the former does not.[15] That seems to me an excellent reason for restricting ourselves to the former compliment.

8

RORTY & ANTIREALISM

Frank B. Farrell

Recent work in philosophy has contributed to what we might call "disenchantment of subjectivity," in that the subject loses its metaphysical depth and autonomy in the way that the world itself, for earlier thinkers, once did. It is important how we read the outcome of that development, and Richard Rorty has given an influential account of one way of reading it. If we stop divinizing both world and self, he says, we are left with a system of causal interactions regarding which it no longer makes much sense to speak of beliefs as attempting to capture how matters stand in the world, and as being constrained in that attempt by the way the world really is. But I think he does not work through those recent investigations of subjectivity to their proper conclusion. They lead not to free-flowing cultural conversations but to the recovery of the world, in two senses. The alienated self of modernity is assured that its concepts are at home in the world as it is, and the world itself recovers from a process of thinning out and contraction that it suffered in relation to the powers of the modern subject. Rorty continues certain basic patterns of thought that run through late medieval and modern philosophy and that exhibit their character especially in the thought that any securing of confidence in the operations of subjectivity requires a deflation of the world as we know it. But we can learn instead, with Wittgenstein and Davidson, that the disenchantment of subjectivity precisely allows us to think of the realm of thought as an openness to the world and to others. Thoughts are what they are, they have content in the first place, only insofar as the world can be brought into play as that upon which thought has a bearing, and as that which an interpreter must consider in order to assign content at all.

Rorty transfers the power of the self to cultural practices, but the larger structure of late medieval and modern philosophy remains. One effect of that way of handling matters is that as the surrounding conditions needed to make sense of subjectivity as having a bearing on the world are eroded, we are left not with an isolated subjectivity but with causal happenings that can no longer count as intentional activity at all. To have a belief requires an engagement with a world rich enough to confer content on mental activities and requires also a subjectivity rich enough to take the world to be a certain way through taking itself to be so taking it. But both of these collapse in Rorty. His cultural conversations lose the conditions for being such, through becoming merely causal. Intentionality and rationality dissolve as one gives up the stance from which the patterns relevant to those phenomena could emerge for our consideration, and could be seen as embodied in our activity. What Rorty would give up as no longer useful turns out to be a necessary support for his own activity, and his own account, to make sense. It is a mistake to think that the disenchantment of subjectivity will lead either to a thinning out of the world or to an undermining of those activities that principally characterize us as subjects. I argue for these conclusions in *Subjectivity, Realism, and Postmodernism*. Here, in a chapter taken from that book, I consider Rorty's position.

Rorty and Davidson

Richard Rorty has written an influential narrative about the dismantling of the modern notion of subjectivity.[1] I think he is wrong in his claims concerning the stance that we are supposedly led to as a result of that history. To show that he is wrong, however, I need to wedge him apart from Davidson, whom he takes to be his most natural ally, since I find many of Davidson's positions persuasive, whereas I am generally in disagreement with the picture offered by Rorty. The attempted link with Davidson is not an incidental one. It is part of Rorty's overall strategy to show that his position, radical though it may seem, is largely motivated by considerations that come out of the work of one of the most honored of contemporary analytic philosophers. But I think this strategy is unsuccessful; there are profound differences between the two thinkers.

When Rorty is trying to defeat his opponents, he describes them as holding a radical position virtually no one holds, and opposes it to the position he claims to share with Davidson. But then when he describes the position he thinks he has established as a result of defeating those opponents, he describes not what he supposedly has in common with Davidson but a more controversial antirealist position. So the frequent misreading of Davidson serves a purpose; it makes an argument appear to go through that really does not, and enlists Davidson's support for an account that he would not, or should not, endorse. There is a deeper basis, I think, for the manner in which Rorty sets up the alternatives we are to consider. I shall argue that his work is embedded in patterns of thought that we have already traced when reviewing religious influences on our metaphysical and epistemic pictures. He presents himself as rejecting such pictures, and in some respects he certainly does so, but without them one would have far less motivation to develop his account, or to accept it once it is developed.

Let me begin by comparing an image of Davidson's with one from Rorty. Davidson speaks of a process of "triangulation":

> If I were bolted to the earth I would have no way of determining the distance from me of many objects. I would only know they were on some line drawn from me toward them. I might interact successfully with objects, but I could have no way of giving content to the question where they were. Not being bolted down, I am free to triangulate. Our sense of objectivity is the consequence of another sort of triangulation, one that requires two creatures. Each interacts with an object, but what gives each the concept of the way things are objectively is the base line formed between the creatures by language. The fact that they share a concept of truth alone makes sense of the claim that they have beliefs, that they are able to assign objects a place in the public world.[2]

I can recognize myself to be a believer, to have a point of view on the world, only through being able to recognize others as having possibly different points of view on that same reality. So only communicators, says Davidson, can have a sense of an objective world, and only they can have beliefs. Rorty says that "in the end, the pragmatists tell us, what matters is our loyalty to other human beings clinging together against the dark, not our hope of getting things right."[3] The two images are similar in their attention to our relations to other believers. But one corner of the Davidsonian triangle is missing in Rorty's picture: the world itself. As we shall see, its disappearance is characteristic of his philosophy; we need to examine why it so readily disappears.

I do not wish to underplay the very considerable agreement between the two thinkers. Rorty happily accepts the Davidsonian attacks on various psychological and semantic reifications: on our notions of meaning, reference, subjectivity, and language. Both reject accounts that would join language to the world through discovering some relation of reference between individual words and things in the world, or some relation of mirroring between representations and sentencelike entities such as facts. Davidson, we saw, also suggests that we give up the notion of subjective representations that stand as epistemic intermediaries between our beliefs and what they are about. So mental states, we may conclude, do not represent the world in either of those two senses (either by mirroring sentencelike worldly entities or by serving as epistemic intermediaries). Therefore there are no representations, at least as far as many traditional uses of *representation* are concerned. (There will remain senses in which we do have representations.)

Rorty agrees with all this, but his conclusion is that without any representing going on, there is no longer any sense to our notion of getting matters right.[4] So we must then be pragmatists and grant that our symbol sequences are meaningful only insofar as they help bring about habits of action that turn out to be useful; to give up reference and representation is to give up the "aboutness" of our statements in any sense richer than that. Davidson's response to the claim that there are no representations is rather different. Beliefs remain for him *about* the world and it is important to him to show, against the skeptic, that they are, very generally, getting matters right. Whereas Rorty says there is no such thing as a language-to-world relationship to worry about, Davidson sees that relationship as a holistic one that cannot be built up out of linkages or isomorphisms at the word or sentence level. Because there is that holistic portrayal of the world roughly as it is, we can understand the large features of reality by studying our ways of talking about it.[5]

Rorty holds, as Davidson does, that our beliefs must generally be correct, but his reasoning is very different. For Davidson the fit is world-driven; it is because of the role the world plays both in causing beliefs and in guiding the identification of beliefs by the interpreter that we are sure of a rough match. For Rorty, in contrast, that matching is guaranteed because the world is little more than a reflection cast by our generally accepted beliefs:

> To sum up this point, I want to claim that "the world" is either the purely vacuous notion of the ineffable cause of sense and goal of intellect, or else a name for the objects that inquiry at the moment is leaving alone; those planks in the boat which are at the moment not being moved about. . . .
>
> Now, to put my cards on the table, I think that the realistic true believer's notion of the world is an obsession rather than an intuition. I also think that Dewey was right in thinking that the only intuition we have of the world as determining truth is just the intuition that we must make our new beliefs conform to a vast body of platitudes, unquestioned perceptual reports, and the like.[6]

Rorty also defines pragmatism as the view that "there are no constraints on inquiry save conversational ones," no wholesale constraints "derived from the nature of the objects."[7] And he says that "our inheritance from, and our conversation with, our fellow-humans" is "our only source of guidance."[8] In all these quotations the only direction of fit at issue is between one's beliefs and the unquestioned beliefs of one's time and place. The "world" is nothing more than the planks on the boat that we are leaving alone for the moment. If the world is defined so as to have its character given by what we believe about it, it will hardly be surprising that our beliefs must be generally true. Rorty will then be correct that *true* is nothing more than an empty compliment that we give to those sentences that are paying their way, that we do not for now see any reason to question. But that is hardly Davidson's position. His triangular picture has us attending to the beliefs of others so that we may have a sense of an objective world that transcends our beliefs about it, and toward which the beliefs of different believers can be thought of as directed. We retain, even in so attending to others, our attentiveness to a world about which we are trying to gain a better picture, and we put ourselves into the sort of relation to that world that will make us more likely to understand what it is like. For

Davidson, the world cannot be a criterion of our belief in the sense of pro-viding sentencelike entities that have already conferred truth in advance on some beliefs and not others; the world, on its own, cannot make our beliefs true. But it remains a criterion in the sense of being that to which our beliefs attempt holistically to accommodate themselves, and taking it as a criterion in that sense affects our practices. Rorty will not allow the world to be any sort of criterion at all for belief; it collapses into that for which it was supposed to be providing the standard. For Rorty the world is just a shadow of our discourse, while, for Davidson, language can be meaningful because of the shadow cast upon it by the antics of what is real.

We can see that difference between the two thinkers in the way they reject the empiricist picture of bringing a statement into a confrontation with the world that makes it either true or false. Both hold that there can be no such confrontation; beliefs can be compared only with other beliefs. Davidson expresses the agreement between the two thinkers as follows: "As Rorty has put it, 'nothing counts as justification unless by reference to what we already accept, and there is no way to get outside our beliefs and our language so as to find some test other than coherence.' About this I am, as you see, in agreement with Rorty."9

But, again, they draw different conclusions. Once we give up the notion of a confrontation with the world, believes Rorty, there is no place at all for distinguishing among beliefs on the basis of their responsiveness to the causal pressure of the world. Beliefs just pop up in our belief systems like bubbles and survive or die through a kind of Darwinism of the epistemic realm. But Davidson thinks the empiricists were on to something with their notion of protocol sentences.10 It may seem that Neurath thought of belief regulation as a matter simply of coherence, with any belief at all a candidate to be thrown into the "machine" to be tested for its coherence with other sentences already in there. But that would be chaotic; every sentence and its negation would thus be candidates. What would be thrown in rather are sentences believed true by scientists. And the training of scientists is aimed precisely at conditioning them to register true beliefs in the presence of sit-uations that cause other scientists to register them; scientists learn what many of their sentences mean in such situations. They are habituated to form sentences in circumstances that make them true because of the very role of those circumstances in making the sentences mean what they do.11 No belief thus becomes self-certifying, but the scientist does give a certain privilege to shared observation statements, and she learns to position herself, through experiments, in situations in which the causal pressure of the world will cause her to register its features in her beliefs.

Perception plays a similar role in Davidson's account of interpretation. Whereas Rorty gives our direction of attentiveness as a sideways one, as we take others' utterances in and interpret them by the pragmatic criterion of helping us get what we want, Davidson says that interpretation cannot even get underway unless we attend to the world and assign the other speaker beliefs on the basis of what in the world occasions his various utterances. Both in the case of the scientist and her training and in the case of interpretation, the world's position in the Davidsonian triangulation, and in the Davidsonian account of belief, disappears for Rorty's analysis. He says, for example, that what makes science different from other fields is just that agreement is easier in science, that more background truths are accepted in advance by its participants.[12] The virtues of science thus have nothing at all to do with the way they bring us into relation to reality's way of doing things; the gulf between the views of Davidson and Rorty remains wide.

It is easy to miss here just what Davidson is objecting to in empiricist philosophies. The empiricist has a strong notion of what it is to bring at least base-level statements into confrontation with truth-conferring circumstances; Davidson clearly believes that that kind of confrontation cannot occur. But he can give up that strong notion of letting experience decide matters for us, and yet still hold that our beliefs direct themselves toward the world and aim at getting things right. From the fact that there is no *naked* confrontation, that a sentencelike entity such as a belief can be compared only with information already in the form of sentences or beliefs, it does not follow that what makes a belief true is that coherence itself. Davidson rather shows us why we should understand, given how the world itself comes into play in the very determination of belief content, that coherence must yield at least a rough correspondence. It is not that lining beliefs up with other beliefs is the end of the story, as it is for Rorty.

Rorty has to skip over much of what Davidson says in order to take him to be in agreement. He says that "for Davidson, Quine's idea of 'ontological commitment' and Dummett's idea of 'matter of fact' are both unfortunate relics of metaphysical thought."[13] But Davidson spends most of the essay "The Method of Truth in Metaphysics" discussing the ontological commitments that arise when one develops a truth theory in the manner that he suggests. He says that "if the truth conditions of sentences are placed in the context of a comprehensive theory, the linguistic structure that emerges will reflect large features of reality," that "postulating needed structure in a language can bring ontology in its wake," that "for large stretches of language, anyway, variables, quantifiers, and singular terms must be construed as referential in function," and that "apparently we are committed to the existence of times if we accept any such sentence as true."[14] The question of ontological commitments is at the basis of much of his work in suggesting translations of natural language sentences into the first-order predicate calculus, such as sentences containing adverbs. (What Davidson attacks, we saw, is not the notion of ontological commitment, but the claim that there are ontological schemes and that statements about what there is in the world must be made relative to them.)

Rorty and the Loss of the World

My claim about Rorty and the disappearance of the world may appear too strong if we see what he says elsewhere. He accepts that "the world is out there," and that "most things in space and time are the effects of causes which do not include human mental states."[15] He holds that there is an objective world that is causing our beliefs and says that he is not a linguistic idealist, that is, one who holds that everything is language or that objects are only linguistic constructs. But we have to consider these claims, and the sense that he can give to them, in the light of his version of pragmatism. All true claims are for him just symbol sequences that are useful in leading to actions and habits that get us what we want; we should not suppose that they represent anything or correspond to anything or refer to anything, as the realist believes. Their significance for him is causal rather than semantic; they are like the animal's horns that help it get what it wants but that represent nothing hornlike in the world.

So when he claims that there is an objective world causing our beliefs, we should not take that statement itself referentially or suppose that he is committing himself ontologically to such a world. What happens rather is that a certain sequence with the words "objective world" and "causing beliefs" appears in his belief space and contributes (or does not) to useful behavior. Whatever we might say in everyday discourse, Rorty's pragmatist will not allow claims about the objective world and its causal powers to be interpreted realistically, as founded on a certain relation of aboutness between those claims themselves and the world. Objectivity and language independence are what we constitute as such from within conversations that should not be thought of as constrained by a reality independent of them. We linguistically project, as the mere shadow of our useful expressions, a world that the very projection allows us to count as independent, and as giving rise to the beliefs that come to appear in us.

Why should we not conclude then that Rorty's pragmatism has collapsed into some form of linguistic idealism? The resistance of the world to thought is simply what thought or our conversational habits count as resistance; there is no further causal independence that is forcing us to accommodate ourselves to its working. There is a difference between the world itself making us think a certain way about it and the appearance of the syntactic shapes "the world's causal power" in a useful statement that cannot be taken referentially, and it seems that Rorty can make sense only of the latter. There is little, then, to make us resist the temptation to think of him as suggesting not a thinking mind but a speaking voice (in his case a communal one) that produces all determinations out of itself, as in Samuel Beckett's novels. (And there is the question as well of why we should call anything that appears in that space a belief.)

Rorty makes it very clear where the determining power is supposed to be coming from and where it is not. He criticizes those who want to see cultural conversation *"guided*, constrained, not left to its own devices."[16] When some vocabularies are claimed to be better than other ones, they are "just better in the sense that they come to *seem* clearly better than their predecessors."[17] We, or at least our ways of talking, are setting the standard defining the objectivity that is their supposed measure. When we speak of standards or criteria that our cultural conversations must meet, these are temporary ones that the conversations impose on themselves, for reasons the sociologist rather than the metaphysician can explore. For the pragmatist, Rorty says, "a criterion . . . *is* a criterion because some particular social practice needs to block the road of inquiry, halt the progress of interpretations, in order to get something done."[18] There is no constraint of objectivity that we do not raise up for ourselves. So objectivity is simply a projection of our practice, what we count as such given our present interests and the inertia of our conversations. The world, as before, has little role to play in such an account. When we are considering "the jargon of Newton versus that of Aristotle . . . it is difficult to think of the world as making one of these better than another."[19] I am reminded here of the idealist Fichte, for whom the objectivity and resistance of the world to the ego are themselves set forth in an infinite self-positing activity of mind; that has become, in Rorty, an infinite self-positing activity of discourse.

It may be suggested here that we should read Rorty as ending up with something of a Kantian position. There is an internal pragmatic stance from which we happily use and accept realist-sounding sentences, with their commitment to objectivity and world guidance and language transcendence. But then there is an external stance from which we recognize the "merely" pragmatic function of all such sentences as we use them. Through understanding that function, we recognize that objectivity cannot be understood in the realist way, but is a projection of our practices. So we become internal pragmatic realists and "transcendental" linguistic idealists.

But Rorty will surely claim that the genuine pragmatist will not allow himself to be forced into that twofold Kantian stance. He will hold that all claims are internal ones, to be judged for their usefulness in our conversations, and that we cannot, nor should we want to, step outside our practices to make overall claims about the status of our claims themselves. But then where has Rorty himself been speaking from in condemning the realist? He will want to say that he has been making one more internal statement concerning the usefulness of a kind of talk. Like a good banker he has examined the statements in use and has recommended that we cut off those "investments" that are not paying their way; the realist statements fall into that category. So the realist cannot be accused of making a general *philosophical* error; he must be shown to be recommending the use of lots of useless sentences.

But if that is Rorty's strategy, his way of carrying it out seems very odd. Suppose we do consider sentences as tools that are useful or not. Tools are useful in some circumstances and not others, for some purposes and not for others. Realist discourse is embedded in very many of our practices, and it is highly unlikely that there will be a general uselessness of such notions that can be decided without a detailed cost-benefit investigation of the particular practices. But Rorty does not even suggest that such an investigation is in order. The pragmatist web of belief ought to be a complex interweave whose threads must be added or removed in a piecemeal fashion. Yet in Rorty there is the sense of a crucial boundary being crossed whenever we get to sentences with an implicit realist commitment. For a genuine pragmatist the classifications into useful and useless concepts will not take place at such a global level; that is where philosophers tend to do their work. There will be no clear boundary that will exhibit itself from that height.

In making global classifications into good and bad sentences from the overall perspective of the philosophical pragmatist, Rorty seems to be accusing his realist opponent of a philosophical error, not a pragmatic one, of not seeing correctly the relation between language and reality that Rorty, from his own external stance, can see correctly. But if he has been right, that stance ought not to be available to him. There is the general Kantian problem here of holding that we can never achieve a stance from which we can talk about the relation between language and reality, while holding (in claiming that objectivity is *merely* phenomenal or *merely* pragmatic, in contrast to a more full-bodied realism) that we can present a version of that relation showing our opponents to be wrong about it. The further problem for Rorty is that he seems to need such a (for him) impossible stance to defeat his opponents. For when we examine our discourse in detail according to the criterion of usefulness, the everyday realist vocabulary seems very useful indeed, useful enough to have survived very well the Darwinian clash of vocabularies in history. So, as a nonphilosophical pragmatist, he ought to be a realist without qualms. It is true, surely, that certain large metaphysical pictures, with their theological underpinnings, are no longer of much use. But Rorty's quarry all along has not so much been those (we should be in agreement with him if it were), but rather the very idea of the world as that against which our beliefs are ultimately measured.

How Rorty Exploits the Alliance with Davidson

I hope it is clear now that Davidson and Rorty are philosophers with quite different beliefs, even if the latter expends a good deal of energy trying to make those differences less visible. He says that Davidson gives us "the first systematic treatment of language which breaks *completely* with the notion of language as something that can be adequate or inadequate to the world or to the self."[20] Yet Davidson, we saw, finds it important to argue, against the skeptic, that our beliefs are indeed adequate in that regard. Rorty, in contrast, is happy with "the world well lost."[21]

Rorty says as well that if we adopt Davidson's account of language, we shall not be tempted to ask about the place of intentionality in a world of causation or about the relation of language and thought.[22] Either Rorty is wrong here or he is making his claim very carelessly. For while Davidson says that there will be no reduction of psychological talk to physicalist talk, and that there can be no strict causal laws picked out at the psychological level of description, he does find it important to show that mental events, under other descriptions, are situated in a determinist causal order.[23] (Rorty pays attention to the adjective but not to the noun in Davidson's "anomalous monism.") Davidson also asks, in an article that is even entitled "Thought and Talk," whether entities have to have a language in order to count as having thoughts and beliefs, whereas Rorty, as we have just seen, says that Davidson will not ask about the relation between language and thought.[24] Rorty believes as well that Davidson has an instrumentalist theory of mental states. Talk about beliefs and intentions, on this view, is an invented vocabulary that has turned out to be rather useful in making sense of the marks and sounds that others produce.[25] Davidson, in contrast, seems to believe that mental states are real states of the individual that our ordinary mentalist vocabulary is able to capture rather well.

Why, then, does Rorty insist on their similarity? It is true that, in some respects, they are quite similar and that Rorty can make good use of Davidson's attacks on traditional conceptions of mind and meaning. But there are two other reasons for that insistence. First, it makes it easier for him to appear to be holding a moderate position. He needs so to appear since he criticizes his opponents not by taking them to be defending the negation of the position he has recommended but by taking them to be defending more radical positions that few thinkers hold and that are the negation rather of the more moderate position that he presents himself as sharing with Davidson. Second, he thinks he can enlist Davidson as a supporter of what we might call a "causal-mutational" account of large changes in the picture we have of the world. I shall look at each of these now.

One quickly becomes familiar with a certain pattern of argument in Rorty. It is suggested that we have a choice of accepting either his position or an outlandish one that few, and certainly not most of those who are disturbed by Rorty's account, will want to support. Let me begin with a quotation given earlier: "To sum up this point, I want to claim that 'the world' is either the purely vacuous notion of the ineffable cause of sense and goal of intellect, or else a name for the objects that inquiry at the moment is leaving alone; those planks in the boat which are at the moment not being moved about."[26] If we do not accept Rorty's account of the world, according to which it is a projection of our currently accepted practices, then our alternative is to conceive of it as an ineffable noumenal source in the manner of Kant: "But this trivial sense in which 'truth' is 'correspondence to reality' and 'depends on a reality independent of our knowledge' is, of course, not enough for the realist. What he wants is . . . the notion of a world so 'independent of our knowledge' that it might, for all we know, prove to contain none of the things we have always thought we were talking about."[27]

The opponent is again presented as accepting, insofar as he is uneasy with Rorty's position, something like a Kantian noumenal world. But consider a modest realism of the following sort. (In *Subjectivity, Realism, and Postmodernism* I make more careful distinctions about sorts of realism, but I need here just to show that there is considerable space to occupy between Rorty's position and the position he assigns to his opponents.) Suppose our beliefs are about a world that transcends what they take it to be. That world conditions our beliefs so that over time they adjust themselves to its own articulations. Perhaps the manner in which the world's way of determining itself emerges for us will depend to some degree on the sort of subjective apparatus we have, and on the interests that make us find some possible boundaries to be more important than others. But even if our subjective apparatus thus plays a role in how the world appears, it is the world itself that is appearing to us, not some substitute realm of appearances. How reality is and how we take it to be cannot vary independently in the Kantian fashion, not because we determine what reality is, but because it determines how an interpreter will fix the semantic content of our statements. Our abilities are limited, and perhaps there are very many features of the universe that are worth having beliefs about and about which we are not able to have any beliefs at all. But the beliefs we do have are largely about features that are really there, and we can hope to extend gradually our conceptual reach so that our picture of how things are becomes more adequate.

Let us grant that considerable work will have to go into filling in that sketch, and in making contrasts with other views more precise. But surely it is an intelligible and stable position that can take its place as one candidate for describing the relation between language and the world. It is also the case that such a position differs, very clearly, both from Rorty's own position and from the position he assigns to his opponents. (Against his position there is regulation of belief by the world; against the other position, there is no commitment to a noumenal world that might be not at all like what we take it to be.) So making those opponents appear to hold unacceptable claims will go no way at all toward making Rorty's own conception more plausible.

Indeed, he maneuvers between his view and the modest realism I have just described when he feels himself vulnerable. He does appear vulnerable, for example, when he says that Davidson "does not want to view sentences as 'made true' by anything," whereas Davidson says that he aims to reestablish our "unmediated touch with the familiar objects whose antics make our sentences and opinions true or false."[28] But he brushes off the apparent inconsistency by claiming that his realist opponent must be making a stronger claim than Davidson's, must indeed be committing himself to a world "which could vary independently of the antics of the familiar objects . . . something rather like the thing-in-itself."[29] But the modest realist would be a fool to accept that redescription of his position. Only Rorty's sliding between Davidson's account and his own makes the more modest response seem unavailable.

A similar sliding occurs when Rorty describes his own position as the generally accepted one that we have access to reality only as already conceptualized, and describes his opponent as one who "thinks that, deep down beneath all the texts, there is something which is not just one more text but that to which various texts are trying to be 'adequate.'"[30] Now we ought to be careful here about making a certain distinction. To say that we do not encounter a bare, unconceptualized reality is not to say that we encounter only texts. Even if the world appears according to the character of our conceptual apparatus, it is the nonconceptual world that is appearing, not the conceptual apparatus itself or one of its cultural artifacts. (The idea that we might be confronting only our own constructions, only texts, again reflects the influence of the theological, self-relational, and demiurgic picture of subjectivity that I have been trying to defeat.) So it is a very modest claim indeed to say that there is something to which our various accounts are trying to be adequate, and that is not itself just another account.

Of course, we do not bring about that adequacy by comparing our account to a reality not yet touched by the character of any conceptual apparatus at all; but we often do succeed in bringing it about nonetheless. Is it some inscrutable world toward which we have thus aimed? No, we go ahead and use our own best picture in describing reality as it is in itself. That is the reality we have been aiming toward, even if other intelligences might describe the same world somewhat differently. So again Rorty has tried to take over a relatively noncontroversial view, that we do not have access to an unconceptualized reality, and to push his opponent into an acceptance of inscrutable noumena. But defeating such an opponent will then be useless when Rorty slides back to his own more radically antirealist stance, for the position of the modest realist still remains on the field.

That pressing of opponents into untenable positions they would be foolish to endorse is ubiquitous. He suggests that his opponents are working out of a legacy of an age for which God's language has already determined truth for the world.[31] They are searching "for some final vocabulary, which can somehow be known in advance to be the common core, the truth of, all the other vocabularies which might be advanced in its place."[32] But I do not know of many thinkers today who expect such a vocabulary to be known in advance or to be final. And the modest realist can easily grant that we need a pluralism of vocabularies in order to give an adequate account of how matters stand, and that there may be different acceptable ways of using such basic terms as *object* and *individual*. In criticizing those who disagree with his "liberal ironism" and who suppose that there are good justifications for our moral values and decisions, Rorty describes such an opponent as believing there are "algorithms" for solving moral dilemmas.[33] But again, no good Aristotelian, and few moral philosophers, would hold that there are such algorithms, or that the adjustment of our ethical beliefs to the world would require that sort of outcome. He also says that those who are afraid of abandoning the language of respect for fact and objectivity believe in science as having a "priestly function" that puts us in touch with a realm that transcends the human.[34] There is, of course, an obvious sense in which the realm of galaxies and quasars and subatomic particles and rain forest flora transcends what is human. But that sense would hardly encourage a belief in any kind of priestly other world. We have seen why he needs this strategy, but we should not be convinced by an argument that is based upon it.

There is a second reason, I said, why Rorty exaggerates his closeness to Davidson. A clear hint of this motivation for distorting Davidson's views comes from his use of Davidson's treatment of metaphor. I need to set the stage for the discussion here by describing Rorty's picture of how our accounts of the world change. He says that the relation between our vocabularies and the world is causal rather than epistemic. Darwin's account of the emergence and decline of species is a causal explanation of that sort: "Davidson lets us think of the history of language, and thus of culture, as Darwin taught us to think of the history of a coral reef. Old metaphors are constantly dying off into literalness . . . . Our language and our culture are as much a contingency, as much a result of thousands of small mutations finding niches (and millions of others finding no niches), as are the orchids and the anthropoids."[35]

Species emerge when conditions are favorable, but there is no rightness as to which ones emerge, and the strategies of the successful ones (horns, speed, mass reproduction, and so forth) do not work because they somehow mirror the built-in metaphysical contours of the world; they just increase the likelihood that the species will propagate. Or we might think of a similar causal explanation of the emergence and decline of geological features and of stable climatic environments. The causal story does not need any norms of rightness or of matching already present contours.

Rorty believes that human vocabularies replace one another and then die off in a similar fashion. Once one is in place, it will fix what is the right thing to say in various circumstances, but in the transition from one vocabulary to the other, there can be no rightness, only the causal story. The distinction between rational and irrational persuasion, between reason and power, breaks down for his account. So when we are dealing with the questions of relations among competing vocabularies, or of historical transitions from one to another, the philosopher has little to say. The literary critic who is sensitive to rhetorical strategies and ambiguities, and who can play off dissimilar texts against one another in interesting ways, will be far more helpful and is coming today to have more power as his abilities in this regard are recognized.

What can Davidson's position on metaphor have to do with that conception? He holds that metaphorical statements have no semantic value as metaphorical.[36] Their meaning is the same meaning they have when taken literally, but such statements also have the pragmatic function of suggesting that we think of matters in new ways. (I think he is wrong on this issue.) Davidson's treatment seems to have the purpose of specifying just what falls within the range of semantic theory and what does not, so as to define the range of phenomena to which semantic theories of the sort he proposes must be sensitive. So Davidson's interest is mainly in keeping the field of semantic investigation free of infiltration by metaphor.

But Rorty thinks he can enlist Davidson as a supporter of the picture of language just given. He says that there are no rational standards of change. We do not get a better picture of the world; some habits of speaking give way to others. So when Davidson makes metaphor nonsemantic, Rorty sees that position as favoring what we might call a mutational view of changes in our dominant vocabularies. Metaphors causally bring about change in such vocabularies, but since they are nonsemantic, there can be no question of truth or inference in the process of adopting them; that process does not occur in accord with rational standards, nor on the basis of an accommodation to the world. Metaphors are literally meaningless, but they are able to cause changes in usage so that once the new vocabulary has taken hold, sentences formed with it can be true or false, according to the rules that the new vocabulary is then in a position to determine.

Now in some respects, to be sure, Rorty gets Davidson right on metaphor. There is that image in Davidson of metaphorical speech dying off into literalness. But I do not see much support in Davidson for transforming that conception of metaphor into a full-scale picture of changes of vocabulary in history, and it seems unlikely that he would agree with Rorty's claim that there are no rational standards being applied when one large theoretical apparatus replaces another. Rorty's picture of changes in our large cultural conversations ignores, as before, the role of the world, while, for Davidson, it is the fact that different conversations or theories are interpretable as being about the same world that guarantees that they are commensurable. Rorty makes a similar use of Davidson's treatment of changes of character, as when a person chooses to remake himself into a different sort of person, with different characteristic desires. In such cases, says Davidson, when the new way of looking at one's life is not yet fully integrated into the rest of one's existence, there may be incompatible belief-desire systems residing within the same person, so that from the point of view of the established belief-desire system, the change to the new one must be irrational; there is no motivation from within the old one to bring about the change, which must appear relative to the old one as the result of causation from outside.[37]

It will be no surprise that Rorty leaps to make use of that account. He sees Davidson as favoring, as he himself does, the view that historical change from one vocabulary to the next is nonrational. But, again, Davidson nowhere indicates that he is sympathetic to such an extrapolation from the individual mind to historical change, and, in the psychological case he mentions, the overall change may well be rational even if it is not so from those standards available from within the belief-desire system being called into question. Then, too, the case of theory change is one of the replacement of some beliefs by other ones, while the Davidsonian analysis cited by Rorty concerns the replacement of some desires by other, and that appears to be a case of a rather different sort. (This is not to deny, of course, that many changes in intellectual history take place through causal processes that have little to do with rational thought.)

If Davidson is a poor supporter of Rorty's picture, we can still ask whether that picture is itself plausible. When we look at the analogy between Darwinian evolution and large-scale changes of belief or vocabulary, it seems to break down right at the start. The standard of success in the rise and fall of species is survival, the increase of one's species at the expense of other ones. By analogy, then, the only measure of success for a set of beliefs is its increased distribution in the total "belief population." But there may well be more believers in astrology today than there are in evolutionary theory, and we shall not take the reproductive success of the former as granting it the privilege that, on Rorty's view, it ought to receive. We go on to ask which of the two theories, if either, is true. If Rorty then switches the relevant field to the total belief population among natural scientists, so that the belief in astrology does much less well, then we need to ask why there should be this sort of preference. Darwinian survival is survival; we do not suppose that survival in, say, England has an automatic privilege in terms of biological distribution. But, of course, the reason why distribution of beliefs among scientists has greater value is that their belief-formation methods, at least in their fields, are generally reliable ways of coming to understand how matters really are.

If Rorty is right, then a scientist, rather than learning proper laboratory techniques, would be better rewarded if he studied the sociology of belief fixation in the scientific community. Adopting a scientific theory is, for Rorty, like adopting a fashionable way of speaking or dressing; one wants to be the sort of person who comes up with new fashions that others will copy. There are academic fields for which that analogy may unfortunately be valid, and one may find even in the natural sciences a willingness to believe what is fashionable. But in the long run the best strategy for getting one's theory generally accepted is to attend to the world, and to discover something about how it works, rather than to attend to strategies of socio-logical manipulation. There is a very good reason why that is the best strat-egy. Future scientists will be attending to the same world and will have their beliefs caused by its happenings, so that the more one's beliefs are sensitive to how matters stand in the world, the more likely it is that future scientists will adopt the same beliefs and will give one credit for one's dis-coveries. The interest in explaining why the universe operates the way it does is continuous across many different vocabularies over centuries. That interest allows the world itself to be a measure of those vocabularies' right-ness in a way that the world cannot be a measure of the "rightness" of the horns of an animal.

Rorty, Davidson, Heidegger

Rorty's allying of himself with Davidson is, we have seen, deeply suspect. Whatever the legitimate points of comparison, the two part company on the basic issue of whether the world disappears as something substantial and independent over against the momentum of our ongoing conversa-tions. Once we have seen that point, then we may become suspicious as well of another alliance that Rorty has claimed: that with Heidegger. I do not want to compare their work in any detail, but it is worth noting that something of the Davidson-Rorty contrast reappears.

Heidegger, like Davidson, is trying to rethink the structure of subjectivi-ty that led to the problems of modern philosophy.[38] He rejects the picture of a subjective determining power that, from a position of independence, constructs or orders or projects its patterns upon a world of objects. Thinking is what it is only through already "belonging to" the world and through letting it manifest its character. It is only in "being toward" the world, in being situated in its surroundings, that I as thinker or experiencer have any real content to my activity; and language, rather than being the embodiment of some conceptual scheme or other, is an "openness" in which things themselves are making their appearance. We do not have to work to bring an alienated subjectivity back in touch with things, because it is by its very nature as subjectivity always in touch with them. The Davidsonian will be uncomfortable perhaps with the language, but should nonetheless recognize genuine analogies there with his own work.

(I should perhaps emphasize that we do not have a simple contrast here but a triangulation. Davidson and Heidegger will also differ in important ways. To take just one case: Although both reject a correspondence between sentences and sentencelike entities in the world, they give different accounts of what it means for us to be already in touch with worldly things. For Davidson we are situated within the world's causal processes and it is generating beliefs in us, so that an interpreter will properly interpret those beliefs by relating them back to their causes. Heidegger describes rather what he calls our "preunderstanding" of things, our nonconceptual manner of being among things through being open to their contexts of significance. Those contexts are neither given to us nor made by us but are what both we and things find ourselves within as a condition for our encounter. We must avoid the one-sidedness that would take them to be no more than projections of a communal subjectivity, yet we must work within our historical preunderstanding in letting what is there to be encountered take hold of us.)

Rorty's use of Heidegger is very much like his use of Davidson. He ignores the way that thinking and speaking are for Heidegger under the sway of Being; the lesson he learns is rather that once correspondence is dismissed as the basis for connecting thought or language to the world, then we are left with the discourses themselves, with linguistic sequences that generate others without the world being there to constrain the process. But that disappearance of the world is the most reliable sign we have that one is working within, rather than genuinely transforming, the patterns of the modern picture of subjectivity. Discourses come to occupy the position of the modern thinker or determiner. They make their own objects and transform the world into a reflection of their patterns.

There is a conflict here between different accusations of going theological. For Rorty, the Heideggerian is like the religious thinker who, having given up God, still needs to feel under the sway of something Godlike. (It is clear that Rorty would make much the same accusation against my own work.) The Heideggerian may say in response that Rorty is employing a theological structure of subjectivity that diminishes the world and makes us lose sight of the way we are at home in it, so that there seems to be an unconstrained self-positing by discourse. Perhaps there is a trace of the search for the divine in Heidegger's rather mystical appeal to Language and Being. But what he has in common with Davidson, as they challenge our picture of subjectivity, stands independently of that sort of language. Rorty is quintessentially and "religiously" modern in holding that if we open ourselves to any constraint at all from the world, we are submitting ourselves to an unacceptable authority that limits the free, self-relating play of subjectivity. Let me develop this notion of Rorty as a "religious" thinker.

Religious Structures in Rorty's Thought

Many of Rorty's arguments, I think I have shown, do not stand up well to analysis. But something else is going on in his work that is worth examining. There are recurring patterns of thought in it that repeat either some of the patterns we described earlier as religious or theological in origin, or some of the characteristic structures of modern philosophy. (The presence of those patterns is not unrelated to the failure of the arguments.) Or so I shall now argue.

Let us begin by noting again Rorty's propensity to see just two alternatives for explaining the success of our beliefs. Either our statements must make themselves adequate to a bare noumenal world, or the only measure of utterances succeeding in what they set out to do is their coherence with the background of accepted beliefs at the time of utterance, the planks in the boat that for the moment we are not trying to change. We saw that there was another candidate, a modest realism, that Rorty habitually ignores. It is as if that stable middle position cannot be achieved in his thinking. Once we turn away from a commitment to a Kantian noumenal world, there seems to be, in Rorty's description of affairs, an irresistible momentum that leads directly to Rorty's version of pragmatism. If we reject that version, he sees us as unable to find a stable position until we arrive at a belief in regulation by an inscrutable thing-in-itself. But why should there be this instability in the middle? Why should the world's onto-logical order and character collapse so readily into one of the two sides: into an unreachable, unconceptualizable noumenon or into an objectivity projected as the shadow of our practices? What is wrong with the world of the modest realist, as described in an earlier section of this chapter?

One will be reminded here of the picture suggested by late medieval nominalism. The Aristotelian natural world is dissolved in the face of the infinite power of God's free willing; we cannot know things as they are, but we can produce pictures of the world that help us cope with it successfully. There, too, the middle collapses. Ontological determinacy must either be a feature of the world as God determines it, inscrutable to us, or it must characterize our useful pictures of the world rather than the world itself. There will be a migration of features either to a noumenal world fixed by God's determinative power or to a subjectivized world fixed by our own, and the world must be regarded by us as a blank and indeterminate realm that is the testing ground for whether our pictures help us to cope or do not. It is important, then, that we not claim too much for our accounts. When we move over the line to realist talk, we are violating our proper lim-its; we are trying to be divine. Rorty's space of possible explanations seems to repeat that late medieval one.

It is true, of course, that Rorty rejects the commitment to noumena; he correctly sees that commitment as an outcome of theological thinking. But once that part of the structure is gone, then our motivation becomes very much unclear for supposing that our conceptions of the world are merely good for coping with it. It is not that one can just remove the noumena and keep the rest of the structure; the two sides went together and were defined by their opposition. Without the pressure of God's omnipotent determining of the world, there will be no demand that the world's own character be eroded until it is an indeterminate realm onto which we pro-ject pictures in order to cope. Then our conceptions of the world can prop-erly count as world-guided; how we take matters to be will be not an instrument for producing useful predictions but an approximate exhibiting of at least some of the world's own features. The middle ground will hold stably against Rorty's bidirectional momentum. When merely coping is contrasted with seeing the world as God does, it makes sense to restrict our capacities to the former. When a realist's claim about an account's getting matters right rather than just helping us to cope is made in the context of theological intentionality, it makes sense to condemn him as violating his proper limits. But if coping is not defined by such a contrast, then why should we continue to define it as "merely" coping? Without the earlier picture, it is no longer tempting to think that there are only the two competing candidates; it was only the notion of a theological intentionality that made the middle position of the modest realist seem to disappear, as he had to appeal to a realm whose determinacy had supposedly been eroded by God's unlimited power, or by the power of human subjectivity, as it takes over God's position in the field.

Rorty supposes that the realist is claiming to be able to describe the world as it is prior to any contact with our perceptual or conceptual apparatus. But again, the modest realist who opposes Rorty will not be fool enough to make any claim of that sort. I may well believe that there might be more sophisticated knowers than human ones who may find my picture of the world a crude one. But what appeal can there be in the notion of a world that might be *completely* different from how it appears to me, and that must be describable apart from the resources of any conceptual apparatus whatever? The strongest motivation, if not the only one, is that there is a kind of knowing, a divine one, completely different from our own, even to the extent that we and God are really knowing different worlds, not just the same world with different degrees of accuracy.

So the late medieval theological positions put in place a structure with characteristic patterns and with built-in directions of force: the eroding of the world's own determinacy; the migration of features to subjectivity; the notion of a noumenal realm that might differ completely from how things appear; the belief that unless we are knowing such a noumenal realm, apart from the working of our own subjectivity, we are not in touch with things as they really are; the restriction of our conceptions to aids for coping with the world; the instability of the middle as the momentum of the structure pushes one either toward a commitment to the noumenal or toward the merely subjective; the notion that what is not immediately given in experience must be something that the mind adds for instrumental reasons. That structure continues in a more secularized form in much of modern philosophy, and Rorty chops off a considerable part of it while assuming that the rest is unchanged.

Note how Rorty makes the same move when he rejects the account given by the logical positivists. They see the world as providing us with an empirical given; that is its contribution to our beliefs. Then we add schemes of linguistic ordering that process the data so as to yield correct predictions about future experiences. We do not suppose that the features present in such schemes pick out features in the world as it really is; they help us to predict and to cope. Rorty acknowledges that attacks on the notion of the empirical given have been successful; *that* side of the picture will then be seen to drop off. But then he retains the other side of the picture as it was:

> One difficulty the pragmatist has in making his position clear, there-fore, is that he must struggle with the positivist for the position of radical anti-Platonist. He wants to attack Plato with different weapons from those of the positivist, but at first glance he looks like just another variety of positivist. He shares with the positivist the Baconian and Hobbesian notion that knowledge is power, a tool for coping with reality. But he carries this Baconian point through to its extreme, as the positivist does not. He drops the notion of truth as correspondence with reality altogether, and says that modern science does not enable us to cope because it corresponds, it just plain enables us to cope.[39]

We have the construction of ways of talking that help us to manage but nothing is given to such ways of talking, from the direction of the world, that constrains how they are to develop. On Rorty's account, the world may help to cause changes in vocabularies, by analogy with the way it causes changes in geological formations, but it is an empty world that falls into insignificance in favor of the momentum of the vocabularies them-selves.

But as before, we want to ask how *half* the positivist structure can remain as it was when its correlate, the empirical given, has disappeared. In Davidson, by way of contrast, the attack on the given is accompanied by a rethinking of the relation of subjectivity to the world. If we do not split up experience into a sensory given and what we then add, we can consider the entire belief-regulation apparatus, as a holistic system, to be sensitive to how matters really are, so that the success of our accounts is not limited to mere coping. While Rorty applauds Davidson's attacks on semantic and mental reifications, he remains committed in a significant way to a reified (linguistic) subjectivity that is positioned over against an emptied-out realm, and that now can go on autonomously, with little or no regulation by that extremely thin world. That is a result one reaches through taking over the modern picture (earlier a theological one), and through naming the positions in it somewhat differently, rather than by rethinking the entire subject-world structure. (Rorty describes a two-step process by which we first "program" ourselves with a language and then let the world cause us to hold beliefs in that language.[40] But is that not a Kantian picture? Are we cut off from the world's guidance during the first "programming" step?)

Fichte claimed that the goal of the self is to see the world as embodying one's own activity. God's activity must ultimately be a self-willing and the Fichtean subject will in some sense imitate the divine self-knowing and self-willing; the world will be a shadow cast by the self as a field for its activity. In Rorty, likewise, the defeat of the myth of the given is accompanied not by the Davidsonian reaffirmation of the world's causal sway over our entire belief system, but by an unconstrained self-relating (of discourses one to another) for which the world is an empty reflection. He complains that "positivism preserved a god in its notion of Science . . . the notion of a portion of culture where we touched something not ourselves."[41] And he makes the following claim: "The wonder in which Aristotle believed philosophy to begin was wonder at finding oneself in a world larger, stronger, nobler than oneself. The fear in which Bloom's poets begin is the fear that one might end one's days in such a world, a world one never made, an inherited world. The hope of such a poet is that what the past tried to do to her she will succeed in doing to the past: to make the past itself . . . bear *her* impress."[42]

We have here the hope of one strand of German idealism, and of the romantic movement that is often associated with it. Rorty, of course, favors Bloom's poet rather than the Aristotelian sage. But Rorty, avowed defender of the disenchantment of subjectivity, has thus turned religious himself. He accuses his opponent of theological yearnings in holding that in thinking about the world we "touch something not ourselves." But my thinking does not have to be taken up into any religious context at all for it to make sense to me that the world I dwell in extends well beyond what my own small purposes make of its arrangements. The universe had gone on for bil-

lions of years before we emerged on this planet and will likely go on for bil-
lions more if an asteroid should wipe us out. On the other hand, there is a
yearning for divinity in Rorty's hope that I shall encounter only myself in
everything I touch. (That was the structure, we saw, of the self-relational
activity of Aquinas's God.) One is hoping for a divine way of being in supposing that all determination will be a self-determining, and that the
boundaries a human discourse runs up against will be boundaries that it has
set for itself. (It may seem inconsistent to attribute to Rorty both a leftover
part of a picture that emphasized our weakness over against God, so that
our beliefs are a matter of coping, and a picture that divinizes subjectivity
through exalting its self-relational powers. But it seems to me that such a
combination of modesty and ambition is what is most characteristic of
modern philosophy. To take over the religious structure means either that
the subject ambitiously takes on a divinized role or that it modestly projects
its schemes upon a world it cannot hope to understand in itself.)

Hegel's version of the idealist program tried to restore the ontological
solidity of the world through a rethinking of that structure of self-relating.
But Rorty gives us the more narcissistic version of encountering only ourselves when we think and talk. To come to grips with the world is just to
encounter our own present cultural artifacts. Instead of the Hegelian
expansion of the understanding of self-relating-in-relating-to-otherness,
Rorty gives us a picture of otherness collapsing into the self-relational activity of conversations feeding off other conversations, so that we never
encounter anything but what we have made. Rorty often seems profoundly
a part of (one strand of) the German romantic tradition. We can see a version of Fichtean self-positing in his talk of "the sense that there is nothing
deep down inside us except what we have put there ourselves, no criterion
that we have not created in the course of creating a practice, no standard of
rationality that is not an appeal to such a criterion, no rigorous argumenta-
tion that is not obedience to our own conventions."[43]

Rorty's pragmatism also continues another structure with religious con-
notations. One of the chief Protestant impulses (at least as Hegel set matters out) is the demand that we not accept what is simply given, from the
world or from tradition or from authorities, but that our own activity of
taking-to-be must be the condition for securing matters as objective and
legitimate. Our labor and our making must transform what we encounter
into what we can recognize as our own. (After being cast out of the garden,

the simple enjoyment of what is real cannot be ours; we must make ourselves real through laboring upon the world.) Since God's presence to us will be inward, at the basis of our making and self-making activities, the role of a noumenal world, as an external realm guaranteed by God's knowing, will become otiose. Our relation with the real will then be understood in terms of work, constitution, transformation, the production of artifacts, insofar as these express our interiority and our personal "calling." Indeed, things can be secured as real only through our labor. Now I think pragmatism in general, and especially Rorty's form of it, retains significant traces of that conception. Sentences are helps to making and changing things in desirable ways; it is our labor that makes matters what they are.

But Rorty, it appears, will have difficulty stating exactly what his position is supposed to be. On his account statements will not have their meaning through the way they are *about* the world, but through the causal interrelations by which they contribute to producing successful or unsuccessful bodily interactions with the environment. The weight of the account comes down on the moment of intervention and reinforcement, and on the moment of perception by which some statements rather mysteriously appear in the system of one's beliefs. But at this point I may repeat an argument given earlier in the chapter. Given the extremely weak sense of the external world that emerges in Rorty's version of pragmatism, we cannot give much weight at all to the notion of genuine causal interventions in the world, and of reinforcements by its causal activity. The world is not sufficiently other; it will be just a projection of our practices themselves, not that which can be genuinely guiding them. The causal interaction with the world is not *real* causal interaction; it is rather that Rorty in his own speaking finds the production of the sounds "causal interaction" to be useful and interesting in the ways they connect to other sounds and to behavior.

What Rorty needs here, it seems, is to be able to stand outside his strict pragmatist posture just long enough to make some general realist claims about the causal interactions between linguistic strings, on the one side, and a world substantial enough and independent enough to contribute to conferring a semantic content upon them. Only after having done so will he have given sufficient sense to the world and its causal power to make the further pragmatic account intelligible. There is a parallel here, I think, with what occurs when you try to separate off a realm of subjectivity and ask what character it has apart from a relationship to a particular world. Doing this yields not an autonomous subjectivity, but the empty running of a syntactic engine. At least on Rorty's account of pragmatism, that realm of subjectivity becomes a network of communal conversations that are supposed to be constituting their referents from out of their own intertextual patterns. But if we have no world with the determinate character that at least a modest realism would grant it, there is nothing substantial enough to cast its shadow on those conversations and make them meaningful. They become patterns of noise in a vacuum.

Now the loss of the world as meaning-conferring is no difficulty if it is God whose presence to and lighting up of the subjective shapes makes them meaningful. Or there will not be a problem if we have divinized subjectivity or Language so that they have on their own, independently of the world, a self-determining power. But the medieval and modern structure of subjectivity comes under enormous pressure that it simply cannot handle when God and his divinized substitutes are removed from it. Rorty continues that structure, and we might say that for him the background platitudes and practices of the culture are supposed to take over the divine role of assuring the meaningfulness of the utterances and thoughts of the individual, since the world has been reduced to an empty frame. But if the foregoing argument is correct, there is nothing to keep them from being meaningless in their turn. The antirealist's erosion of the world, at least in Rorty's version, turns out to erode as well the semantic content of his sayings. (A partial antirealism, concerning ethical beliefs, for example, would not suffer from the same defect.)

Let me return to the "Protestant" emphasis on labor, making, and constituting, on our securing the real as such through our working upon it. Rorty's pragmatism, I suggested, continues that emphasis; sentences must pay their way in the work they accomplish. To say that they mirror the world is, for Rorty, to take the determinacy of the world as already given, as another external "authority" to be obeyed instead of what we ourselves, from the inside, take to be worth obeying. (The realist is then, for Rorty, like the Catholic who wants to be under the authority of the Pope instead of taking responsibility for his own epistemic projects.) In the earlier religious model there is an assimilation of knowing and making. Something is determinate either because God has made it so or because we have; God knows the world as it is because he made it, while we know the substitute world that we have constructed through the application of our labor to the raw material of experience. As before, Rorty removes half of the picture and keeps the rest as it was. There is no noumenal world that God has created, and no raw material that we are given to work upon as demiurges, but still we ourselves know only what we have made, the cultural artifacts upon which we have labored. But once we remove the religious and theological incentives for that conception, once we no longer take the model of God's creation as a metaphor for the relation of thought and reality, then we shall not so readily accept that relation of knowing and making. The removal of God from the scene, and the consequent demotion of the model of divine creation, will cause us to rethink the entire picture of the relation of subjectivity to the world. Then we shall not be left with our making, coping, and laboring as what remains after God's laboring disappears. We can instead think of our knowing as allowing the world to display its own character, even if our ways of thinking and seeing let the world become visible in some ways rather than others. Perhaps the articulations of the world need to be actualized in our thinking, or in the thinking of other sorts of believers, in order to count as genuine articulations. But they are features of a world whose self-exhibiting we may enjoy as thinkers.

If Rorty does appeal to the pragmatist notions of labor and economy, of making sentences pay their way, he also transforms the structure that supported that manner of thought. There is no longer the "calling" from God that sets up a proper field for our labor, and there is no longer the raw material of "givenness" that constrains what that labor will be able to accomplish. Without those two constraints the Protestant work ethic turns into textual play, as (in America) the search for a religious justification has turned for many into a search for a sexual or therapeutic one.

Rorty, Disenchantment, and Modern Institutions

As we remove the various effects of religious and theological ideas on thinking about the self, there will be a temptation to see our political and epistemic institutions as no longer having a kind of basis that once was available. It will be said that these institutions that developed in the modern era did so in tandem with practices of self-formation, and with conceptions of selfhood and subjectivity that can no longer be honored. Rorty himself believes strongly in the virtues of our modern liberal political and ethical institutions.[44] He believes that the support seemingly given once by philosophers' arguments to these institutions was illusory, but he also thinks that it does not matter. Philosophical thinking does not make much of a difference to practice anyway, and humans can learn to live very well with the notion that their institutions have no deeper support or justification than their own habits of commitment to them. (Sometimes he is less sure that such a society will do well.)

We may see this case as parallel to the loss of divine support for our forms of ethical life. It is worth noting, of course, that for hundreds of millions of individuals it is still religion that forms the strongest basis for moral beliefs, and surely there are many instances where a lessening of religious influence has led to a weakening of habits of living morally. But one of the great modern projects was to give a new basis for ethical life by appealing to various conceptions of subjectivity. It is an important fact of recent history that this new basis, expressed especially in appeals to human rights, equal treatment, civil and political liberties, and democracy, has been able to ground firm commitments to at least some ethical institutions even in those who are not at all religious. It is perhaps unsurprising that these conceptions of subjectivity retained aspects of the earlier religious and theological forms of thought. There was, for example, the Kantian notion of a self that determines rational principles for its life from a stance outside of space and time; and there are Kantian accounts that retain that sort of stance without the metaphysics. The question now is whether our practices can endure the loss of such religious pictures of the self and its activity, as they once endured the loss of religion itself as a support.

Now I think Rorty is correct that the disenchantment of subjectivity does not have to be threatening to such institutions. (In my way of seeing matters, our Enlightenment practices were not simply creatures of those metaphysical pictures and can thus survive their disappearance.) But I think, in contrast, that Rorty's version of pragmatism can be dangerous in regard to them. The problem is a double one: the dissolving of the world as that to which our practices must accommodate themselves in order to get matters right, and the dissolving of the self-relating subject into a mere construction of social practices and linguistic codes. (For Rorty, "the human self is created by the use of a vocabulary."[45]) Rorty believes that either we must make a very controversial metaphysical commitment to a noumenal world and a noumenal self-willing, or we must accept, as he does, that there is no further support for our practices beyond the fact that we support them.

But, again, Rorty seems not radical enough in rethinking the structures of modern thought. One modern idea was to try to derive from the resources of subjectivity itself the standards that reality and rational practice, as well as political and ethical life, must satisfy. Now as the disenchantment of subjectivity undermines that project, there are two responses available. One, Rorty's, is to retain the modern picture of an impoverished world whose determinacy must come from the self-relational structure of subjectivity, while granting that what comes from the subjective side must be, after disenchantment, a mere preference for some fashions over others. Rules of argument, human rights, liberal institutions, ethical habits will, like fashions in clothing, have their only backing in our activity of backing them, an activity that could just as well have settled on many other preferences. (It should be said, however, that in at least one sense, Rorty is not a relativist about such matters. Even if our commitment to our institutions has no deeper grounding than that, we shall quite properly take for granted the shape that such a commitment gives to our lives and our communities.)

The other response is that we need to rethink the picture of subjectivity as projecting its determinations on the real. Rorty goes only part way in his process of disenchantment. A more fully naturalized subjectivity will be one whose identity we will be able to specify only by seeing it as accommodating itself to real features of the world. Rather than being a result of habits or fashions we just *happen* to accept, or being derivable from the very nature of subjectivity, our epistemic and ethical practices can be seen as part of a holistically adjusted process of gradually getting things right. So an alternative to trying to find support in an increasingly less potent and less divine subjectivity is to return to the world, though in a more sophisticated fashion than in traditional realism. In *Subjectivism, Realism, and Postmodernism* I give considerable attention to showing that this alternative is a plausible one, and that the world can thus regulate our ethical beliefs. If this conception is plausible, then Rorty's position is much less so.

I think Rorty is wrong in supposing that we could accept the fashion analogy and still have the kind of commitment we need to our epistemic and ethical and political institutions. It is hardly the case that we must discover Platonic or Kantian foundations for them, nor do we have to suppose that there is no place for invention on our part, for our interests to give some degree of shaping to what we may take getting things right to be. But I think we need also the sense that epistemic goodness and ethical goodness are at least as much discovered as made, that they transcend the peculiarities of our practices and regulate to an important degree the adjusting of those practices to what is epistemically or ethically the case.

It is true, I grant, that the issue of whether Rorty's "fashion" model of our ethical and epistemic practices will undermine them is an empirical question about what human beings are like. We do not know now what attitudes those in the future must have toward their practices if they are to have the needed commitment to them to keep them going. It will be said that the English have a passionate commitment to the practices and the exact rules of cricket, even if cricket has no basis other than their own setting of the rules. But we need to ask whether our engagement in a communal ethical life could be of this sort, whether we could accept the analogy that our commitment to human rights follows just from the rules we happen to play by and happen to like very much, since they help give a sense to our Westernness, in the way that cricket helps give a sense to Englishness. I think we shall demand that some deeper basis remain after reflection, and that we understand our ethical thought to be a responding to ethical considerations that are only partly constituted by what we do. And there is the question of whether, even if we could succeed with an understanding of our commitment as cricketlike, our understanding of what we are about as ethical individuals will have been impoverished. For we shall have failed to grasp in just what the importance of being ethical lies. It is not just an interesting game that we have happened to invent.

The success of the institutions of the West can be measured for Rorty only by subjective criteria. Western science and political forms of life do not have their prestige because they have discovered more about how nature is articulated and about what forms of community best suit human beings. Europeans rather have been very good at changing their vocabularies and reinventing themselves rapidly.[46] Presumably Europe became a fashion leader in such vocabularies, and so managed to keep its cultural hegemony, because it could keep coming up with new vocabularies faster than those in the rest of the world could copy them. But surely there is a large difference between Eastern Europeans' adoption of the Western legal system and democratic institutions and their copying of Western clothing and rock music. It is true that within the fashion model we might decide to make our commitment to some fashions much more important than our commitments to others. But how would we thereby have made it comprehensible that others must, in order to get matters at least roughly right, follow us in making those same fashions (human rights, for example, and greater equality of opportunity) more important? Why is there that limitation on their freedom? Could it really be the case that there is no deeper rightness here than that the trend-setting West has happened to make those fashions extremely important for joining "our" club?

Rorty favors a "poeticized" culture, in which there is a split between a privatized Nietzschean self-inventing and a public world characterized by the liberal institutions of the modern West.[47] But that split between private and public worlds is again a staple of modern thought. It is true that the emphasis on an active interiority that sets the standard for how reality can or should appear often leads, among modern thinkers, to vigorous demands on the political order. But it is also likely that there will be a separating out of this private self-relating from the world. As an early modern self, an individual will not want the public life of the ancient polis; his concern will be rather to have political institutions that do a good job of preserving the sphere of private self-making, so that he can carry out the calling that is his through his being open to God's presence to his interiority, and for which inner attitude is more important than public status. Kierkegaard expresses a later version of this outcome. My public performances as a member of an institution seem to count very little for him. What matters is my inner choosing to be a self, to take myself as a choosing self seriously. That sort of attentiveness to the self will not be immune to narcissism; but the Kierkegaardian self avoids that outcome because in taking over one's subjectivity, one's self-relating, in the most serious possible way, one automatically becomes closer to God and thus gains a career for the self that is grounded in an other.

In Rorty we seem to have something like the Kierkegaardian structure without the saving relationship to an eternal divinity. There are the public liberal institutions that one favors but a participation in which is not assigned a very high value. Then there is the private Nietzschean self-inventing, the production of interesting and novel vocabularies that may or may not find successful replication in the culture. As in Locke's notion of a calling, Rorty praises bourgeois liberal society precisely because without it, "people will be less able to work out their private salvations."[48]

Participation in public life does not seem to have any value in itself. Rorty praises Derrida for having been the first to recognize that philosophy can only be private ironic play rather than the carrying out of a public responsibility; Derrida has given up even the appearance of giving arguments, of trying to get matters right, of discovering foundations for the institutions we believe in.[49] But then there is little to stop that play from turning into an empty narcissism.

Rorty, while speaking favorably of utopian politics, has little to say about the normal processes of self-revision that have become embodied in Western societies. On his view, as self-invention becomes private, we simply accept our liberal institutions without trying to justify their character. Since what is moral is defined by our practices, it is impossible to ask whether ours is a moral society, and our allegiance to liberal institutions is like our allegiance to friends or heroes in that it does not require, and cannot have, justification in a common language.[50] But allegiance to a friend may require such a justification (if he becomes a neo-Nazi, for example) and allegiance to a hero may as well (if he turns out to be a vicious racist). In Hegel the self relational structure of subjectivity becomes a demand placed on political institutions, that they develop until their own structure is suitable for forming a community of citizens who can be both rational and free. But in Rorty the activity of the self-inventing, self-determining self has become cut off from that relation to political life (a familiar pattern by now). So institutions become inert, simply accepted, divorced from that which needs to ground the self-revising processes of the modern order. And while he speaks of Nietzschean self-making, the self-determining activity of the modern self seems to become in Rorty a playful, ironic consumption of linguistic codes, more passive than active in relation to the world. There is a split-off, self-relational activity that has little to do with the public order except insofar as, by accident, it happens to throw up a new vocabulary into the ongoing conversation. As the subjective world becomes a realm for an empty sort of play, there is a withering not only of public life but of the very notion that we might improve our lot through rational self-reflection regarding our institutions.

So I think that Rorty continues modern structures more than he subverts them. Simply to show that Rorty gives us a later version of modern philosophy instead of rethinking it is not to show thereby that he is wrong. It is to show only that he fails by his own standards; he is trapped within an older fashion, an older vocabulary, as the narrative has moved on. But if my arguments have been valid, it is by more than his own standards that he fails. Rorty is missing what is significant about recent work in philosophy and has learned the wrong lessons. When we apply ourselves thoroughly to rethinking the subject-world structure of modern philosophy, we end up not losing the world but recovering it, not in narcissistic play but in a project of increasing our sensitivity to what the world is like and to what is right and wrong.

RESPONSE TO FRANK FARRELL

Frank Farrell's *Subjectivity, Realism and Postmodernism The Recovery of the World*, from which the above chapter is excerpted, is unusual in two respects. It treats "analytic" and "Continental" philosophers with equal respect and care, and it tries to put the work of both within a large historical narrative. It is the sort of book I hope we get more of—one that moves easily back and forth between Hegel and Davidson, and between Dennett and Derrida, while maintaining a consistent point of view and developing a strong, focused line of argument. I particularly admire Farrell's thoughtful and original use of Blumenberg's account of the Ockhamite origins of Bacon, Descartes, and the modern world.

Farrell raises both exegetical and philosophical issues in his discussion of my work. The exegetical ones concern what Farrell calls my "misreading" and "distortion" of Davidson. This is the less important set of issues, and I shall discuss them only briefly, in order to get on to the more interesting philosophical ones.

Farrell is quite right that I often take a Davidsonian doctrine and extrapolate from it in directions Davidson does not go, and in which (for all I know, and for all my readers should care) he may not wish to go. This is most obviously the case in my use of Davidson's reconstruction of Freud—his interpretation of unconscious motives and beliefs in terms of the utility of several distinct, conflicting, belief-and-desire schemes for explaining the behavior of a single organism. Farrell correctly says that Davidson "nowhere indicates that he is sympathetic to [Rorty's] extrapolation from the individual mind to historical change" (171). But I do not think it matters whether Davidson would or would not be sympathetic to such an extrapolation. If you borrow somebody's good idea and use it for a different purpose, is it really necessary to clear this novel use with the originator of the idea?

The same goes for Davidson's doctrine of metaphor, which I use—and Davidson does not—to (in Farrell's words) break down "the distinction between rational and irrational persuasion, and between reason and power" (169). Farrell says that he "does not see much support in Davidson for transforming [Davidson's] conception of metaphor into a full-scale picture of changes of vocabulary in history" (170). Nor do I, but I think that the absence of such support is irrelevant to the value of my account of long-term historical change in vocabulary. My account can, I should like to think, stand on its own feet, and be judged on its own. He also says that "it seems unlikely that he [Davidson] would agree with Rorty's claim that there are no rational standards being applied when one large theoretical apparatus replaces another" (170). Maybe, but I do not see that Davidson's silence on the issues debated between Kuhn and his critics should inhibit me from using Davidsonian ideas to formulate arguments on Kuhn's side.

The most important exegetical question Farrell raises about my use of Davidson, however, is whether Davidson shares Farrell's own realist intuitions. I think that Davidson's position allows him to go either Farrell's way or mine, and that the evidence is ambiguous. Passages can be cited on both sides. Farrell cites Davidson as saying "We can accept objective truth conditions as the key to meaning, a realist view of truth, and we can insist that knowledge is of an objective world independent of our thought or language."[1] I can cite him as saying "It is futile either to reject or to accept the slogan that the real and the true are 'independent of our beliefs'" and also as saying "Realism, with its insistence on radically nonepistemic correspondence, asks more of truth than we can understand."[2] I can also cite him (and frequently have cited him) as saying "It is good to be rid of representations, and with it of the correspondence theory of truth."[3]

But there is little point in trotting out such competing texts, or in either of us trying to wrap ourselves in Davidson's mantle. The two of us admire Davidson equally, and we can both employ Davidsonian ideas as we debate the question of whether we should enhance or suppress the realist intuitions to which Farrell appeals. We can do so without worrying about whether Davidson himself would take sides, or would remain neutral. So from here on I shall forget about exegesis, though not about Davidson.

Farrell thinks of me as losing the world and glorifying the self, and as under the sway of the Ockhamist train of thought whose influence Blumenberg has highlighted—the train of thought which, by exalting God's omnipotence, began the process of "eroding . . . the world's own determinacy; the migration of features to subjectivity" (176; see also *Subjectivity*, 1–4). His title, which features "the recovery of the world," contrasts with that of a paper of mine called "The World Well Lost." He explains that his initial motivation for writing his book was a belief that I have "given an unreliable account of recent philosophy" (*Subjectivity*, xi).

I think that Farrell is right to criticize that paper, and various other papers of mine, for suggesting that the only alternatives are a radical subjectivism in which the self projects schemes out upon a featureless reality (what Putnam has satirized as "the cookie-cutter view") on the one hand, and an unknowable noumenon on the other (175). But "The World Well Lost" was written twenty-three years ago. Lately I have been trying to mark out a position that does not take sides between subject and object, mind and world, but that instead tries to erase the contrast between them. I have, so to speak, been trying to lose *both* us and the world. Whereas Farrell reads me as trying to glorify us at the expense of the world, and hopes to rectify the balance with a "modest realism," I want to stop using the us-world contrast, and thus to get rid of the realism-antirealism issue.

I agree with Arthur Fine that the problem is to find a way of thinking that neither preserves the realistic intuitions to which Farrell, like Gouinlock and Lavine, is attached nor substitutes antirealist intuitions of the sort to which I used to be more attached than I now think I should be.[4] I should like to see James and Dewey as having attempted to get us beyond the dualism of subject and object, a dualism that both tempts us into thinking we have to choose between realism and antirealism and makes us frightened of a menace called "relativism"—a menace whose danger Farrell, like many of my other critics, thinks I do not sufficiently appreciate.[5]

I think that Davidson's account of the need for "triangulation" in order to have intentionality makes it hard to be either a realist or an antirealist. Farrell and I are both fans of this notion (158, and see *Subjectivity*, 113–14). I agree with Farrell when he says that we must reject an account of "the world's metaphysical character" as "a reflection of logical structure, and specifically of the structure of a language as it is available to an interpreter." But I disagree with him when he goes on to say that we must instead insist "The world must already be there, with its own well-developed contours, as a condition for counting speech as meaningful, as more than a stream of noise."[6]

If I ever suggested that the world's metaphysical structure was a "reflection of logical structure," then I was wrong. For as I (now, at least) see the matter, the picture of the mind projecting structure onto an unstructured world is just as bad as the idea of the world projecting structure onto, or into, language. I should like to reject the whole set of optical metaphors—projecting as well as mirroring, reflecting, or shadowing—and thus to reject the question Which comes first, subject or object? This means rejecting the question Whose contours were there first? Language's or the world's? Whose contours are reflecting whose? Rejecting such questions seems to me the cash value of rejecting what Davidson calls "the dogma of scheme and content."

There seems to me to be a conflict between the following two sentences, which occur in Farrell's account of the "realism" he attributes to Davidson:

> We err if we think we can divide up the contributions of world, language, and interpreter, so as to specify what the contribution of one of those sources would be, in independence of the others. A correct account of what the world is like whose articulations our language is capturing depends on what worldly contours that very language makes prominent; a correct account of what that language is like already takes for granted a well-articulated world as what is casting its shadow upon the language to make it meaningful. (*Subjectivity*, 78)

I entirely agree with the first sentence, but, because I do, it is hard for me to see what words like *articulations, contours,* and *well-articulated* could mean in this context. If there is to be any issue about realism on which Farrell and I disagree, then these words must convey more than just: we would not have the language and the beliefs we do were the world not as it is. Anybody naturalistic enough to accept Davidson's account of meaning, as we both have, is going to believe *that*. But I take shadowing an articulation to be a much richer, and much more dubious, notion than being under the causal sway of something not ourselves.

I have argued that, if one is content to think of the relations between human organisms, their beliefs, and the rest of the universe in merely causal terms, rather than dragging in representational relations in addition to causal ones, questions about realism and antirealism will not arise.[7] Farrell's use of "shadowing" and of "well-articulated" seems to me to drag in representational relations. Putting Davidson exegesis to one side, the philosophical issue between Farrell and me is: once one gives up on the project of isolating *which* articulations are ours and which the world's, does the question of whether the world's articulations are "encountered" or "projected" any longer need to be asked? If we cannot say anything about any *specific* contours or articulations, is there any point in talking of such things at all?

Farrell says such things as "our beliefs generally capture the world as it is and, at least holistically, are made true or false by it" (*Subjectivity*, 115). I think that "generally" and "at least holistically" take back what was supposed to given by terms like *contours* and *well-articulated*. For the former terms suggest, I think correctly, that no answers to the question *Which* contours? is ever going to be given. Yet the latter terms invite that question. The "modesty" of what Farrell calls his "modest realism" seems to consist in not answering that question. The "realist" part seems to consist in insisting that it is a good, or at least a meaningful question.[8]

I want to say that pragmatism can help us get beyond realism and antirealism by insisting that if something does not work in practice, it does not work in theory.[9] If there can be no project that consists in separating out the various shadows apparently cast upon language by the world, and then figuring out which are real shadows cast by real contours as opposed to pseudo-shadows that are due to something in language itself, then there is no point in saying that "a well-articulated world" casts "its shadow upon the language to make it meaningful." This picture is as empty as the one that Farrell attributes to me: the picture of a the world as a "substratum upon which linguistic distinctions are projected" (*Subjectivity*, 77–78). Both pictures pose unanswerable riddles: the question What was language like before it became meaningful by having the world's shadow cast on it? is just as bad as What was the substratum like before those linguistic distinctions got projected?

I take the moral of Davidson's account of triangulation to be that I, the other language-users, and the rest of the universe all are what we are because the other two sides of the triangle are what they are, *and* that there is no point in trying to break down "are what they are" into more specific processes of projecting or reflecting. This is because there is no way of examining any of these three sides in isolation from each other, in order to see who is doing what to whom. To fully accept this moral would be to stop talking about realism and antirealism and, more generally, to stop asking questions about our relationship to rest of the universe.

That would mean ceasing to be religious either in the way in which Farrell thinks I am religious (making human beings quasi-divine by giving them the power to create quasi worlds by projecting) or the way in which I think Farrell is religious (making human beings quasi-divine by giving them the power to mirror reality rather than merely interacting with it). Farrell is quite right in saying that I would accuse him of being the sort of thinker "who, having given up on God, still needs to feel under the sway of something Godlike" (174).[10]

Farrell says that "Rorty is quintessentially and 'religiously' modern in holding that if we open ourselves to any constraint at all from the world, we are submitting ourselves to an unacceptable authority that limits the free, self-relating play of subjectivity" (174). I would rejoin that Farrell seems quintessentially and "religiously" pre-Romantic in thinking that if we lose the sense of reflecting, mirroring, displaying something not ourselves—lose the sense that we are getting things right—we reduce ourselves to meaninglessness.[11] The realistic intuitions which he defends seem to me to have no practical function, and his insistence on them seems to have a purely spiritual function. If we both got off our "religious" high horses we might be able to agree that nobody's language has ever been or ever will be unconstrained by the world, and that nobody will ever be able to be interestingly specific about what these constraints are and how they work.

Farrell would, however, disagree with my claim that his modest realism has a purely spiritual function. For he thinks that "realist discourse is embedded in very many of our practices" and that I owe my audience a "detailed cost-benefit investigation of the particular practices" (163). This is because, presumably, the utility of our present practices depends upon the realistic discourse embedded in them. I do not see such embedding. Like Fine, I think that most of our practices (notably those of expert cultures such as natural science) swing free of the glosses which philosophers put upon them, and that there is no point in quizzing either carpenters or physicists about their views on the relation between language and reality.[12]

But there is a sense in which I agree with Farrell that the question at hand is ultimately spiritual, and that the adoption of my view would be a real change in people's self-image. For when people step outside of their expert cultures—when they stop acting as carpenters or physicists and start getting reflective in religious or philosophical ways—they do, alas, start wondering about whether we are shadowing, displaying, mirroring, and representing something. I wish they did not. I think that if we could get rid of *both* Farrell's sense that we are meaningless unless we are getting something not ourselves right, *and* the Nietzschean sense that we are meaningless unless we create a world in our image (the Romanticism that Farrell attributes to me), then our spiritual state would be better than it is now. Whereas Farrell sees the interesting choice as between a modest realism and an anarchic subjectivism (Ockham as humanized by Nietzsche), I see it as between continued worry about realism versus antirealism and benign neglect of traditional religious and philosophical topics.

I think that pragmatism is as counterintuitive as antirealism, even though I think that it is very different from antirealism. (By analogy, atheism used to be [around 1450] as counter-intuitive as Protestantism, even though it is very different from Protestantism.) I also think that a world of pragmatic atheists—people who thought realism versus antirealism as little worth thinking about as Catholicism versus Protestantism—would be a better, happier world than our present one. But this is, of course, just a guess. I do not have an original argument for pragmatism, but I do think that James and Dewey suggested a new, inspiring, spiritually edifying self-image—one that is well worth a try.

9

PHILOSOPHY & THE FUTURE

Richard Rorty

Philosophers became preoccupied with images of the future only after they gave up hope of gaining knowledge of the eternal. Philosophy began as an attempt to escape into a world in which nothing would ever change. The first philosophers assumed that the difference between the flux of the past and the flux of the future would be negligible. Only as they began to take time seriously did their hopes for the future of this world gradually replace their desire for knowledge of another world.

Hans Blumenberg has suggested that philosophers began to lose interest in the eternal toward the end of the Middle Ages, and that the sixteenth century, the century of Bruno and Bacon, was the period in which philosophers began trying to take time seriously. Blumenberg is probably right, but this loss of interest only became fully self-conscious in the nineteenth century. This was the period in which Western philosophy, under the aegis of Hegel, developed detailed and explicit doubts not only about Platonic attempts to escape from time but about Kantian projects of discovering ahistorical conditions for the possibility of temporal phenomena. It was also the period in which it became possible, thanks to Darwin, for human beings to see themselves as continuous with the rest of nature—as temporal and contingent through and through, but none the worse for that. The combined influence of Hegel and Darwin moved philosophy away from the question "What are we?" to the question "What might we try to become?"

This shift has had consequences for the philosophers' image of themselves. Whereas Plato and even Kant hoped to survey the society and the culture within which they lived from an outside standpoint, the standpoint of ineluctable and changeless truth, later philosophers have gradually abandoned such hopes. Just insofar as we take time seriously, we philosophers have to give up the priority of contemplation over action. We have to agree with Marx that our job is to help make the future different from the past, rather than claiming to know what the future must necessarily have in common with the past. We have to shift from the kind of role that philosophers have shared with priests and sages to a social role that has more in common with the engineer or the lawyer. Whereas priests and sages can set their own agendas, contemporary philosophers, like engineers and lawyers, must find out what their clients need.

Since Plato invented philosophy precisely in order to escape from transitory needs, and to rise above politics, taking time, Hegel, and Darwin seriously has often been described as "giving up on" or "ending" philosophy. But giving up on Plato and Kant is not the same as giving up on philosophy. For we can give better descriptions of what Plato and Kant were doing than these men were able to give of themselves. We can describe them as responding to the need to replace a human self-image which had been made obsolete by social and cultural change with a new self-image, a self-image better adapted to the results of those changes. We can add that philosophy cannot possibly end until social and cultural change ends. For such changes gradually render large-scale descriptions of ourselves and our situation obsolete. They create the need for new language in which to formulate new descriptions. Only a society without politics—that is to say, a society run by tyrants who prevent social and cultural change from occurring—would no longer require philosophers. In such societies, where there is no politics, philosophers can only be priests in the service of a state religion. In free societies, there will always be a need for their services, for such societies never stop changing, and hence never stop making old vocabularies obsolete.

John Dewey—a philosopher who, like Marx, admired Hegel and Darwin equally—suggested that we will, in the course of dropping the self-image common to Plato and Kant, the image of a knower of unconditional ahistorical necessities, come to see philosophy as springing "from a conflict of inherited institutions with incompatible contemporary tendencies. . . . That which may be pretentiously unreal when it is formulated in metaphysical distinctions," Dewey said, "becomes intensely significant when connected with the struggle of social beliefs and ideals."[1]

Dewey took seriously Hegel's famous remark that philosophy paints its gray on gray only when a form of life has grown old. For Dewey, this meant that philosophy is always parasitic on, always a reaction to, developments elsewhere in culture and society. Dewey construed Hegel's insistence on historicity as the claim that philosophers should not try to be the avant-garde of society and culture, but should be content to mediate between the past and the future. Their job is to weave together old beliefs and new beliefs, so that these beliefs can cooperate rather than interfere with one another. Like the engineer and the lawyer, the philosopher is useful in solving particular problems that arise in particular situations—situations in which the language of the past is in conflict with the needs of the future.

Let me offer three examples of such conflict. The first is the need to reconcile the moral intuitions clothed in the language of Christian theology with the new scientific world-picture that emerged in the seventeenth century. In that century and the next, philosophers tried to find a way of seeing moral intuitions as something other than the commands of an atemporal yet anthropomorphic divinity—a divinity whose existence was hard to reconcile with the mechanized world-picture offered by Galileo and Newton. Seen from this angle, the systems of Leibniz, Kant, and Hegel are so many suggestions about how to reconcile Christian ethics and Copernican-Galilean science—how to keep these two good things from interfering with each other.

My second example is the Darwinian suggestion that we think of human beings as more complex animals, rather than as animals with an extra added ingredient called "intellect" or "the rational soul." This suggestion casts doubt not only on the hope to escape from time but also on the distinction between adapting to reality and knowing reality. Darwin made philosophers realize that they would have to redescribe human activities in a way that required no sudden discontinuities in evolutionary development. This meant redescribing the relation between biological and cultural evolution in ways that blurred the distinction between Nature and Spirit—a distinction that everyone from Plato through Hegel, except for occasional eccentrics like Hobbes and Hume, had taken for granted.

The new demands on philosophers created by Darwin's successful explanation of the origin of humanity were interwoven with those created by my third example of extraphilosophical novelty: the emergence of mass democracy. Unlike the first two, this third novelty came from political experience rather than scientific ingenuity. Mass democracy—the successful working out in practice of the suggestion that all those affected by political decisions should have the power to influence those decisions—endangers the Platonic distinction between the rational pursuit of truth by the wise and the flux of passion characteristic of the many. When taken together with Darwin's blurring of the human-animal distinction, the practice of mass democracy casts doubt on a whole range of further distinctions: those between the cognitive and the non-cognitive, reason and passion, logic and rhetoric, truth and utility, philosophy and sophistry. One of the assignments that the success of mass democracy gave to philosophers was to restate these distinctions in terms of the political difference between free and forced consensus rather than in terms of the metaphysical distinction between the unconditioned and the conditional.

The systems of Dewey, Bergson, and Whitehead were attempts to reach an accommodation with Darwin, to keep what was useful in the old dualisms while restating them in, so to speak, thoroughly temporalized language. Russell's and Husserl's efforts to partition culture by drawing a line between a priori philosophical questions and a posteriori empirical questions were another such attempt: they tried to make a democratic culture safe for transcendental philosophy by making Darwin irrelevant to Kant.

Seen in this way, the contrast between Dewey and Russell, or between Bergson and Husserl, is not a contrast between two attempts to represent our ahistorical nature and situation accurately, but rather between two attempts to mediate between historical epochs, to reconcile old and new truth. Dewey and Russell were equally devoted to Newtonian mechanics, Darwinian biology, and mass democracy. Further, neither thought that philosophy could provide foundations for any of these three. Both thought that the question was how to change familiar ways of speaking so as not to presuppose a metaphysics, or a metaphysical psychology, that conflicted with these three cultural developments. Their differences were about means rather than ends—about how radically one had to change the descriptions that Plato and Kant had given of human beings in order to preserve the useful elements in their work while discarding what had become obsolete.

If we adopt Dewey's image of the philosopher's task, however, we have to drop both the Marxist distinction between science and ideology and the distinction, deployed by both Russell and Husserl, between the a priori and the a posteriori. More generally, we have to drop all attempts to make philosophy as autonomous an activity as it was thought to be before philosophers began taking time seriously. Dewey, but not Russell, can adopt Locke's suggestion that the role of the philosopher is that of an underlaborer, clearing away the rubbish of the past in order to make room for the constructions of the future. But Dewey would have admitted, I think, that the philosopher is occasionally able to fuse this janitorial role with the role of prophet. Such a combination is found in Bacon and Descartes, both of whom combined the attempt to clear away Aristotelian rubbish with visions of a utopian future. Similarly, the effort of Dewey to get philosophy out from under Kant, of Habermas to untangle it from what he calls "the philosophy of consciousness," and of Derrida to liberate it from what he calls "the metaphysics of presence" are intertwined with prophecies of the fully democratic society whose coming such extrication will hasten.

Ceasing to worry about the autonomy of philosophy means, among other things, no longer wanting to draw nice clear lines between philosophical questions and political, religious, aesthetic, or economic questions. Philosophy will not play the modest but essential role that Dewey assigned it, and so will not succeed in taking time seriously, unless we philosophers are willing to accept a certain deprofessionalization and to acquire a certain insouciance about the question of when we are doing philosophy and when we are not. We shall have to stop worrying about the purity of our discipline and stop dramatizing ourselves, not only in the grandiose way in which Hegel and Marx dramatized themselves, but even in the less spectacular way in which Russell and Husserl dramatized themselves.

If we stop preening ourselves on our position at the top of the hierarchy of disciplines, stop identifying our professional practices with "rational thought" or "clear thought," we shall be in a better position to grant Dewey's point that our discipline is no more able to set its own agenda than is engineering or jurisprudence. Such an admission would help us dispense with the idea that scientific or political developments require "philosophical foundations"—the idea that judgment must remain suspended on the legitimacy of cultural novelties until we philosophers have pronounced them authentically rational.

Philosophers who specialize in antifoundationalism, however, often see themselves as revolutionaries rather than as rubbish-sweepers or visionaries. Then, alas, they become avant-gardist. They start saying that our language and our culture need radical change before our utopian hopes can be realized, and that the philosophers are just the people to initiate such changes. This insistence on radicality is foundationalism turned on its head. It is the insistence that nothing can change unless our philosophical beliefs change. The philosophical avant-gardism common to Marx, Nietzsche, and Heidegger—the urge to make all things new all at once, to insist that nothing can change unless everything changes—seems to me one of two contemporary tendencies within philosophy that should be discouraged.

The other tendency is, as I have already suggested, the urge toward professionalization: the urge to keep our discipline intact and autonomous by narrowing its scope. This defensive maneuver is apparent whenever one finds a philosopher saying that he intends to confine himself to "the problems of philosophy," as if there were a well-known list of such problems, a list handed down from heaven and kept intact from generation to generation. Such an attempt to escape from time and change, to forget Hegel and affiliate oneself to Kant, is widespread in the Anglophone philosophical community, the community that describes itself as practicing "analytic" philosophy.

Hilary Putnam seems to me right in saying that much analytic philosophy has degenerated into quarrels between philosophy professors' differing "intuitions"—intuitions about questions that are, as Putnam says, "far from having either practical or spiritual significance."[2] The desire to harmonize pre-existent intuitions has replaced the task of asking whether the vocabulary in which these intuitions are stated is a useful one. This refusal reinforces the conviction that philosophical problems are eternal, and suited to be studied by a discipline that works independently of social and cultural change. Such a refusal, and such a conviction, were characteristic of the period in the history of philosophy that we now refer to as "decadent scholasticism." Whenever philosophers begin to pride themselves on the autonomy of their discipline, the danger of such scholasticism recurs.

Just as much Anglophone philosophy has become overprofessionalized, non-Anglophone philosophy is frequently overambitious and avant-gardist. It attempts the sort of radical critique that Marx offered of the so-called bourgeois culture of the nineteenth century—a critique offered in the same tones of high disdain that Marxists have made so familiar. Disgust with both the scholastic character of analytic philosophy and the impossibly high pretensions of avant-gardist non-analytic philosophy, however, has led to a third danger: that of chauvinism. Occasionally one finds philosophers saying that their own country, or their own region, requires a distinctive phi-losophy: that each nation needs a philosophy of its own, to express its own unique experience, just as it needs its own national anthem and its own flag. But whereas novelists and poets can usefully create a national litera-ture, a literature in which the youth can find embedded a narrative of the emergence and development of the nation of which they are citizens, I doubt that there is any analogous task to be performed by philosophers. We philosophers are good at building bridges between nations, at cos-mopolitan initiatives, but not at telling stories. When we do tell stories, they tend to be bad ones, like the stories that Hegel and Heidegger told the Germans about themselves—stories about the superior relation in which a certain country stands to some supernatural power.

I hope that we philosophy professors can find a way to avoid all three temptations: the revolutionary urge to see philosophy as an agent of change rather than of reconciliation, the scholastic urge to retreat within discipli-nary boundaries, and the chauvinistic urge. It seems to me that we might do so if we adopt Dewey's notion of our job as one of reconciliation of the old with the new, and of our professional function as serving as honest bro-kers between generations, between areas of cultural activity, and between traditions. This sort of reconciliatory activity cannot, however, be carried out in the manner of what Lévi-Strauss once disdainfully called "UNESCO cosmopolitanism," the sort of cosmopolitanism that is content with the sta-tus quo and defends it in the name of cultural diversity. Such cosmopoli-tanism was, when UNESCO was founded in the 1940's, prudently and respectfully silent about Stalinism; nowadays it remains prudently and respectfully silent about religious fundamentalism and about the blood-stained autocrats who still rule much of the world. The most contemptible form of such cosmopolitanism is the sort that explains that human rights are all very well for Eurocentric cultures, but that an efficient secret police, with subservient judges, professors, and journalists at its disposal, in addi-tion to prison guards and torturers, is better suited to the needs of other cultures.

The alternative to this spurious and self-deceptive kind of cosmopoli-tanism is one with a clear image of a specific kind of cosmopolitan human future: the image of a planetwide democracy, a society in which torture, or the closing down of a university or a newspaper, on the other side of the world is as much a cause for outrage as when it happens at home. This cosmopolis may be, in nonpolitical matters, as multicultural and heterogeneous as ever. But in this utopian future cultural traditions will have ceased to have an influence on political decisions. In politics there will be only one tradition: that of constant vigilance against the predictable attempts by the rich and strong to take advantage of the poor and weak. Cultural tradition will never be permitted to override Rawl's "difference principle," never permitted to excuse inequality of opportunity.

If such a utopia ever comes into being, we philosophers will probably have had a marginal, minor, but nevertheless helpful role in creating it. For, just as Aquinas had to mediate between the Old Testament and Aristotle, as Kant had to mediate between the New Testament and Newton, as Bergson and Dewey had to mediate between Plato and Darwin, as Gandhi and Nehru had to mediate between the language of Locke and Mill and that of the Bhagavad Gita, so somebody will have had to mediate between the egalitarian language of this kind of politics and the explicitly inegalitarian languages of many different cultural traditions. Somebody will have had to weave egalitarian politics gently and patiently into the language of traditions that insist on a distinction between the rational or inspired few, and the disorderly or confused many. Somebody will have had to persuade us to modify our habit of basing political decisions on the difference between people like us, the paradigmatic human beings, and such dubious cases of humanity as foreigners, infidels, untouchables, women, homosexuals, halfbreeds, and deformed or crippled people. Such distinctions are built into our cultural traditions, and thus into our vocabularies of moral deliberation, but utopia will not arrive until the peoples of the world become persuaded that these distinctions do not much matter.

This persuasion is going to be gradual and gentle and piecemeal, not revolutionary and wholesale. But such gentle and gradual persuasion is possible. For even though mass democracy may be a specifically European invention, the idea of a democratic utopia finds resonance everywhere. Within each cultural tradition there are stories of the many seeing farther than the wise, of the tradition-sanctioned cruelty of the high yielding to the sense of injustice felt by the low. Within every such tradition there are stories of successful intermarriage with members of despised groups, of ancient hatreds overcome by patience and civility. Every culture, no matter how parochial, contains material which can be woven into utopian images of a planetwide democratic political community.

It is self-contradictory to think of imposing democracy by force rather than persuasion, of forcing men and women to be free. But it is not self-contradictory to think of persuading them to be free. If we philosophers still have a function, it is just that sort of persuasion. Once upon a time, when we thought more about eternity and less about the future than we do now, we philosophers defined ourselves as servants of truth. But recently we have spoken less about truth and more about truthfulness, less about bringing truth to power than about keeping power honest. I think that this is a healthy shift. Truth is eternal and enduring, but it is hard to be sure when you have it. Truthfulness, like freedom, is temporal, contingent, and fragile. But we can recognize both when we have them. Indeed, the freedom we prize most is the freedom to be honest with one another and not be punished for it. In a thoroughly temporalized intellectual world, one in which hopes for certainty and changelessness have disappeared altogether, we philosophers would define ourselves as servants of that sort of freedom, as servants of democracy.

To think of ourselves in that way would be to avoid the dangers of scholasticism, or avant-gardism, and of chauvinism. It would be to agree with Dewey that "philosophy can proffer only hypotheses, and that these hypotheses are of value only as they render men's minds more sensitive to the life about them."[3] In a fully temporalized intellectual world, contributing to such sensitivity would be just as respectable a goal for an academic discipline as contributing to knowledge.

NOTES

INTRODUCTION

1. Richard Rorty, *The Linguistic Turn* (Chicago: University of Chicago Press, 1967), 33.

2. Richard Rorty, *Philosophy and the Mirror of Nature* (Oxford: Blackwell, 1980), 7.

3. Richard Rorty, *Objectivity, Relativism, and Truth* (Cambridge: Cambridge University Press, 1991), 99.

4. The two independent essays by Rorty in this volume, "Dewey Between Hegel and Darwin" and "Philosophy and the Future," represent both outlooks.

5. John Dewey, *Reconstruction in Philosophy and Essays, The Middle Works of John Dewey, 1899–1924*, ed. Jo Ann Boydston et al. (Carbondale: Southern Illinois University Press, 1976–83), 12:91–92.

6. Frank B. Farrell, *Subjectivity, Realism, and Postmodernism—The Recovery of the World* (Cambridge: Cambridge University Press, 1994), xi.

CHAPTER I

1. James Kloppenberg, *Uncertain Victory* (New York, Oxford University Press, 1985), 90.

2. David Hollinger, *In the American Province* (Bloomington, Indiana University Press, 1985), 16-17

3. Hollinger, *American Province*, 42. Hollinger distinguishes this cluster as one of "three interpenetrating layers" which make up "pragmatism as a presence in the discourse of American intellectuals." The other two are "a theory of meaning and truth" and "a range of general ideas stereotypical of American life."

4. Charles S. Peirce, *Collected Papers*, 6:492.

5. Outside the school of neo-Whiteheadians centering around Charles Hartshorne, one of the few contemporary philosophers who has a good word to say for panpsychism is Thomas Nagel—a thinker who has no use whatever for pragmatism, and thinks it the root of much philosophical evil.

6. Peirce *Collected Papers*, 5:314.

7. The locus classicus for this distinction is Peirce's two papers "Questions Concerning Certain Faculties Claimed for Man" and "Some Consequences of Four Incapacities" (*Collected Papers*, 5:213–317). See the discussion of these papers in John Murphy, *Pragmatism: From Peirce to Davidson* (Boulder, Colo.: Westview, 1990). Murphy's presentation helps one see the connection between such contemporary holist philosophies of knowledge as Davidson's and Peirce's claim that "at no one instant in my state of mind is there cognition or representation, but in the relation of my states of mind at different instants there is" (5.289).

8. What Davidson calls "the crucial step from the nonpropositional to the propositional" is not taken by looking where Locke and James looked—at the way in which experience supposedly sorts itself out, gradually changing from a buzzing

confusion to a coherent inner discourse. Rather, it is taken by watching organisms interact with their environment and then formulating a theory that ascribes propositional attitudes to them, on the sole basis of "information about what episodes and situations in the world cause an agent to prefer that one rather than another sentence be true." (The passages quoted are from Davidson, "The Structure and Content of Truth," *Journal of Philosophy* 87 [June 1990]: 325, 322). The question of "the origin of intentionality" is, from a Davidsonian point of view, no more mysterious than the question of how organisms began tossing around marks and noises in predictable sequences.

9. Manfred Frank, *What is Neostructuralism?* trans. Sabine Wilke and Richard Gray (Minneapolis, University of Minnesota Press, 1989), 87.

10. Frank, *Neostructuralism*, 93. See also 217, where Frank says "the linguistic turn consists in the transferral of the philosophical paradigm of consciousness onto that of the sign." (I myself would have said "the sentence" rather than "the sign," in order to exclude the sorts of iconical and indexical signs which Peirce included in his semiotic. This would accord with what Frank, following Tugendhat, says about propositional attitudes being "the basic form of all intentional consciousness" at 219. He there quotes Tugendhat as saying "the question of consciousness dissolves into the question of propositional understanding"; I take that dissolution to be the crucial difference between the philosophers' talk of "experience" circa 1900 and their talk of "language" circa 1990.)

11. Frank, *Neostructuralism*, 87.

12. Frank, *Neostructuralism*, 7.

13. William James, *Pragmatism* (Cambridge: Harvard University Press, 1978), 106.

14. James, *Pragmatism*, 35.

15. John Dewey, *Experience and Nature*, in his *Later Works of John Dewey, 1925–1953*, ed. Jo Ann Boydston, et al. (Carbondale: Southern Illinois University Press, 1981–90), 1:29–30.

16. Dewey, *Later Works*, 1:199.

17. John Dewey, *On Experience, Nature and Freedom*, ed. Richard Bernstein (Indianapolis: Bobbs-Merrill, 1960), 86–87.

18. I have mounted criticisms of Dewey's *Experience and Nature* along these lines myself, in "Dewey's Metaphysics" (in my *Consequences of Pragmatism*).

19. See E. B. McGilvary, "The 'Chicago Idea' and Idealism," reprinted in Dewey, *Early Works*, 4:317–27, esp. 322, where McGilvary says that the scheme produced by Dewey's redefinitions "is beautifully simple, and if you adhere to it, you get rid of some very disagreeable questions [i.e., the traditional epistemological problems about the relation of thought to reality] which force themselves on you if you refuse to adopt it. But if the questions referred to are asked with a view to determining whether the new way of ideas comports with facts, then we have a different matter on our hands."

20. John Dewey, "A Short Catechism Concerning Truth," *Middle Works,*

1899–1924, ed. Jo Ann Boydston, et al. (Carbondale: Southern Illinois University Press, 1976–83), 6:5.

21. James, *Pragmatism*, 96: "Where our ideas cannot copy definitely their object, what does agreement with that object mean?"

22. See James, *Pragmatism*, 97, 103.

23. James, *Pragmatism*, 102.

24. Dewey, "Short Catechism," 5–6.

25. See Kloppenberg, *Uncertain Victory*, 65.

26. See *Hegel's Philosophy of Mind*, trans. William Wallace (Oxford, Oxford University Press, 1971), 17 (sec. 383, *Zusatz*): "God has revealed that his nature consists in having a Son, i.e., in making a distinction within himself, making himself finite, but in his difference remaining in communion with himself . . . so that the Son is not the mere organ of the revelation but is himself the content of the revelation." Compare the polemic against the "idea of knowledge as an instrument, and as a medium" in the introduction to *The Phenomenology of Spirit*. Hegel thought that whenever you had a picture of knowledge as a matter of relating (via an organ or a medium) two independently existing entities (the Subject and the Object) you automatically brought about the sort of skepticism which culminates in the Kantian claim that things-in-themselves are unknowable, and that Absolute Idealism was thus the only alternative to skepticism. For a sample of the early Dewey's version of this Hegelian line of thought, see chapter 9 ("Stages of Knowledge. Intuition," in *Psychology* (*Early Works*, vol. 2), especially 212: "The true self-related must be the organic unity of the self and the world, of the idea and the real, and this is what we know as God. It must be remembered that this intuition is one like in kind to the other intuitions, and involves the process of mediation as much as they. . . . Every concrete act of knowledge involves an intuition of God." *Psychology* insouciantly mingles Absolute Idealism with Wundtian empirical psychology—mingling metaphysics with psycho-physical correlation in just the way that James, at the outset of *The Principles of Psychology*, said he would avoid. Dewey gave up on God *qua* Absolute Idea not long after writing that book. But the themes of the need to insist on continuity to avoid skepticism, and of cognitive development as continuous with animal and infantile feeling and as consisting in ever-expanding relationality, continue to be sounded throughout Dewey's later work.

27. John Dewey, "The Influence of Darwinism on Philosophy," *Middle Works*, 4:8–9.

28. See "Influence of Darwinism," 7.

29. Dewey, "Short Catechism," 9.

30. John Dewey, "The Present Position of Logical Theory," *Early Works*, 3:134.

31. Ibid., 134–35.

32. Ibid., 135.

33. Ibid., 138–39.

34. Ibid., 140.

35. See Dewey's "The Intellectualist Criterion of Thinking," *Early Works*, 4:58

for a polemic against F. H. Bradley's "intellectualist" claim that "Thinking is the attempt to satisfy as *special* impulse." The same claim appears in contemporary critics of pragmatism like Bernard Williams, whose notion of "the absolute conception of reality" incorporates almost all the features that Dewey thought undesirably "intellectualist." See J. E. Tiles, *John Dewey* (London: Routledge, 1988), chapter 5, for a very useful account of Williams as Dewey's antithesis. For the a similar comparison, see my "Is Natural Science a Natural Kind?" in *Construction and Constraint: The Shaping of Scientific Rationality*, ed. E. McMullin (Notre Dame: Notre Dame University Press, 1988), 49–74.

36. See Charles Taylor, *Hegel* (Cambridge: Cambridge University Press, 1975) 24, 539 40.

37. See John Dewey, "Moral Theory and Practice," *Early Works*, 3:104, on "the movement of German ethics from Kant to Hegel." See also "Poetry and Philosophy," *Early Works*, 3:118 for a criticism of "the Stoics, Kant and Matthew Arnold" as holding a "conception of the individual as shut off from real communion with nature and with fellow-man, and yet as bearing himself a universal principle"—a conception to which Robert Browning stands as the antithesis. Although the "Poetry and Philosophy" essay does not mention Hegel, it seems reasonable to suppose that Dewey saw Hegel standing to Browning as Kant to Arnold.

38. John Dewey, *Human Nature and Conduct,* in *Middle Works*, 14:196.

39. Ibid., 195.

40. Note that this is true not only for onward-and-upward stories like Hegel's but for stories of decline from greatness like Heidegger's. Only because we have reached our present nadir can a Heidegger arise and draw the redemptive moral of this decline: "Wo aber Gefahr ist, wächst das Rettende auch."

41. The doctrine that evil is just out-of-date good is as central to Dewey as it was to Hegel. See, e.g., "Outlines of a Critical Theory of Ethics" (*Early Works*, 3:379): "Goodness is not remoteness from badness. In one sense, goodness is based upon badness; that is, good action is always based upon action good once, but bad if persisted in under changing circumstances." See also *Human Nature and Conduct (Middle Works*, 14:193): "The worse or evil is a rejected good. In deliberation and before choice no evil presents itself as evil. Until it is rejected, it is a competing good. After rejection, it figures not as a lesser good, but as the bad of that situation."

42. John Dewey, *Reconstruction in Philosophy*, in *Middle Works*, 12:94.

CHAPTER 2

Note to epigraph: Richard Rorty, *Consequences of Pragmatism* (Minneapolis: University of Minnesota Press, 1982), 173–74.

1. Ibid., 736–37.

2. *Philosophy and the Mirror of Nature* (Princeton, N.J.: Princeton University Press, 1979).

Response to Hartshorne

1. Both left the University of Chicago about the time I did (Hartshorne for Emory, Carnap for UCLA). My fellow philosophy students and I sometimes felt indignant that McKeon reigned over all he surveyed from a large, bow-windowed, solitary study in the stacks of Classics, while Carnap and Hartshorne each shared their gloomy rooms in Swift Hall with two or three assistant professors. Much as I admired McKeon's immense learning and his synoptic imagination, it was hard to avoid the feeling that, in departmental and university politics, he threw his weight around too much.

2. "Pragmatism, Categories and Language," *Philosophical Review* 70 (April 1961), 197–223.

3. Hartshorne and I both have spent appreciable portions of our lives looking for birds. He is an expert on their song, whereas I, being pretty well tone-deaf, am restricted to their visual appearances.

4. As I did in *Contingency, Irony and Solidarity*, I am here using "poet" in a wide sense—one wide enough to include much-footnoted Plato. I have never seen the point of Heidegger's distinction between *Dichter* and *Denker*.

5. I shall not discuss panpsychism here, because all I have to say about it is contained in "The Subjectivist Principle and the Linguistic Turn," in *Alfred North Whitehead: Essays on His Philosophy*, ed. George L. Kline (Englewood Cliffs, N.J.: Prentice-Hall, 1963), 134–57. That essay—an invocation of Sellars against Whitehead—is thirty-odd years old, but I still agree with most of it.

6. In a famous footnote to *Pragmatism*, James quotes W. S. Franklin as saying that "the healthiest notion" of physics is as "the science of the ways of taking hold of bodies and pushing them."

7. William James, *The Varieties of Religious Experience* (Cambridge: Harvard University Press, 1985), 384.

8. I am not sure that I did not first hear these words of Blake's from Hartshorne's lips. I am quite sure that he was the first person I heard quote the great passage from "Tintern Abbey": "And I have felt / A presence that disturbs me with the joy / Of elevated thoughts; a sense sublime / Of something far more deeply interfused."

9. This is Whitehead's official label for "creativity" in the first chapter of *Process and Reality*.

10. The trouble with that Carnapian slogan, as many people have remarked, is that it assumes that language is only properly used when used for the purpose of constructing a unified science—a notion of propriety that persisted on into Quine's *Word and Object* but was never much more than an expression of the positivists' poetic preferences.

11. This attitude may seem hard to reconcile with the Santayanesque one—metaphysics as poetic vision—that I enunciated earlier. But I think that the two can be brought together by saying that we never know whether a difference in doctrine or terminology will make a difference to practice until we have kicked it around for

a while—until it is a theme on which a reasonable number of variations have been tried out. But after a while we may begin to feel that the difference—e.g., the difference between Kant and Fichte, or between Bergson and Whitehead, or between Fodor and Dennett—has had its day, and has not suggested any novel practices, poetic or otherwise. Then James's attitude of "Who needs it? What good is it doing us?" becomes appropriate.

12. I take this Hegel, *pace* Hance and Pippin, to be the good Hegel, the one from whom we can still learn. After the *Phenomenology*, it seems to me, something went horribly wrong, something that led him to start writing *The Science of Logic* and the *Encyclopedia*.

13. It is misleading because it gives rise to the metaphysical pseudo-problem: what *is* that reality?

CHAPTER 3

An earlier version of this essay was presented as the presidential address at the 1994 annual meeting of the Society for the Advancement of American Philosophy.

1. *John Dewey and Arthur F. Bentley: A Philosophical Correspondence, 1932–1951*, ed. Sidney Ratner and Jules Altman (New Brunswick, N.J.: Rutgers University Press, 1964), 11.

2. Dewey and Bentley, *Philosophical Correspondence*, 264. Dewey's comment is with reference to their collaboration on *Knowing and the Known*, (Boston: Beacon Press, 1949); also in *John Dewey, The Later Works*, vol. 16 (Carbondale: Southern Illinois University Press, 1989).

3. Arthur F. Bentley, *The Process of Government: A Study of Social Processes* (Chicago: University of Chicago Press, 1908), 178.

4. Arthur F. Bentley, *Behavior, Knowledge, Fact* (Bloomington, In.: Principia Press, 1935), 183.

5. Bentley, *Behavior, Knowledge, Fact*, 183.

6. Dewey and Bentley, *Philosophical Correspondence*, 92–94.

Response to Lavine

1. See "Science and Solidarity" and "Is Natural Science a Natural Kind?" reprinted in my *Objectivity, Relativism and Truth* (Cambridge: Cambridge University Press, 1991).

2. See "Science and Solidarity" and "Is Natural Science a Natural Kind?" reprinted in my *Objectivity, Relativism and Truth*.

3. I give my reasons for thinking this in "Twenty-five years after," an appendix to the second edition of my anthology *The Linguistic Turn* (Chicago: University of Chicago Press, 1992).

CHAPTER 4

Note to epigraph: Alasdair MacIntyre, "Epistemological Crises, Dramatic Narrative and the Philosophy of Science," *Monist* 60 (1977): 461.

1. The above passages are from William James, "Philosophical Conceptions and Practical Results," reprinted in *The Writings of William James,* ed. John J. McDermott (Chicago: University of Chicago Press, 1977), 347–49.

2. William James, *Pragmatism,* in *The Writings of William James,* 378.

3. Charles S. Peirce, "What Pragmatism Is," *Monist* 15 (1905). Reprinted in *Charles S. Peirce: Collected Papers,* ed. Charles Hartshorne and Paul Weiss (Cambridge: Harvard University Press, 1934), 5:415. In relating his narrative of the "origins" of pragmaticism, Peirce stresses how he learned philosophy "out of Kant." One way of appreciating the differences and tensions among the "classical pragmatists" is by telling the story of the philosophic traditions that most significantly influenced them. James felt a deep affinity for the empiricists (and, at a later date, Bergson). Kant was the decisive influence on Peirce, just as Hegel was for Dewey.

4. John Dewey, "The Development of American Pragmatism," reprinted in *The Philosophy of John Dewey,* ed. John J. McDermott (Chicago: University of Chicago Press, 1981), 43.

5. Peirce, *Collected Papers,* 5:429.

6. Dewey, "Development of American Pragmatism," 43.

7. Ibid., 44.

8. Ibid., 56.

9. John Dewey, "From Absolutism to Experimentalism," in *The Philosophy of John Dewey,* 11.

10. Dewey, "The Development of American Pragmatism," 56.

11. Ibid., 58.

12. See: "Philosophy in the Conversation of Mankind," in *Philosophical Profiles* (Philadelphia: University of Pennsylvania Press, 1986); "One Step Forward, Two Steps Backward: Rorty on Liberal Democracy and Philosophy" and "Rorty's Liberal Utopia" in *The New Constellation: The Ethical Political Horizons of Modernity/Postmodernity* (Cambridge: MIT Press, 1992).

13. Morton White begins his article "The Analytic and the Synthetic: An Untenable Dualism" by declaring:

John Dewey has spent a good part of his life hunting and shouting at dualisms: body-mind, theory-practice, precept-concept, value-science, learning-doing, sensation-thought, external-internal. They are always fair game and Dewey's prose rattles with fire whenever they come into view. . . . The writer must confess to a deep sympathy with Dewey on this point. Not that distinctions ought not to be made when they are called for, but we ought to avoid making those that are unnecessary or unfounded. It is in this spirit that I wish to examine one form of a distinction which has come to dominate so much of contemporary philosophy. (Reprinted in *Pragmatism and the American Mind* [New York: Oxford University Press, 1973], 121–22).

14. Wilfrid Sellars, "Empiricism and Philosophy of Mind," in *Science, Perception and Reality* (New York: Humanities Press, 1963), 170.

15. In the 1987 "After Thoughts" of his famous article "A Coherence Theory of

Truth and Knowledge," Davidson writes: "Rorty urges two things: that my view of truth amounts to a rejection of both coherence and correspondence theories and should properly be classed as belonging to the pragmatist tradition, and that I should not pretend that I am answering the skeptic when I am really telling him to get lost. I pretty much concur with him on both points." Davidson's article with his "After Thoughts, 1987" is reprinted in *Reading Rorty*, ed. Alan Malachowski (Cambridge: Basil Blackwell, 1990), 134.

16. Hilary Putnam, *Realism with a Human Face* (Cambridge: Harvard University Press, 1990), xi.

17. Cornel West, *The American Evasion of Philosophy: A Genealogy of Pragmatism* (Madison: University of Wisconsin Press, 1989).

18. For my contribution to this ongoing debate, see "Pragmatism, Pluralism, and the Healing of Wounds," in *The New Constellation;* and "The Resurgence of Pragmatism" *Social Research* 59 (Winter 1992).

19. See *Philosophy, Social Theory, and the Thought of George Herbert Mead*, ed. Mitchell Aboulafia (Albany: State University of New York Press, 1991), which includes articles by Dmitri Shalin, Hans Joas, Mitchell Aboulafia, and others who stress the relation between Mead's pragmatism and his democratic commitment. See also Robert B. Westbrook, *John Dewey and American Democracy* (Ithaca, N.Y.: Cornell University press, 1991).

20. Richard Rorty, "Trotsky and the Wild Orchids" in *Wild Orchids and Trotsky*, ed. Mark Edmundson (New York: Penguin, 1993), 45. See also Richard Rorty, "Intellectuals in Politics," *Dissent*, Fall 1991.

21. For my critical reservations about Rorty's understanding of politics, see *The New Constellation*.

22. Hilary Putnam, "A Reconsideration of Deweyan Democracy," in *Pragmatism in Law and Society*, ed. Michael Brint and William Weaver (Boulder, Colo: Westview, 1991).

23. See also Richard Rorty's critical comments on West's "prophetic pragmatism" in "The Professor and the Prophet," in *Transition: An International Review* 52 (1991).

24. For further discussion of the revived interest and development of pragmatism, see "The Resurgence of Pragmatism."

Response to Bernstein

1. For example, I seem doomed to be referred to as a "postmodernist", even though the only time I used that term—in the title of an article called "Postmodernist Bourgeois Liberalism"—I was trying to make a joke. No matter how much I squirm, I now cannot get the label off. But that does me no harm, and it may be of use to the people who stick it on. I can, more or less, see why they do so, and I can see that the people they are bunching me with do share quite a few enemies and attitudes. For polemic against the idea that there have been important movements called "modernism" and "postmodernism" see my "Campaigns and

Movements," *Dissent* 42 (Winter 1995): 55–60.

2. I am very glad that Bernstein cites Morton White in his paper. White is a neglected figure in the history of American analytic philosophy, and his *Towards Reunion in Philosophy* still seems to me the best discussion of the relations between American pragmatism and the movement which shoved if off stage.

3. I think that micro-neurology, parallel distributed processing simulation of mental functioning, and a Freudian understanding of the role of phantasy in mental life will eventually help philosophers to accomplish this process. I have learned a great deal about the first two from books by Daniel Dennett. I think Freud has been rendered more available for work in this area by Marcia Cavell's linguistification of the Freudian unconscious in her *The Psychoanalytic Mind: From Freud to Philosophy* (Cambridge: Harvard University Press, 1993).

CHAPTER 5

An earlier version of this paper, entitled "Pragmatism Reconsidered," was the Roy Wood Sellars Lecture at Bucknell University, April 18, 1983.

1. The most recent instance with which I am familiar is his discussion of Allan Bloom's *Closing of the American Mind* in "That Old-Time Philosophy," *New Republic*, 4 April 1988, 28–33.

2. See Gary Brodsky, "Rorty's Interpretation of Pragmatism," *Transactions of the Charles S. Peirce Society* (hereafter *TPS*) 17 (1982): 311–38; James Campbell, "Rorty's Use of Dewey," *Southern Journal of Philosophy* 22 (1984): 175–287; Ralph Sleeper, "Rorty's Pragmatism: Afloat in Neurath's Boat, But Why Adrift?" *TPS* 21 (1985): 9–20 and *The Necessity of Pragmatism: John Dewey's Conception of Philosophy* (New Haven and London: Yale University Press, 1986), *passim*; Abraham Edel, "A Missing Dimension in Rorty's Use of Pragmatism," *TPS* 21 (1985): 21–37; Thomas M. Alexander, "Richard Rorty and Dewey's Metaphysics of Experience," *Southwest Philosophical Studies* 5 (1980): 24–35, and *John Dewey's Theory of Art, Experience, and Nature: The Horizons of Feeling* (Albany: State University of New York Press, 1987), *passim*; and Raymond D. Boisvert, *Dewey's Metaphysics* (New York: Fordham University Press, 1988), *passim*, but esp. the conclusion. On the whole, Brodsky regards Rorty's interpretation as valid. The other writers are more critical.

3. He refers to the "bad ('metaphysical') parts of Dewey" in *Consequences of Pragmatism* (Minneapolis: University of Minnesota Press, 1982), 214, and throughout the article "Dewey's Metaphysics," where "backsliding" is used, in the same volume.

4. "'[L]ogic,' conceived as Dewey conceived of it, is a subject not worth developing" (Rorty, "Comments on Sleeper and Edel," *TPS* 21 [1985]: 41).

5. This is the title of chapter 7 of *The Necessity of Pragmatism*.

6. See esp. "Rorty's Use of Dewey," 182–86.

7. Alexander refers to philosophies like Rorty's as "the pastime of academic intellectual czars and their faddists" (*John Dewey's Theory of Art, Experience, and Nature*,

263).

8. *Rorty, Consequences of Pragmatism,* 203–8.

9. *Rorty, Consequences of Pragmatism,* chapter 1, "The World Well Lost."

10. Richard Rorty, "Solidarity or Objectivity?" in *Post-Analytic Philosophy,* ed. John Rajchman and Cornel West (New York: Columbia University Press, 1985), 7.

11. Ibid., 6–7.

12. See esp. Richard Rorty, "The Contingency of Language," *London Review of Books,* 17 April 1986, 3–6.

13. Rorty writes, "To have a meaning is to have a part in a language-game. Metaphors, by definition, do not." If a new metaphor is "savoured," rather than "spat out," it may in time gain currency and find "a familiar place in the language-game." Then it has meaning and is hence a *dead* metaphor. The histories of art, science, philosophy, and moral sense are the histories of successive metaphors. And, "the world does not provide us with any criterion to choose between alternative metaphors" ("The Contingency of Language," 6).

14. Richard Rorty, *Philosophy and the Mirror of Nature* (Princeton, N.J.: Princeton University Press, 1979), 330–31.

15. Rorty admits to this. See "Comments on Sleeper and Edel," 39.

16. John Dewey, *The Quest for Certainty,* in *John Dewey: The Later Works, 1925–1953* (Carbondale and Edwardsville: Southern Illinois University Press, 1984), 4:160. References to Dewey's works are taken from *Early Works* (1882–1898), *Middle Works* (1899–1924), and *Later Works* (1925–1953), all of which are published by Southern Illinois University Press and edited by Jo Ann Boydston.

17. Ibid., 177.

18. John Dewey, *A Common Faith,* in *Later Works,* 9:23–24.

19. John Dewey, *Logic: The Theory of Inquiry,* in *Later Works,* 12:84.

20. Ibid., 102.

21. Rorty, *Consequences of Pragmatism,* 204. The quotation is taken from *Human Nature and Conduct,* in *Middle Works,* 14:136.

22. *Ibid.,* 204, 207. The second quotation is taken from *Human Nature and Conduct,* in *Middle Works,* 14:136.

23. "The Place of Intelligence in Conduct" is the title of Part III of *Human Nature and Conduct.* Emphasis added.

24. Rorty, *Consequences of Pragmatism,* 51.

25. See esp. chapter 3 of *Art as Experience,* in *Later Works,* vol. 10, in which Dewey points out that the *experience* of cognitive thinking has aesthetic qualities, but the *conclusions* of such thinking are not judged with aesthetic criteria. A similar statement is made in chapter 9 of *Experience and Nature,* in *Later Works,* vol. 1.

26. John Dewey, "The Reflex Arc Concept in Psychology" is in *Early Works,* 5:96–109. See also, for example, *Experience and Nature,* chapter 8, and *Logic: The Theory of Inquiry,* chapters 8 and 25.

27. "I hold that my *type* of theory is the only one entitled to be called a corre-

spondence theory of truth" (Dewey, "Propositions, Warranted Assertibility, and Truth," *Later Works*, 14:180). The "correspondence" he has in mind is analogous to the way in which "a key answers to conditions imposed by a lock." Just as a key satisfies the requirements that it addresses, a warranted hypothesis is a *"solution* [that] answers the requirements of a *problem"* (179).

28. Dewey, *Human Nature and Conduct*, 127.

29. Dewey, *Experience and Nature*, 100.

30. Dewey, *The Quest for Certainty*, 132.

31. Alexander's *John Dewey's Theory of Art, Experience, and Nature* should finally put this belief to rest for good. See esp. chapter 2. Boisvert's *Dewey's Metaphysics* is similarly devastating. See esp. the first three chapters.

32. John Dewey, "Does Reality Possess Practical Character?" in *Middle Works*, 4:141. Emphasis added.

33. This is the subject of chapter 4 of *The Quest for Certainty*.

34. Dewey, *Logic: The Theory of Inquiry*, 277.

35. Rorty, *Consequences of Pragmatism*, xix.

36. Ibid., 86–87.

37. Dewey, *Experience and Nature*, 146.

38. See esp. *Experience and Nature*, chapter 5 and *Logic: The Theory of Inquiry*, chapter 3. It is not clear that the theory of the development of meanings articulated in *Human Nature and Conduct* is wholly consistent with that of his subsequent writings, but the question is immaterial here, for in any case meanings are objective and are determined by interaction.

39. Dewey, *Experience and Nature*, 101.

40. Dewey, *Quest for Certainty*, 109.

41. John Dewey and Arthur F. Bentley, *Knowing and the Known* (Boston: Beacon Press, 1949), 121.

42. Richard Rorty, "From Logic to Language to Play," *Proceedings and Addresses of the American Philosophical Association* 59 (1986): 753.

43. Rorty, *Consequences of Pragmatism*, 80.

44. For a fuller analysis of the nature of social intelligence, see my *Excellence in Public Discourse: John Stuart Mill, John Dewey, and Social Intelligence* (New York: Teachers College Press, 1986), esp. chapter 5.

45. Dewey, *Liberalism and Social Action*, in *Later Works*, 11:32.

46. Ibid., 39.

47. When it is not in league with Rorty's radical historicism, contemporary moral theory is slipping back into the harness of the classic tradition. For a brief criticism from the pragmatic point of view, see my essay, "Philosophy and Moral Values: The Pragmatic Analysis," in *Pragmatism: Its Sources and Prospects*, ed. Robert J. Mulvaney and Philip M. Zeltner (Columbia: University of South Carolina Press, 1981), 99–119.

Response to Gouinlock

1. Sidney Hook, *Pragmatism and the Tragic Sense of Life* (New York: Basic Books, 1974), 22.

2. Hook, *Pragmatism,* 19.

3. The definition I cited there (from the revised edition of *How We Think,* 8:118) was "active, persistent and careful consideration of any belief or supposed form of knowledge in the light of the grounds that support it and the further conclusions to which it tends."

4. Charles S. Peirce, "The Fixation of Belief," in *Collected Papers,* 5:238 (section 5.382). Hilary Putnam has recently criticized David Lewis for resuscitating this method for use in metaphysics. See Putnam, *Renewing Philosophy* (Cambridge: Harvard University Press, 1992), 138–39. I entirely agree with Putnam's point that "the function of philosophers is not simply to endorse existing ways of living but neither is it to play skeptical games" (though, alas, Putnam tends to lump me in with the "fashionably postmodernist" skeptical game players). As I say below in "Philosophy and the Future," I think that function is to help to prevent old intuitions from getting in the way of human happiness by forming a "crust of convention." If that opinion is enough to enlist me as an adherent of "scientific method," so much the better. If not, I need to know more about the enlistment requirements than Gouinlock tells me, or than I have been able to glean from Dewey's own writings.

5. Ibid., 242–43 (sec. 5.384).

6. Dewey, "The Present Position of Logical Theory," *Early Works,* 3:138.

7. I doubt that the philosopher who became famous for the doctrine of the "means-end continuum" would have had much time for rational-choice theory.

8. See Kitcher's *The Advancement of Science* (New York and Oxford: Oxford University Press, 1993). At 189 Kitcher puts forward a criterion for the rationality of "processes of cognitive modification," but he offers no examples of such processes. What he does offer are specific arguments from Galileo and Darwin, arguments whose acceptance did, to be sure, lead to such progress. To apply his criterion of rationality we should need just what the positivists failed to provide us: a way of abstracting out generic processes from specific arguments, so that Galileo's argument in the *Dialogue Concerning the Two Chief World Systems,* for example, could be seen as offering an example of a "cognitive process" that recurs in Darwin's arguments. One can entirely agree with Kitcher that "Galileo's *Dialogue* . . . encapsulates a process of reasoning which is strikingly better designed for promoting cognitive progress than any available alternatives" (209), but this leaves us still unable to specify what *methodological* lesson Darwin could have learned from Galileo.

Kitcher has said that "normative epistemology can survive a naturalistic metamorphosis" ("The Naturalists Return," *Philosophical Review* 101 [January 1992]:114). I think it will do so only if Kitcher and his fellow naturalists can put forward an example of an epistemic norm which is neither specific to what Kuhn calls a "disciplinary matrix" nor so general as to seem trivial and commonsensical.

9. See my "Holism, Intrinsicality, and the Ambition of Transcendence" in

Dennett and his Critics: Demystifying Mind, ed. Bo Dahlbom (Oxford: Blackwell, 1993), 184–202.

10. Gouinlock quotes this last desideratum from Dewey and Bentley's *Knowing and the Known*. He also quotes their rejection of a "no man's land" between the organism and its "environmental objects." I see it as the great virtue of Davidson's linguistification of Dewey's antirepresentationalism that it enables us to get rid of "experience" as the name of such an intermediary. It describes causal transactions between the environment and the linguistic behavior of speakers which are mediated only by, e.g., nerves and light waves.

11. Reprinted in my *Consequences of Pragmatism* (Minneapolis: University of Minnesota Press, 1982).

12. That phrase actually sums up neatly what Davidson says in his Dewey Lectures about "triangulation" as the "ultimate source of both objectivity and communication." See "The Structure and Content of Truth," *Journal of Philosophy*, 87 (1990): 325.

CHAPTER 6

1. John Dewey, *The Quest for Certainty: A Study of Relation of Knowledge and Action* (New York: Minton, Balch, 1929), 63.

2. Richard Rorty, "Lumps and Texts," in Richard Rorty, *Objectivity, Relativism, and Truth* (Cambridge: Cambridge University Press, 1991), 90.

3. Richard Rorty, "Inquiry as Recontextualization: An Anti-Dualist Account of Interpretation," in Rorty, *Objectivity, Relativism, and Truth*, 109.

4. See Richard Rorty, "The World Well Lost," in Richard Rorty, *Consequences of Pragmatism* (Minneapolis: University of Minnesota Press, 1982), 16.

5. Richard Rorty, "Epistemological Behaviorism and the De-Transcendentalization of Analytic Philosophy," in *Hermeneutics and Praxis*, ed. Robert Hollinger (Notre Dame: University of Notre Dame Press, 1985), 89.

6. Rorty, "The World Well Lost," 16.

7. Rorty, "Epistemological Behaviorism," 90.

8. Richard Rorty, "Strawson's Objectivity Argument," *Review of Metaphysics* 24 (December 1970): 207–44.

9. Rorty, "Strawson's Objectivity Argument," 240.

10. Ibid., 237.

11. Ibid., 242–43.

12. Rorty, "The World Well Lost," 4.

13. Cf. Robert B. Pippin, *Hegel's Idealism: The Satisfactions of Self-Consciousness* (Cambridge: Cambridge University Press, 1989), 91, 277–78.

14. Allen Wood, *Hegel's Ethical Thought* (Cambridge: Cambridge University Press, 1990), 5–6.

15. Karl Löwith, *From Hegel to Nietzsche: The Revolution in Nineteenth-Century Thought*, trans. David E. Green (New York: Holt, Rinehart and Winston, 1964), 115; and Karl Löwith, *Nature, History and Existentialism and Other Essays in the*

Philosophy of History, ed. Arnold Levison (Evanston, Ill.: Northwestern University Press, 1966), 46–50.

16. This point has been forcefully argued by Robert Pippin in *Hegel's Idealism.* The most influential exponent of nonmetaphysical interpretations of Hegel has been Klaus Hartmann. See Klaus Hartmann, *Studies in Foundational Philosophy* (Amsterdam: Editions Rodopi, 1988). See also Terry Pinkard, *Hegel's Dialectic* (Philadelphia: Temple University Press, 1988).

17. G. W. F. Hegel, preface to *Phenomenology of Spirit,* in *Hegel: Texts and Commentary,* trans. and ed. Walter Kaufmann (Notre Dame: University of Notre Dame Press, 1977), 90.

18. Thus in the *Encyclopedia Logic* Hegel argues that "Kant's examination of the categories suffers from the grave defect of viewing them, not absolutely and for their own sake, but in order to see whether they are *subjective* or *objective*" (G. W. F. Hegel, *Hegel's Logic. Part One of the Encyclopedia of the Philosophical Sciences [1830],* trans. William Wallace [Oxford: Clarendon Press, 1975], 67).

19. "Thoughts, according to Kant, although universal and necessary categories, are *only our* thoughts—separated by an impassable gulf from the thing, as it exists apart from our knowledge. But the true objectivity of thinking means that the thoughts, far from being merely ours, must at the same time be the real essence of the things, and of whatever is an object to us" (Hegel, *Hegel's Logic,* 67–68).

20. Rorty, "Strawson's Objectivity Argument," 231.

21. See Immanuel Kant, *Critique of Pure Reason,* B823.

22. Hegel, *Hegel's Logic,* 66.

23. See Tom Rockmore, *Hegel's Circular Epistemology* (Bloomington: Indiana University Press, 1986); and Tom Rockmore, "Hegel's Circular Epistemology as Antifoundationalism," *History of Philosophy Quarterly* 6 (January 1989): 101–13.

24. Hegel, *Hegel's Logic,* 223.

25. This discussion is based on Richard Cobb-Stevens's phenomenological (Husserlian) critique of Frege in his *Husserl and Analytic Philosophy* (Dordrecht: Kluwer, 1990), 26–27.

26. See Richard Rorty, "Pragmatism Without Method," in Richard Rorty, *Objectivity, Relativism and Truth,* 63–64.

27. Ibid., 64.

28. Ibid., 65.

29. Richard Rorty, "The Contingency of Language," in Richard Rorty, *Contingency, Irony, and Solidarity* (Cambridge: Cambridge University Press, 1989), 17.

30. Richard Rorty, "Is Derrida a Transcendental Philosopher?" in Richard Rorty, *Essays on Heidegger and Others* (Cambridge: Cambridge University Press, 1991), 127.

31. Ibid.

Response to Hance

1. In the first chapter of his *Subjectivity, Realism and Postmodernism* (Cambridge: Cambridge University Press, 1994), Frank Farrell offers an interesting parallel between Hegel (as read by Pippin) and Davidson. Both, he rightly says, try to secure correspondence of reality to thought "without depending on a comparison of thought and the world" and without appealing to "theories of reference, of epistemic anchorage, of construction by a scheme" (27). However, as I say below in my response to Farrell, I do not think that Davidson should be read as attempting to "guarantee the correspondence of our categories to what is real."

2. My favorite remark of Kierkegaard's about Hegel is that if he had ended books like *Science of Logic* and *Encyclopedia of Philosophical Sciences* with the remark that "this was all just a thought experiment," he would have been the greatest thinker who ever lived. Kierkegaard went on to say that, as it was, he was a buffoon. The epithet is too harsh, but the spirit of the remark seems right.

3. Note Hance's claim that "only thought itself (nonrepresentationally conceived) deserves the title of thing-in-itself" (111). I do not think that anything should be burdened with this title, a title which can be thought of as honorific only if one had been sufficiently bitten by the epistemological bug to insist on asking Is X really real? rather than simply For what is talk of X useful? The former was a Greek question, and I think that Plato and Aristotle invented the problematic which Descartes and Locke picked up on and ran with. So I cannot accept Hance's suggestion that epistemology is a specifically modern aberration, and that Plato, Aristotle, and Hegel avoided the mistakes common to Descartes, Locke, and Kant.

4. I also disagree that "the appeals to existence, facticity, and materiality" in such movements as pragmatism, existentialism, and deconstructionism are "an attempt to revitalize the theory of intuition" (109). I see them as attempts to set aside Knowledge as the most important human accomplishment in favor of such alternatives as happiness and honesty. Insofar as advocates for pragmatism and naturalism favor a world-picture of particulars, that is because they think it a very useful picture for many of our purposes, not because they think it can be privileged, by an act of intuition, as metaphysically correct.

CHAPTER 7

This essay is adapted from chapter 9 of my *Evidence and Inquiry: Towards Reconstruction in Epistemology* (Oxford, England and Cambridge, Mass.: Blackwell, 1993).

1. My thanks to David Stove for reporting this dialogue.

2. All page references in the text of section I of this paper are to Richard Rorty, *Philosophy and the Mirror of Nature* (Princeton, N.J.: Princeton University Press, 1979). Rorty is by no means the first, of course, to argue that epistemology is misconceived; cf., for example, L. Nelson, "The Impossibility of a 'Theory of Knowledge,'" first published in German in 1908, reprinted in English in *Socratic Method and Critical Philosophy* (New York: 1969), 185–205.

3. See Rorty, "Unfamiliar Noises: Hesse and Davidson on Metaphor,"

Proceedings of the Aristotelian Society 61 (Supplement, 1987); and cf. Susan Haack, "Surprising Noises: Rorty and Hesse on Metaphor," *Proceedings of the Aristotelian Society* 88 (1987–88): 179–87, and "Dry Truth and Real Knowledge: Epistemologies of Metaphor and Metaphors of Epistemology," in *Approaches to Metaphor,* ed. J. Hintikka (Dordrecht, the Netherlands: Kluwer, 1994), 1–22.

4. See Susan Haack, *Evidence and Inquiry: Towards Reconstruction in Epistemology* (Oxford: Blackwell, 1993), chapter 1.

5. See *Evidence and Inquiry,* chapter 4, for detailed development of the found-herentist theory of justification, including the articulation of the interaction of causal and evaluative elements referred to above.

6. See Wilfrid Sellars, "Empiricism and Philosophy of Mind," in *Science, Perception and Reality* (New York: Humanities Press, 1963), 127–96.

7. See W. V. Quine, "Two Dogmas of Empiricism," *From a Logical Point of View* (New York: Harper and Row, 1963), 20–46.

8. At any rate, everything in Davidson's work before 1987 is strongly opposed to any such idea. Perhaps, in "Afterthoughts, 1987" in *Reading Rorty,* ed. Alan Malachowski (Oxford: Blackwell, 1990), Davidson sounds a little wobbly, describing himself, on 134, as a "pragmatist" about truth. By his Dewey Lectures of 1990, "The Structure and Content of Truth," *Journal of Philosophy* 87 (1990): 279–328, however, though he has repudiated the idea that Tarski's is a correspondence theory, it is once again clear that he is by no stretch of the imagination sympathetic to "pragmatism" in Rorty's vulgar sense. (On Tarski and correspondence, cf. Susan Haack, "Is It True What They Say About Tarski?" *Philosophy* 51 (1976): 323–36; and "'Realism,'" *Synthese* 73 (1987): 275–99.).

9. Richard Rorty, *Contingency, Irony and Solidarity* (Cambridge: Cambridge University Press, 1989), 73.

10. An accusation made explicitly in Richard Rorty, *Essays on Heidegger and Others,* (Cambridge: Cambridge University Press, 1991), 86.

11. All page references in the text of section II of this paper are to Stephen P. Stich, *The Fragmentation of Reason* (Cambridge: Bradford Books, MIT Press, 1990).

12. Richard Rorty, *Objectivity, Relativism and Truth* (Cambridge: Cambridge University Press, 1991), 21.

13. Stich gets this conceit from Stephen R. Schiffer, "Truth and the Theory of Content," in *Meaning and Understanding,* ed. Parret and Bouverese (Berlin: Walter de Gruyter, 1981).

14. B. Hallen and J. Sodipo, *Knowledge, Belief and Witchcraft* (London: Ethnographica, 1986).

15. Bertrand Russell, "Knowledge, Error and Probable Opinion," in *The Problems of Philosophy* (Oxford: Oxford University Press, 1912).

16. As does A. I. Goldman in "Stephen P. Stich: *The Fragmentation of Reason,*" *Philosophy and Phenomenological Research* 51 (1991): 190–91.

17. S. P. Stich, "The Fragmentation of Reason: A Précis of Two Chapters," *Philosophy and Phenomenological Research* 51 (1991): 179.

18. C. S. Peirce, *Collected Papers,* ed. Charles Hartshorne, Paul Weiss, and Arthur Burks (Cambridge: Harvard University Press, 1931–58), 8:143.

19. Ibid., 1:34, 1:235, 2:135.

20. William James, *Pragmatism,* ed. F. Burkhardt and F. Bowers (Cambridge: Harvard University Press, 1975) 107ff.; *The Meaning of Truth,* ed. F. Burkhardt and F. Bowers (Cambridge: Harvard University Press, 1975) 3, 143. Cf. Susan Haack, "Can James's Theory of Truth Be Made More Satisfactory?" *Transactions of the Charles S. Peirce Society* 20 (1984): 269–78.

21. William James, *The Will to Believe* (New York: Dover, 1956), 11: "*Our passional nature . . . must decide an option between propositions, whenever it is a genuine option that cannot by its nature be decided on intellectual grounds.*" See also James's letter to Kallen in R. B. Perry, *The Thought and Character of William James* (Cambridge: Harvard University Press, 1948) 249.

22. James, *Pragmatism,* 112.

23. Cf. Susan Haack, "Pragmatism," in *Handbook of Epistemology,* ed. E. Sosa and J. Dancy (Oxford: Blackwell, 1992), 351–57, for a more detailed analysis of the epistemologies of pragmatism, and "Philosophy/philosophy, an Untenable Dualism," *Transactions of the Charles S. Peirce Society* 29, no.3 (1993): 411–26 for a detailed critique of Rorty's interpretation of Peirce.

In the text I have confined my discussion to James, whom both Rorty and Stich, I believe, seriously misinterpret. Scholars may observe that, although Stich's one quotation from James (*The Fragmentation of Reason,* 160, quoting James's *Pragmatism,* 42), is carefully, and tendentiously, edited in an attempt to make James appear to say what Stich says he does, even the bowdlerized version makes clear James's commitment to the instrumental value of truth.

A more difficult question, pressed upon me by Sidney Ratner, is how closely Rorty's anti-epistemological stance resembles Dewey's critique, in *The Quest for Certainty* (New York: G. P. Putnam's Sons, 1960), of the "spectator theory of knowledge." For now, I shall say only that Dewey seems to me quite ambiguous, but that one (though not the only) way to read him is as urging a more naturalistic epistemology—and that on this interpretation, of course, he is quite unlike Rorty.

Response to Haack

1. I have sometimes used Wittgensteinian pejoratives like "nonsense," and "meaningless," etc., but I regret having done so. I think Wittgenstein was wiser when he said that you can give anything a sense if you want to. Epistemologists have given various questions sense in the same way as astrologers and theologians gave their questions sense: by embedding them in a coherent language-game. But questions about the utility of all three language-games persist.

2. In her *Evidence and Inquiry: Towards Reconstruction in Epistemology* (Oxford: Blackwell, 1993) (chapter 9 from which the present essay is adapted) Haack seems to me to try and fail to imagine the end of inquiry where she sketches a Peirce-like "hypothetical ideal theory." In chapter 10 of her book, she employs the notion of

"all other relevant propositions" (214), a notion that seems to me to suggest, unrealistically, that we might somehow know that there was no point in new descriptions of the world, in the creation of new truth-value candidates. If, as I should urge, there always is such a point, then the list of relevant propositions will never be closed, but will expand forever. Relevance will always be up for grabs, because the logical space within which relevance is to be judged will keep changing.

The upshot of Haack's book, at pages 220–21, is that "if any truth-indication is possible for us, satisfaction of the foundherentist criteria is the best truth-indication we can have." This seems to me like saying "if life has any meaning, then continuing to breathe is the best way of engaging in meaningful activity we have." Since both satisfying foundherentist criteria and breathing are very difficult to stop doing—no matter what one may think about truth-indicativeness or about the meaningfulness of life—I do not see that Haack's epistemological inquiries have done much for us.

3. I suspect that Haack too thinks this about Davidson. But I am not sure I grasp her account of Davidson. I am puzzled by her claims that Davidson is "wrong to present his interpreter as seeking 'a correlation of sentences held true with sentences held true'" (*Evidence and Inquiry*, 66), that his principle of charity "directs the interpreter to interpret his respondents as holding true [$p*$] just in case, in fact, p," and that "if a limited, fallible interpreter happens to be mistaken about whether p, he will not have conformed to the truth-oriented principle of charity" (ibid., 68). The latter claim especially seems to me a misunderstanding of the way Davidson wishes the principle of charity to be applied.

4. Another name for what I cannot seem to locate is "a certain relation of aboutness." See Farrell's chapter, "Rorty and Antirealism," 161–62: "Rorty's pragmatist will not allow claims about the objective world and its causal powers to be interpreted realistically, as founded on a certain relation of aboutness between those claims themselves and the world. . . . There is a difference between the world itself making us think a certain way about it and the appearance of the syntactic shapes 'the world's causal power' in a useful statement that cannot be taken referentially, and it seems that Rorty can make sense only of the latter." I had thought myself as capable of aboutness and referentiality as the next philosopher, but in both cases Farrell notices a deficiency. These deficiencies are doubtless due to my inability to spot E.

Again, I had thought that my lively appreciation of the utility of expressions like "the world's causal power" and "Look out, you're about to be hit by a truck!" was enough to keep me in touch with reality, but Farrell says that in my view we encounter "only ourselves when we think and talk" (*Subjectivity, Realism, and Postmodernism*, 139). Apparently one needs an extra ingredient—referentiality? aboutness? transcendence?—to add to utility, in order to break out from what Farrell calls "narcissism."

5. Haack, *Evidence and Inquiry*, 207.

6. "My conjecture is that the very deep-seated disagreements which have encouraged the idea that standards of evidence are culture-relative—or, in the intra-

scientific form of the variability thesis, paradigm-relative—may be explicable in a similar way; as lying, that is, in a complex mesh of further disagreements in background beliefs, rather than in any deep divergence of standards of evidence" (Haack, *Evidence and Inquiry*, 207). I quite agree, and I suspect Kuhn and other proponents of "the variability thesis" would, too.

7. So, do I adopt Haack's own "foundherentist" epistemology? Well, I agree with her criticisms of foundationalism, and I accept her crossword-puzzle metaphor, as well as most of her criticisms of Goldman, Stich, et al. My only problem with her foundherentism is that it seems merely verbally different from coherentism. What Haack calls "an experience, playing a causal role" seems to me just what coherentists like Davidson call "a non-inferential belief, playing a justificational role." I do not see that the difference is worth arguing about. I do not see why the word justification needs to be stretched, as Haack recommends, to include causes as well as reasons, so as to make "justification not after all purely logical" (*Evidence and Inquiry*, 71). As I see it, Davidson has already done justice to the role of appropriate causation in the formation of justified belief by recognizing that observation of the causal context of the speaker's holdings-true is essential to the interpreter's decisions about what beliefs to attribute to the speaker.

8. Haack, *Evidence and Inquiry*, 203. I suspect that people to whom *E* is more visible understand better than I what Haack means by "substantial" truth. These people doubtless also understand what other philosophers mean by "realist truth"— something they oppose to a second-rate, relatively insubstantial sort of truth. One of the things that allies me with Davidson is that he has the same trouble with this substantial-insubstantial distinction that I do.

9. Haack is not the only person to make this very common suggestion. See "Is Truth the Goal of Inquiry?" in which I criticize Crispin Wright for making it.

10. I suppose that somebody could answer the latter questions with "in order to survive," but I think that such an answer would miss the point. The questioner was doubtless aware that cessation of breath or eating means failure to survive, and was asking about the worth of survival.

11. Haack is more or less right in suggesting that I am prepared to turn sociologist of knowledge (139). But I should prefer to say "historian, sociologist, and moralist of knowledge," where *moralist* means something like "somebody with suggestions about the costs and benefits of changing your sense of relevance in specific ways." A "moralist of knowledge" in this sense is pretty much the same thing as what is sometimes called a "culture critic." Culture critics like Carlyle, Ortega, and Heidegger have argued that we moderns have a worse sense of relevance than our ancestors, whereas those like Macauley and Dewey have argued that we have a better one. There is much to be said on both sides.

12. This is a point I tried to make in my "Is Natural Science a Natural Kind?": see *Objectivity, Relativism and Truth*, 60–62, on "scientificity as moral virtue."

13. *Evidence and Inquiry*, 207.

14. See my introduction to *The Later Works of John Dewey*, 8:xv–xvi.

15. One of the disagreements between Haack and myself is that she thinks that epistemology is a natural and obvious topic of reflection, whereas I think that it survives nowadays only because some philosophy professors still think it important to take epistemic skepticism seriously—a spiritual exercise I find profitless. Once you get rid of the skeptic (in the way, for example, in which Michael Williams gets rid of Barry Stroud in the former's *Unnatural Doubts*), then I think you have little motive for waxing epistemological (unless you get a kick out of refuting once again, as Haack seems to me to do successfully, the foundationalists, the reliabilists, and the reductionists). I see James and Dewey (and even Peirce at his best—in the anti-Cartesian "Capacities" papers—despite the empty bombast of passages like the one Haack quotes at 147 as having done an especially good job of dissuading us from taking the skeptic seriously. They do so by asking us to worry more about relevance and less about rigor (or, *pace* Lavine and Gouinlock, more about consequences than about method).

CHAPTER 8

1. Richard Rorty, *Philosophy and the Mirror of Nature* (Princeton, N.J.: Princeton University Press, 1979.)

2. Donald Davidson, "Rational Animals," in *Actions and Events*, ed. Ernest LePore and Brian McLaughlin (Oxford: Basil Blackwell, 1985), 480.

3. Richard Rorty, *Consequences of Pragmatism* (Minneapolis: University of Minnesota Press, 1982), 166.

4. Rorty favors the view that "great scientists invent descriptions of the world which are useful for purposes of predicting and controlling what happens, just as poets and political thinkers invent other descriptions of it for other purposes. But there is no sense in which any of these descriptions is an accurate representation of the way the world is in itself." Rorty, *Contingency, Irony, and Solidarity* (Cambridge: Cambridge University Press, 1989), 4.

5. Donald Davidson, *Inquiries into Truth and Interpretation* (Oxford: Clarendon Press, 1984), 199.

6. Rorty, *Consequences of Pragmatism*, 15, 13–14.

7. Ibid., 165.

8. Ibid., 166.

9. Donald Davidson, "A Coherence Theory of Truth and Knowledge," in *Truth and Interpretation*, 310. His citation of Rorty is from Rorty, *Philosophy and the Mirror of Nature*, 178.

10. Donald Davidson, "Empirical Content," in *Truth and Interpretation*, 320–32.

11. Ibid., 331–32.

12. Rorty, *Consequences of Pragmatism*, 141.

13. Rorty, "Pragmatism, Davidson and Truth," in *Truth and Interpretation*, 353.

14. Davidson, *Inquiries*, 201, 207, 210, 211.

15. Rorty, *Contingency, Irony, and Solidarity*, 5.

16. Rorty, *Consequences of Pragmatism*, xxxix.

17. Ibid., xxxvii.

18. Ibid., xli.

19. Rorty, *Contingency, Irony, and Solidarity*, 5.

20. Ibid., 10.

21. Rorty, "The World Well Lost," *Journal of Philosophy* 69 (1972): 649–65.

22. Rorty, *Contingency, Irony, and Solidarity*, 11–12.

23. For Davidson's view that reasons are causes, see the essays "Actions, Reasons, and Causes," and "How Is Weakness of the Will Possible?" in Davidson, *Essays on Actions and Events* (Oxford: Clarendon Press, 1980). For his view that the mental is irreducible to the physical, even if all mental events are physical ones, see the essays "Mental Events," "The Material Mind," and "Psychology as Philosophy" in the same volume. Very helpful is the summary by Ernest LePore and Brian McLaughlin in *Actions and Events*, ed. LePore and McLaughlin, 3–13, and the essay by McLaughlin, 331–66, in the same volume.

24. Davidson, "Thought and Talk," in *Inquiries*, 155–70.

25. "To say that it is a language user is just to say that pairing off the marks and noises it makes with those we make will prove a useful tactic in predicting and controlling its future behavior" (Rorty, *Contingency, Irony, and Solidarity*, 15).

26. Rorty, *Consequences of Pragmatism*, 15.

27. Ibid. 14.

28. Rorty, "Pragmatism, Davidson and Truth," 333; Davidson, *Inquiries*, 198.

29. Rorty, "Pragmatism, Davidson and Truth," 354, n. 58.

30. Rorty, *Consequences of Pragmatism*, 154, xxxvii.

31. Rorty, *Contingency, Irony, and, Solidarity*, 5.

32. Rorty, *Consequences of Pragmatism*, xlii.

33. Rorty, *Contingency, Irony, and Solidarity*, xv.

34. Ibid., 21.

35. Ibid., 16.

36. That is his conclusion in "What Metaphors Mean," in *Inquiries*, 245–64.

37. See Donald Davidson,, "Paradoxes of Irrationality," in *Philosophical Essays on Freud*, ed. R. Wollheim and J. Hopkins (Cambridge: Cambridge University Press, 1982), 305.

38. A similar contrast between Rorty and Heidegger is given in John Caputo, "The Thought of Being and the Conversation of Mankind: The Case of Heidegger and Rorty," in *Hermeneutics and Praxis*, ed. Robert Hollinger (Notre Dame: University of Notre Dame Press, 1985), 248–71.

39. Rorty, *Consequences of Pragmatism*, xvii.

40. Rorty, *Contingency, Irony, and Solidarity*, 6.

41. Rorty, *Consequences of Pragmatism*, xliii.

42. Rorty, *Contingency, Irony, and Solidarity*, 29.

43. Rorty, *Consequences of Pragmatism*, xlii.

44. See his essays "The Contingency of a Liberal Community" and "Private Irony and Liberal Hope" in Rorty, *Contingency, Irony, and Solidarity*, 44–95.

45. Rorty, *Contingency, Irony, and Solidarity*, 7.

46. Ibid., 78.

47. Ibid., 65–66.

48. Ibid., 84–85.

49. Ibid., 125.

50. Ibid., 59, 54.

Response to Farrell

1. Donald Davidson, "A Coherence Theory of Truth and Knowledge," in *Truth and Interpretation*, ed. Ernest LePore (Oxford: Blackwell, 1986), 307.

2. Donald Davidson, "The Structure and Content of Truth," *Journal of Philosophy* 87 (June 1990): 305, 309. At the latter passage Davidson also says that "we should not say that truth is correspondence, coherence, warranted assertability, ideally justified assertability, what is accepted in the conversation of the right people, what science will end up maintaining, what explains the convergence on single theories in science, or the success of our ordinary beliefs. To the extent that realism and antirealism depend on one or another of these views of truth we should refuse to endorse either." At the former he says that "correspondence" is an idea without content."

The reader who wishes to pursue the exegetical question should consult Davidson's response to my "Pragmatism, Davidson and Truth" in his "Afterthoughts, 1987" appended to "A Coherence Theory" (*Reading Rorty*, ed. Alan Malachowski (Oxford: Blackwell, 1987), 134–37), and also his criticisms of my interpretation of him at 281–88 of "Structure and Content. . . ." I reply to the latter in my "Is Truth a Goal of Inquiry? Davidson vs. Wright," forthcoming in *The Philosophical Quarterly*. (Note also Susan Haack's claim that despite Davidson's "wobbling" in "Afterthoughts" he has made clear, in "Structure and Content," that he "is by no stretch of the imagination sympathetic to 'pragmatism' in Rorty's vulgar sense" [222, note 8]. I do not find this as clear as Haack does.)

Bjorn Ramberg—whose *Donald Davidson's Philosophy of Language* (Oxford: Blackwell, 1989) both Farrell and I admire—has remarked that by now there is a fairly striking contrast between a British interpretation of Davidson (most fully expounded in Simon Evnine's *Donald Davidson* [Stanford: Stanford University Press, 1991]), which is both metaphysical and sympathetic to realism, and a North American interpretation which offers what Ramberg calls "a pragmatic reading of Davidson." (See Ramberg, "Interpreting Davidson," *Dialogue* 23 (1993): 565–571.) Farrell's account of Davidson occupies, so to speak, a mid-Atlantic position.

3. Donald Davidson, "The Myth of the Subjective," in *Relativism*, ed. M. Krausz (Notre Dame: Notre Dame University Press, 1989), 165. The sentence quoted continues: "for it is thinking there are representations which engenders

thoughts of relativism." I interpret this to mean: if you drop the metaphor of "representation" you will not think in terms of alternative conventions of representation, and thus will not be able to use the standard perspectivalist metaphoric employed by such authors as Nietzsche.

4. See Fine's "The Natural Ontological Attitude" and "And Not Antirealism Either" in his *The Shaky Game* (Chicago: University of Chicago Press, 1986). At 149 Fine says that "NOA [the Natural Ontological Attitude] is . . . basically at odds with the temperament that looks for definite boundaries demarcating science from pseudoscience" and that it "is inclined to reject *all* interpretations, theories, construals, pictures, etc. of truth."

This last passage seems to me in accord with Davidson's remarks on what we should not say about truth (see note 3 above).

5. See my "Putnam and the Relativist Menace," *Journal of Philosophy* 90 (Sept: 1993).

6. These last two quotations are both from *Subjectivity, Realism and Postmodernism*, 78.

7. See the "Introduction" to my *Objectivity, Relativism and Truth* (Cambridge: Cambridge University Press, 1991).

8. The immodest realists include, conspicuously, fans of elementary physical particles, such as John Locke and David Lewis. These two philosophers have no doubt about which contours were projected from our side and which were already out there.

9. I owe this phrasing to Paul Ziff.

10. I could back up this accusation by citing the concessions that he makes to Nagel's criticism of Davidson (in the "Thought and Reality" chapter of Nagel's *View From Nowhere*) at 89–90. Farrell says that, pace Davidson, there might be beings of "vastly superior intelligence" who use "forms of individuation and classification that our brain machinery simply isn't competent to understand." This agreement with Nagel seems to me to betoken a yearning for a God's-eye view, and a fear that we may not have it (for the forms of individuation and classification which we thought were shadows cast on our language might turn out to be merely pseudo-shadows). For my own view of Nagel's treatment of Davidson, see my "Holism, Intentionality, and the Ambition of Transcendence" in *Dennett and his Critics: Demystifying Mind*, ed. Bo Dahlbom (Oxford: Blackwell, 1993), 184–202.

11. See 133, where Farrell says that our "interest in explaining why the universe operates the way it does" . . . "allows the world itself to be a measure of [our] vocabularies' rightness in a way that the world cannot be a measure of the 'rightness' of the horns of an animal." At 132 he explains the success of science as by saying that it helps us come "to understand how things really are," and suggests that if one has my "Darwinian" view of the function of beliefs one must test a belief by its prevalence. I have argued in some detail that this is a pseudo-explanation of the success of science, and that the test of a belief, on a Darwinian view, is its utility *to us*. Farrell's claim that, in my view, the "only measure for a set of beliefs is its increased

distribution in the total 'belief population'" seems based on the assumption that a belief is analogous to a species rather than to a tool used by members of a species. Tools, like beliefs and specialized bodily organs, can become obsolete, and eventually vanish—but they have survival value in their niche at their time.

12. See Fine, *The Shaky Game*, 148: "The realisms and antirealisms seem to treat science as a sort of grand performance, a play or opera, whose production requires interpretation and direction. They argue among themselves as to whose 'reading' is best. I have been arguing that if science is a performance, then it is one where the audience and crew play as well. . . . Such a performance is not susceptible to a reading or interpretation in any global sense, and it picks out its own interpretations, locally, as it goes along."

CHAPTER 9

1. John Dewey, *Reconstruction in Philosophy*, (*The Middle Works of John Dewey: 1899–1924*, ed. Jo Ann Boydston et al. (Carbondale: Southern Illinois University Press, 1976–83), 12:94.

2. Hilary Putnam, *Renewing Philosophy* (Cambridge: Harvard University Press, 1992), 139.

3. Dewey, *Reconstruction in Philosophy*, 91–92.

BIBLIOGRAPHY OF RICHARD RORTY'S WORKS
Published as of December 31, 1994

BOOKS

(Bold type indicates that a translation in that language has been published. Regular type indicates that a translation is in preparation but has not yet appeared, prior to 1995.)

Philosophy and the Mirror of Nature. Princeton: Princeton University Press, 1979.
  Trans.: **Chinese, German, Italian, Spanish, Portuguese, French, Serbo-Croat, Japanese, Polish**, Greek, Bulgarian.
Consequences of Pragmatism. Minneapolis: University of Minnesota Press, 1982.
  Trans.: **Italian, Japanese, Serbo-Croat, French**, Spanish.
Contingency, Irony, and Solidarity. Cambridge: Cambridge University Press, 1989.
  Trans.: **German, Italian, Spanish, Dutch, Danish, French, Portuguese, Hungarian**, Polish, Greek, Turkish, Chinese, Serbo-Croat.
Objectivity, Relativism, and Truth. Vol. 1 of *Philosophical Papers.* 2 vols.
  Cambridge: Cambridge University Press, 1991. Trans.: **Italian**, French, Hungarian.
Essays on Heidegger and Others. Vol. 2 of *Philosophical Papers.* 2 vols. Cambridge:
  Cambridge University Press, 1991. Trans.: **Italian, Spanish, French**, Hungarian.
(Co-editor with Edward N. Lee and Alexander P. O. Mourelatos.) *Exegesis and Argument: Essays in Greek Philosophy Presented to Gregory Vlastos.* Amsterdam:
  Van Gorcum, 1973.
(Co-editor with Jerome B. Schneewind and Quentin Skinner.) *Philosophy in History.*
  Cambridge: Cambridge University Press, 1985. Partial trans.: **Spanish**.
(Editor.) *The Linguistic Turn.* Chicago: University of Chicago Press, 1967; second,
  enlarged edition 1992.

COLLECTIONS OF ARTICLES IN FOREIGN TRANSLATION

Solidarität oder Objectivität? Ditzingen: Reclam Verlag, 1988. (Contains: 1.
  Solidarity or Objectivity; 2. The Priority of Democracy to Philosophy; 3. Freud
  and Moral Reflection.)
Solidariteit of Objectiviteit: Drie filosofische essays. Meppel, Uitgeverij Boom, 1990.
  (Dutch translation of the three essays included in *Solidarität oder Objectivität?*)
Rentaito Jiyuno Tetsugaku: Nigenronno Gensoo Koete (Philosophy of/for Solidarity and Freedom: Beyond the Illusions of Dualisms). Tokyo: Iwanami Shoten, 1988.
  (Contains: 1. Science as Solidarity; 2. Texts and Lumps; 3. Pragmatism without
  Method; 4. The Historiography of Philosophy: Four Genres; 5. The Priority of
  Democracy to Philosophy; 6. Pragmatism, Davidson, and Truth.)

Verite sans Pouvoir: la Philosophie sans Authorite. Paris: Editions de l'Eclat, 1990. (Contains: 1. Pragmatism, Davidson, and Truth; 2. Science as Solidarity; 3. Is Natural Science a Natural Kind? 4. Deconstruction and Circumvention.)

Heidegger, Wittgenstein en Pragmatisme. Amsterdam: Uitgeverij Kok Agora, 1992. (Contains: 1. Pragmatism without Method; 2. Texts and Lumps; 3. Inquiry as Recontextualization; 4. Philosophy as science, as metaphor, and as politics; 5. Heidegger, Contingency, and Pragmatism; 6. Wittgenstein, Heidegger, and the Reification of Language.)

Eine Kultur ohne Zentrum: Vier phiosophische Essays. Stuttgart: Reclam, 1993. (Contains: 1. Is Natural Science a Natural Kind? 2. Non-Reductive Physicalism; 3. Heidegger, Kundera, and Dickens; 4. Deconstrution and Circumvention.)

Chung Wei Literary Monthly 22, no. 7 (December 1993). (A Rorty issue containing Chinese translations of: 1. Trotsky and the Wild Orchids; 2. A Pragmatist View of Rationality and Cultural Difference; 3. Feminism and Pragmatism; 4. Deconstruction; 5. Comments on Eco.)

Hou Zhe Xue Wen Hua (Towards a Post-Philosophical Culture). Shanghai: Shang Hai Yi Wen Chu Ban She, 1991. (Contains Chinese translations of: 1. Introduction to *Consequences of Pragmatism;* 2. Philosophy as Science, as Metaphor and as Politics; 3. Is Natural Science a Natural Kind? 4. Deconstruction; 5. Anti-Essentialism and the Literary Left; 6. The Priority of Democracy to Philosophy; 7. Postmodernist Bourgeois Liberalism; 8. Pragmatism, Davidson and Truth; 9. Pragmatism, Relativism and Irrationalism; 10. Science as Solidarity.)

La Svolta Linguistica. Milan: Garzanti, 1994. (Contains Italian translations of: 1. Metaphysical Difficulties of Linguistic Philosophy; 2. Why does language matter to philosophy?—ten years later; 3. Twenty-five years later.)

ARTICLES AND REVIEWS

Initials of book titles in parentheses indicate that the piece was reprinted in *Consequences of Pragmatism* (CP) or *Objectivity, Relativism, and Truth* (ORT) or *Essays on Heidegger and Others* (EHO).

1959a. Review of *Experience and the Analytic: A Reconsideration of Empiricism,* by Alan Pasch. *International Journal of Ethics* 70 (October 1959): 75–77.

1960a. Review of *Modern Science and Human Freedom,* by David L. Miller. *International Journal of Ethics* 70 (April 1960): 248–49.

1960b. Review of *John Dewey: His thought and Influence,* ed. John Blewett. *Teacher's College Record* 62 (October 1960): 88–89.

1961a. "The Limits of Reductionism." In *Experience, Existence and the Good,* ed. Irwin C. Lieb (Southern Illinois University Press, 1961), 100–116.

1961b. "Pragmatism, Categories and Language." *Philosophical Review* 70 (April

1961): 197–223.

1961c. "Recent Metaphilosophy." *Review of Metaphysics* 15 (December 1961): 299–318.

1961d. Review of *Introduction to the Philosophy of History*, by Raymond Aron. *New Leader* (25 December 1961): 18–19.

1962a. Review of *American Pragmatism: Peirce, James and Dewey*, by Edward C. Moore. *International Journal Of Ethics (Ethics)* 72 (January 1962): 146–47.

1962b. "Second Thoughts on Teaching Communism." *Teacher's College Record* 63 (April 1962).

1962c. "Realism, Categories, and the 'Linguistic Turn,'" *International Philosophical Quarterly* 2 (May 1962): 307–22.

1962d. Review of *The Value Judgement*, by William D. Lamont. *Journal for the Scientific Study of Religion* 2 (Fall 1962): 139–40.

1963a. "Matter and Event." In *The Concept Of Matter*, ed. Ernan McMullin (Notre Dame: Notre Dame University Press, 1963), 497–524. A revised version appears in *Explorations in Whitehead's Philosophy*, ed. Lewis S. Ford and George L. Kline (New York, Fordham University Press, 1983), 68–103.

1963b. "The Subjectivist Principle and the Linguistic Turn." In *Alfred North Whitehead: Essays on His Philosophy*, ed. George L. Kline (Englewood Cliffs, N.J.: Prentice-Hall, 1963), 134–57.

1963c. "Empiricism, Extensionalism and Reductionism." *Mind* 72 (April 1963): 176–86.

1963d. Review of *Understanding Whitehead*, by Victor Lowe. *Journal Of Philosophy* 60 (25 April 1963): 246–51.

1963e. Review of *Utopian Essays and Practical Proposals*, by Paul Goodman. *Teacher's College Record* 64 (May 1963): 743–44.

1963f. Review of *Reason and Analysis*, by Brand Blanshard. *Journal Of Philosophy* 60 (12 September 1963): 551–57.

1963g. "Comments on Prof. Hartshorne's Paper." *Journal Of Philosophy* 60 (10 October 1963): 606–8.

1964a. Questions to Weiss and Tillich in *Philosophical Interrogations, interrogations of Martin Buber, John Wild, Jean Wahl, Brand Blanshard, Paul Weiss, Charles Hartshorne, Paul Tillich*, ed. Beatrice and Sidney Rome (New York: Holt, Rinehart and Winston, 1964), 266–67, 369–70, 392–93.

1964b. Review of *Clarity is Not Enough: Essays in Criticism of Linguistic Philosophy*, by Hywel D. Lewis. *International Philosophical Quarterly* 4 (1964): 623–24.

1964c. Review of *Chauncy Wright and the Foundations of Pragmatism*, by Edward H. Madden. *Philosophical Review* 73 (April 1964): 287–89.

1965a. "Mind-Body Identity, Privacy, and Categories." *Review of Metaphysics* 19

(September 1965): 24–54.

1966a. "Aristotle." *The American Peoples' Encyclopedia*, ed. Walter D. Scott (Chicago: Spencer Press, 1966), 2:399–400.
1966b. Review of *Charles Peirce and Scholastic Realism: A Study of Peirce's Relation to John Duns Scotus*, by John F. Boler. *Philosophical Review* 75 (January 1966): 116–19.

1967a. Introduction. In *The Linguistic Turn*, ed. Richard Rorty (Chicago: University of Chicago Press, 1967).
1967b. "Intuition." In *Encyclopedia of Philosophy*, ed. Paul Edwards (New York: Macmillan, 1967), 4:204–12.
1967c. "Relations, Internal and External." In *Encyclopedia of Philosophy*, ed. Paul Edwards (New York: Macmillan, 1967), 7:125–33.
1967d. Review of *Metaphysics, Reference and Language*, by James W. Cornman. *Journal Of Philosophy* 64 (23 November 1967): 770–74.
1967e. "Do Analysts and Metaphysicians Disagree?" *Proceedings of The Catholic Philosophical Association* 41 (1967): 39–53.

1970a. "Cartesian Epistemology and Changes in Ontology." In *Contemporary American Philosophy*, ed. John E. Smith (New York: Humanities Press, 1970), 273–92.
1970b. Review of *Science and Metaphysics: Variations on Kantian Themes*, by Wilfrid Sellars. *Philosophy* 45 (March 1970): 66–70.
1970c. "Incorrigibility as the Mark of the Mental." *Journal of Philosophy* 67 (25 June 1970): 399–429.
1970d. "Wittgenstein, Privileged Access, and Incommunicability." *American Philosophical Quarterly* 7 (July 1970): 192–205.
1970e. "In Defense of Eliminative Materialism." *Review of Metaphysics* 24 (September 1970): 112–21.
1970f. "Strawson's Objectivity Argument." *Review of Metaphysics* 24 (December 1970): 207–44.

1971a. Review of *The Origins of Pragmatism: Studies in the Philosophy of Charles Sanders Peirce and William James*, by Alfred J. Ayer. *Philosophical Review* 80 (January 1971): 96–100.
1971b. "Verificationism and Transcendental Arguments." *Nous* 5 (Fall 1971): 3–14.

1972a. Review of *Nihilism*, by Stanley Rosen. *Philosophy Forum* 11 (1972): 102–8.
1972b. "Indeterminacy of Translation and of Truth." *Synthese* 23 (March 1972): 443–62.
1972c. "Dennett on Awareness." *Philosophical Studies* 23 (April 1972): 153–62.

1972d. "Functionalism, Machines, and Incorrigibility." *Journal Of Philosophy* 69 (20 April 1972): 203–20.

1972e. "The World Well Lost." *Journal of Philosophy* 69 (26 October 1972): 649–65. (CP)

1973a. "Genus as Matter: A Reading of Metaphysics Z–H." In *Exegesis and Argument: Essays in Greek Philosophy Presented To Gregory Vlastos*, ed. Richard Rorty, Edward N. Lee, and Alexander P. O. Mourelatos (Assen: Van Gorcum, 1973), 393–420.

1973b. "Criteria and Necessity." *Nous* 7 (November 1973): 313–29.

1974a. "Matter as Goo: Comments on Grene's Paper." *Synthese* 25 (September 1974): 71–77.

1974b. "More on Incorrigibility." *Canadian Journal Of Philosophy* 4 (September 1974): 195–97.

1975a. Review of *The Anxiety of Influence: A Theory of Poetry*, by Harold Bloom. *University: A Princeton Quarterly* 66 (Fall, 1975): 17.

1976a. "Professionalized Philosophy and Transcendalist Culture." *Georgia Review* 30 (1976): 757–69. (CP)

1976b. "Keeping Philosophy Pure." *Yale Review* 65 (Spring 1976): 336–56. (CP)

1976c. "Realism and Reference." *The Monist* 59 (July 1976): 321–40.

1976d. "Realism and Necessity: Milton Fisk's *Nature and Necessity*." *Nous* 10 (September 1976): 345–54.

1976e. Review of *On Human Conduct*, by Michael Oakeshott, and *Knowledge and Politics*, by Roberto Mangabiera Unger. *Social Theory and Practice* 4 (Fall 1976): 107–16.

1976f. "Overcoming the Tradition: Heidegger and Dewey." *Review of Metaphysics* 30 (December 1976): 280–305. (CP)

1977a. "Dewey's Metaphysics." In *New Studies in the Philosophy of John Dewey*, ed. Steven Cahn (Hanover, N.H.: University of New England Press, 1977), 45–74. (CP)

1977b. "Wittgensteinian Philosophy and Empirical Psychology." *Philosophical Studies* 31 (March 1977): 151–72.

1977c. Review of *Why Does Language Matter To Philosophy?*" by Ian Hacking. *Journal of Philosophy* 74 (July 1977): 416–32.

1977d. "Derrida on Language, Being and Abnormal Philosophy." *Journal of Philosophy* 74 (November 1977): 673–81.

1978a. "Epistemological Behaviorism and the De-Transcendentalization of Analytic Philosophy." *Neue Hefte Fur Philosophie* 14 (1978): 117–42. Also in

Hermeneutics and Praxis, ed. Robert Hollinger (Notre Dame: University of Notre Dame Press, 1985), 89–121.

1978b. "From Epistemology to Hermeneutics," *Acta Philosophica Fennica*, 30 (1978): 11–30. (CP)

1978c. "A Middle Ground Between Neurons and Holograms?" *Behavioural and Brain Sciences* 2 (1978): 248.

1978d. "Philosophy as a Kind of Writing: An essay on Derrida," *New Literary History* 10 (August 1978): 141–60. (CP)

1979a. "Transcendental Argument, Self-reference, and Pragmatism." In *Transcendental Arguments and Science*, ed. Peter Bieri, Rolf P. Hortsman, and Lorenz Kruger (Dordrecht: D. Reidel, 1979), 77–103.

1979b. "The Unnaturalness of Epistemology." In *Body, Mind and Method: Essays in Honor of Virgil C. Aldrich*, ed. Donald Gustafson and Bangs Tapscott (Dordrecht: D. Reidel, 1979), 77–92.

1980a. "Idealism, Holism, and the `Paradox of Knowledge.'" In *The Philosophy of Brand Blanshard*, ed. Paul A. Schilpp (La Salle, Ill.: Open Court, 1980), 719–38.

1980b. "On Worldmaking." Review of *Ways of Worldmaking*, by Nelson Goodman. *Yale Review* 69 (1980): 276–79.

1980c. "Searle and the Secret Powers of the Brain." *Behavioral and Brain Sciences* 3 (1980): 445–46.

1980d. "Freud, Morality, and Hermeneutics." *New Literary History* 12 (August 1980): 177–85.

1980e. "Pragmatism, Relativism and Irrationalism," *Proceedings and Addresses of the American Philosophical Association* 53 (August 1980): 719–38. (CP)

1980f. "Reply to Dreyfus and Taylor." *Review of Metaphysics* 34 (September 1980): 39–46.

1980g. (With Hubert L. Dreyfus and Charles Taylor.) "A Discussion." *Review of Metaphysics* 34 (September 1980): 47–55.

1980h. "Kripke vs. Kant." Review of *Naming and Necessity*, by Saul Kripke. *London Review of Books*, 4 September 1980, 4–5.

1981a. "From Epistemology to Romance: Cavell on Scepticism." *Review of Metaphysics* 34 (1981): 759–74. (CP)

1981b. "Method, Social Science, and Social Hope." *Canadian Journal Of Philosophy* 11 (1981): 569–88. (CP)

1981c. "Is There a Problem about Fictional Discourse?" *Funktionen Des Fictiven: Poetic und Hermeneutik*, vol. 10 (Munich: Fink Verlag, 1981). (CP)

1981d. "Nineteenth-Century Idealism and Twentieth-Century Textualism." *The Monist* 64 (1981): 155–74. (CP)

1981e. "Reply to Professor Yolton." *Philosophical Books* 22 (1981): 134–35.

1981f. Review of *American Sociology and Pragmatism*, by J. David Lewis and Richard L. Smith. *Review of Metaphysics* 35 (1981): 147.

1981g. Review of *The Calling Of Sociology and Other Essays*, by Edward Shils. *Review of Metaphysics* 35 (1981): 167–68.

1981h. "Beyond Nietzsche and Marx." Review of three books by or about Foucault. *London Review of Books*, 19 February 1981, 5–6.

1981i. "Being Business." Review of *A Heidegger Critique*, by Roger Waterhouse. *Times Literary Supplement* (3 July 1981): 760.

1982a. Introduction. In *Consequences of Pragmatism* (University of Minnesota Press, 1982). Reprinted as "Pragmatism and Philosophy." In *After Philosophy*, ed. Kenneth Baynes, James Bohman, and Thomas McCarthy (Cambridge: MIT Press, 1987), 26–66. Abridged version appeared as "The Fate of Philosophy," *New Republic* (18 October 1982): 28–34.

1982b. "Hermeneutics, General Studies, and Teaching." *Synergos* 2 (1982): 1–15.

1982c. "Philosophy in America Today." *American Scholar* 51 (1982): 183–200. (CP)

1982d. "Persuasive Philosophy." Review of *Philosophical Explanations*, by Robert Nozick. *London Review of Books*, 20 May 1982, 10–11.

1982e. "From Philosophy to Post-Philosophy" (interview). *Radical Philosophy* (August 1982): 10–11.

1982f. "Comments on Dennett." *Synthese* 53 (November 1982): 181–87.

1982g. "Contemporary Philosophy of Mind." *Synthese* 53 (November 1982): 323–48. Reprinted as "Mind as Ineffable." In *Mind in Nature*, ed. Richard Elvee (Nobel Conference 17, 1982), 60–95.

1982h. "Brute and Raw Experience." Review of *Philosophy in the Twentieth Century*, by Alfred J. Ayer. *New Republic* (6 December 1982): 33–36.

1983a. "Pragmatism Without Method." In *Sidney Hook: Philosopher of Democracy and Humanism*, ed. Paul Kurtz (Buffalo: Prometheus Books, 1983), 259–73. (ORT)

1983b. "The Pragmatist." Review of *A Stroll with William James*, by Jacques Barzun. *New Republic* (9 May 1983): 32–34.

1983c. "Against Belatedness." Review of *The Legitimacy of the Modern Age*, by Hans Blumenberg. *London Review of Books*, 16 June 1983, 3–5.

1983d. "Unsoundness in Perspective." Review of *Nietzsche*, by Richard Schacht, and *Nietzsche and Philosophy*, by Gilles DeLeuze. *Times Literary Supplement* (17 June 1983): 619–20.

1983e. "What Are Philosophers For?" *The Center Magazine* (September–October 1983): 40–44.

1983f. "Postmodernist Bourgeois Liberalism." *Journal of Philosophy* 80 (October

1983): 583–89. (ORT)

1984a. "The Historiography of Philosophy: Four Genres." In *Philosophy in History*, ed. Richard Rorty, Jerome B. Schneewind, and Quentin Skinner (Cambridge: Cambridge University Press, 1984), 49–75.

1984b. (Co-author.) Introduction. In *Philosophy in History*, ed. Richard Rorty, Jerome B. Schneewind, and Quentin Skinner (Cambridge: Cambridge University Press, 1984).

1984c. "Heidegger Wider den Pragmatisten." *Neue Hefte fur Philosophie* 23 (1984): 1–22. (EHO)

1984d. "Solidarity or Objectivity?" *Nanzan Review of American Studies* 6 (1984): 1–19. Also in *Post-Analytic Philosophy*, ed. John Rajchman and Cornel West (New York: Columbia University Press, 1985), 3–19. (ORT)

1984e. "Signposts Along the Way That Reason Went." Review of *Margins of Philosophy*, by Jacques Derrida. *London Review of Books*, 16 February 1984, 5–6.

1984f. "Habermas and Lyotard on Post-Modernity." *Praxis International* 4 (April 1984): 32–44. Also in *Habermas and Post-Modernity*, ed. Richard J. Bernstein (Cambridge: Polity Press, 1985), 161–76. (EHO)

1984g. "What's It All About?" Review of *Intentionality*, by John Searle. *London Review of Books*, 17 May 1984, 3–4.

1984h. "A Reply To Six Critics." *Analyse & Kritik* 6 (June 1984): 78–98.

1984i. "Life at the end of Inquiry." Review of *Realism and Reason: Philosophical Papers III*, by Hilary Putnam. *London Review of Books*, 2 August 1984, 6–7.

1984j. "Deconstruction and Circumvention." *Critical Inquiry* 11 (September 1984): 1–23. (EHO)

1985a. Review of *Traditional and Analytical Philosophy: Lectures on the Philosophy of Language*, by Ernst Tugendhat. *Journal of Philosophy* 82 (1985): 720–29.

1985b. "Texts and Lumps." *New Literary History* 17 (1985): 1–15. (ORT)

1985c. "Comments On Sleeper and Edel." *Transactions of the Charles S. Peirce Society* 21 (Winter 1985): 40–48.

1985d. "Philosophy Without Principles." *Critical Inquiry* 11 (March 1985): 132–38. Also in *Against Theory*, ed. W. J. T. Mitchell (Chicago: University of Chicago Press, 1985), 132–38.

1985e. "The Humanities: Asking Better Questions, Doing More Things" (interview). *Federation Review* 8 (March–April 1985): 15–19.

1985f. "Feeling His Way." Review of *The War Diaries of Jean-Paul Sartre November 1939–March 1940. New Republic* (15 April 1985): 32–34.

1985g. "Le Cosmopolitanisme sans Emancipation: Reponse a Jean-Francois Lyotard." *Critique* (May 1985): 569–80, 584. (ORT)

1985h. "Absolutely Non-Absolute." Review of *Philosophical Papers*, by Charles Taylor. *Times Literary Supplement* (6 December 1985): 1379–80.

1986a. "Beyond Realism and Anti-Realism." In *Wo steht die Analytische Philosophie heute?* ed. Ludwig Nagl and Richard Heinrich (Vienna: R. Oldenbourg Verlag, Munich, 1986), 103–15.

1986b. "Foucault and Epistemology." In *Foucault: A Critical Reader*, ed. David C. Hoy (Oxford: Blackwell, 1986), 41–49.

1986c. "Freud and Moral Reflection." In *Pragmatism's Freud: The Moral Disposition of Psychoanalysis*, ed. Joseph H. Smith and William Kerrigan (Baltimore: Johns Hopkins University Press, 1986), 1–27. (EHO)

1986d. "From Logic to Language to Play." *Proceedings and Addresses of the American Philosophical Association* 59 (1986): 747–53.

1986e. Introduction. In *John Dewey: The Later Works, vol. 8: 1933*, ed. Jo Ann Boydston (Carbondale, Southern Illinois University Press, 1986).

1986f. "Philosophie als Wissenschaft, als Metapher, und als Politik." In *Die Krise der Phaenomenologie und die Pragmatik des Wissenschaftsfortschritt*, ed. Michael Benedikt and Rudolf Burger (Vienna: Verlag der Oesterreichischen Staatsdruckeri, 1986): 138–49. Subsequently published in the English original in EHO.

1986g. "Pragmatism, Davidson and Truth." In *Truth and Interpretation. Perspectives on the Philosophy of Donald Davidson*, ed. E. LePore (Oxford: Blackwell, 1986), 333–68. (ORT)

1986h. "Should Hume Be Answered or Bypassed?" In *Human Nature and Natural Knowledge: Essays Presented to Marjorie Grene*, ed. Alan Donagan, Anthony N. Perovich, Jr., and Michael V. Wedin. (Dordrecht: D. Reidel, 1986), 341–52.

1986i. "Comments on Toulmin's 'Conceptual Communities and Rational Conversation,'" *Archivio di Filosofia* (1986): 189–93.

1986j. "The Higher Nominalism in a Nutshell, A Reply to Henry Staten." *Critical Inquiry* 12 (1986): 462–66.

1986k. "On Ethnocentrism: A Reply to Clifford Geertz." *Michigan Quarterly Review* 25 (1986): 525–34. (ORT)

1986l. "The Contingency of Language." *London Review of Books*, 17 April 1986, 3–6. (Ch. 1 of *Contingency, Irony and Solidarity.*)

1986m. "Freedom as Higher Than Being." *Working Papers: Critique of Modernity* (ed. Robert Langbaum) 1 (April 1986): 16–26.

1986n. "The Contingency of Selfhood." *London Review of Books*, 8 May 1986, 11–14. (Ch. 2 of *Contingency, Irony and Solidarity.*)

1986o. "Sex and the Single Thinker." Review of *Sexual Desire: A Moral Philosophy of the Erotic*, by Roger Scruton. *New Republic* (2 June 1986): 34–37.

1986p. "The Contingency of Community." *London Review of Books*, 24 July 1986, 10–14. (Ch. 3 of *Contingency, Irony and Solidarity.*)

1986q. "Interview with Richard Rorty." *Journal of Literary Studies / Tydskrif Vir Literatuurwetenskap* 2 (November 1986): 9–13.

1987a. "Non-Reductive Physicalism." In *Theorie der Subjektivitaet*, ed. Konrad Cramer, et al (Frankfurt: Suhrkamp, 1987), 278–96. (ORT)

1987b. "Science as Solidarity." In *The Rhetoric of the Human Sciences*, ed. John S. Nelson, A. Megill, and D. N. McCloskey (Madison: University of Wisconsin Press, 1987), 38–52. (ORT)

1987c. "Unfamiliar Noises: Hesse and Davidson on Metaphor." *Proceedings of the Aristotelian Society* (suppl.) 61 (1987): 283–96. (ORT)

1987d. "Waren die Gesetze Newtons schon vor Newton Wahr?" In *Jahrbuch des Wissenschaftkollegs zu Berlin*, 1987. (Trans.: Italian.)

1987e. "Nominalismo e Contestualismo." *Alfabeta* 9 (September 1987): 11–12.

1987f. "Posties." Review of *Der Philosophische Diskurs der Moderne*, by Jurgen Habermas. *London Review of Books*, 3 September 1987, 11–12.

1987g. "Thugs and Theorists: A Reply to Bernstein." *Political Theory* 15 (November 1987): 564–80. (Trans.: French.)

1988a. "Is Natural Science a Natural Kind?" In *Construction and Constraint: The Shaping of Scientific Rationality*, ed. Ernan McMullin (Notre Dame: Notre Dame University Press, 1988), 49–74. (ORT)

1988b. "The Priority of Democracy to Philosophy." In *The Virginia Statue of Religious Freedom*, ed. Merill Peterson and Robert Vaughan (Cambridge: Cambridge University Press, 1988), 257–88. (ORT)

1988c. "Representation, Social Practice, and Truth." *Philosophical Studies* 54 (1988): 215–28. (ORT)

1988d. Review of *The Limits of Analysis*, by Stanley Rosen, *Independent Journal of Philosophy*, 5/6 (1988): 153–54.

1988e. "Unger, Castoriadis and the Romance of a National Future." *Northwestern University Law Review* 82 (Winter 1988): 335–51. (EHO)

1988f. "I Professori Sono Meglio dei Torturatori" (interview). *Alpfabeta* 10 (March 1988): 5.

1988g. "That Old-Time Philosophy" (on Allan Bloom's *The Closing of the American Mind*) *New Republic* (4 April 1988): 28–33.

1988h. "Taking Philosophy Seriously." Review of *Heidegger et le Nazisme*, by Victor Farias. *New Republic* (11 April 1988): 31–34.

1989a. "Identité Morale et Autonomie Privée." In *Michel Foucault Philosophe: Recontre Intenationale* (Paris: Editions du Seuil, 1989), 385–94. (English original appeared as 1990g. Also translated into Spanish.) (EHO)

1989b. "Philosophy as Science, as Metaphor and as Politics." In *The Institution of Philosophy: A Discipline in Crisis?* ed. Avner Cohen and Marcello Dascal (La Salle, Ill.: Open Court, 1989), 13–33. (English original of 1986f.) (EHO)

1989c. "Two Meanings of 'Logocentrism': A Reply to Norris." In *Redrawing the Lines: Analytic Philosophy, Deconstruction and Literary Theory*, ed. Reed Way Dasenbrock (Minneapolis: University of Minnesota Press, 1989), 204–16. (EHO)

1989d. "Social Construction and Composition Theory: A Conversation with Richard Rorty." *Journal of Advanced Composition* 9 (1989): 1–9.

1989e. Review of *Connections to the World: The Basic Concepts of Philosophy*, by Arthur C. Danto, *New York Newsday Books*, 19 March 1989.

1989f. "Education Without Dogma." *Dissent* 36 (Spring 1989): 198–204. (Also as "Education, Socialization and Individuation" and accompanied by "Replies to Commentators," in *Liberal Education* 75 (October 1989); also in shortened form as "Truth and Freedom in Education," in *Harper's*, June 1989.

1989g. "Is Derrida a Transcendental Philosopher?" *Yale Journal of Criticism* 2 (April 1989). (EHO)

1989h. "Comments on Castoriadis' 'The End of Philosophy.'" *Salmagundi*, no. 82–83 (Spring–Summer 1989): 24–30.

1989i. "Philosophy and Post-Modernism." *Cambridge Review* 110 (June 1989): 51–53.

1989j. Review of *Interpreting Across Boundaries*, ed. Eliot Deutsch, *Philosophy East and West* 39 (July 1989): 332–37.

1989k. "Wittgenstein e Heidegger: due percorsi incrociati." *Lettere Intenazionale* 22 (Ottobre–Dicembre, 1989): 21–26. (In English in *The Cambridge Guide to Heidegger*, ed. Charles Guignon, Cambridge University Press, 1993.) (EHO)

1989l. "The Humanistic Intellectual: Eleven Theses." *ACLS Occasional Papers*, no. 11 (November, 1989).

1990a. "Consciousness, Intentionality and Pragmatism." In *Modelos de la Mente*, ed. Jose Quiros (Madrid: 1990).

1990b. "Twenty-five years after," a postscript to 1967a. Published (in Spanish translation) along with 1967a and 1977c, in *El Giro Linguistico*, trans. G. Bello (Barcelona: Ediciones Paidos, 1990); subsequently published in English in the second edition of *The Linguistic Turn*.

1990c. "The Dangers of Over-Philosophication—Reply to Arcilla and Nicholson." *Educational Theory* 40 (1990): 41–44.

1990d. "Two Cheers for the Cultural Left." *South Atlantic Quarterly* 89 (1990): 227–34.

1990e. "Another Possible World" (on Heidegger's Nazism). *London Review of Books*, 8 February 1990, 21.

1990f. "Foucault/Dewey/Nietzsche." *Raritan* 9 no. 4 (Spring 1990): 1–8

1990g. "Truth and Freedom: A Reply to Thomas McCarthy." *Critical Inquiry*, 16 (Spring 1990): 633–43.

1991a. "The Banality of Pragmatism and the Poetry of Justice." In *Pragmatism in Law and Society*, ed. Michael Brint and William Weaver (Boulder, Colo.: Westview Press, 1991), 89–97. (This article had previously appeared in *Southern California Law Review*.)

1991b. "Comments on Taylor's 'Paralectics.'" In *On the Other: Dialogue and/or*

Dialectics, ed. Robert P. Scharlemann (Lanham, Md.: University Press of America, 1991), 71–78. (Working paper #5 of the University of Virginia Commitee on the Comparative Study of the Individual and Society.)

1991c. "Pragmatismo." In *Dicionario do Pensiamento Contemporanaio*, ed. Manuel Maria Carrilho (Lisbon: Publicacoes Dom Quixote, l991), 265–78.

1991d. "Just One More Species Doing Its Best." Review of four books about John Dewey. *London Review of Books*.

1991e. "The Philosopher and the Prophet." Review of *The Genealogy of Pragmatism*, by Cornel West. *Transition*, no. 52, (1991): 70–78.

1991f. "Feminism and Pragmatism," *Michigan Quarterly Review* (Spring l991): 231–58.

1991g. "The Guru of Prague." Review of three books by Jan Patocka. *New Republic* (1 July 1991): 35–40.

1991h. "Nietzsche, Socrates and Pragmatism," *South African Journal of Philosophy* 10 (August 1991): 61–63.

1991i. "Intellectuals in Politics," *Dissent* 38 (Autumn 1991): 483–90.

1991j. "Blunder Around for a While." Review of *Consciousness Explained*, by Daniel Dennett. *London Review of Books*, 21 November 1991, 3–6.

1991k. "Philosophers, Novelists, and Intercultural Comparisons: Heidegger, Kundera, and Dickens." In *Culture and Modernity: East-West Philosophic Perspectives*, ed. Eliot Deutsch (Honolulu: University of Hawaii Press, 1991), 3–20. (EHO)

1992a. Introduction. Vladimir Nabokov, *Pale Fire* (New York: Everyman's Library, l992).

1992b. "The pragmatist's progress." In *Interpretation and Overintepration*, by Umberto Eco et al. (Cambridge: Cambridge University Press, l992), 89–108.

1992c. "Reponses de Richard Rorty" (to Jacques Bouveresse, Vincent Descombes, Thomas MacCarthy, Alexander Nehamas, and Hilary Putnam). In *Lire Rorty*, ed. Jean-Pierre Cometti (Paris: Editions de l'Eclat, l992), 147–250.

1992d. "Robustness: A Reply to Jean Bethke Elshtain." In *The Politics of Irony*, ed. David W. Conway and John E. Seery (New York: St. Martin's Press, l992), 219–23.

1992e. "Trotsky and the Wild Orchids." *Common Knowledge* 1, no. 3 (Winter 1992): 140–53. (Previously appeared in French translation in *Lire Rorty* (see item l992c above); also in *Wild Orchids and Trotsky: Messages from American Universities*, ed. Mark Edmundson (New York: Viking, l993).

1992f. "The Politicization of the Humanities." *UVa Alumni Journal* (Winter l992).

1992g. "Love and Money," *Common Knowledge* 1, no. 1 (Spring 1992): 12–16.

1992h. "Reply to Andrew Ross," *Dissent* 39 (Spring l992): 265–67.

1992i. "We Anti-Representationalists." Review of *Ideology: An Introduction*, by Terry Eagleton, *Radical Philosophy* 60 (Spring 1992): 40–42.

1992j. "The Intellectuals at the End of Socialism," *Yale Review* 80, nos. 1 & 2 (April 1992): 1–16. An abbreviated version of this article appeared under the title "For a More Banal Politics," in *Harper's* (May 1992): 16–21.

1992k. "Nietzsche: Un philosophe pragmatique." *Magazine Litteraire* (April 1992): 28–32. (Trans. of "Bloom's Nietzsche," a piece not yet published in English.)

1992l. "What Can You Expect from Anti-Foundationalist Philosophers? A Reply to Lynn Baker." *Virginia Law Review* 78 (April 1992): 719–27.

1992m. "The Feminist Saving Remnant." Review of *The Rise and Fall of the American Left*, by John Patrick Diggins. *New Leader* 1–15 June 1992, 9–10.

1992n. "A Pragmatist View of Rationality and Cultural Differences," *Philosophy East and West* 42, no. 4 (October 1992): 581–96. (Trans.: Italian, Polish.)

1992o. "Dewey entre Hegel et Darwin," *Rue Descartes*, nos. 5–6 (Novembre 1992): 53–71. (The English original appeared as 1994j.)

1993a. "An Antirepresentationalist View: Comments on Richard Miller, van Fraassen-Sigman, and Churchland" and "A Comment on Robert Scholes' 'Tlon and Truth.'" In *Realism and Representation*, ed. George Levine (Madison: University of Wisconsin Press, 1993), 125–33, 186–89.

1993b. "Holism, Intentionality, and the Ambition of Transcendence." In *Dennett and his Critics: Demystifying Mind*, ed. Bo Dahlbom (Oxford: Blackwell, 1993), 184–202.

1993c. "Human Rights, Rationality and Sentimentality." In *On Human Rights: The 1993 Oxford Amnesty Lectures*, ed. Susan Hurley and Stephen Shute (New York: Basic Books, 1993), 112–34. (A shortened version, without the footnotes, appeared in *Yale Review* 81, no. 4 (October 1993). 1–20.

1993d. "Centers of Moral Gravity: Comments on Donald Spence's 'The Hermeneutic Turn,'" *Psychoanalytic Dialogues* 3, no. 1 (1993): 21–28.

1993e. "On Democracy, Liberalism and the Post-Communist Challenge" (interview). *Mesotes: Zeitschrift fuer philosophischen Ost-West Dialog* 4 (1992): 491 500.

1993f. "'Paroxysms and Politics." Review of *The Passion of Michel Foucault*, by James Miller. *Salmagundi* no. 97 (Winter, 1993): 61–68.

1993g. "Feminism, Ideology and Deconstruction: A Pragmatist View," *Hypatia* 8 (Spring, 1993): 96–103.

1993h. "Du Pragmatisme en Politique" (interview). *Le Banquet* (2eme Semestre 1993, no. 3): 135–47.

1993i. "Intersubjectividad y libertad" (interview). *Theoria: Revista de Filosofia* 1, no. 1 (July 1993): 113–22.

1993j. Review of *Ideals and Illusions: On Reconstruction and Deconstruction in Contemporary Critical Theory*, by Thomas McCarthy. *Journal of Philosophy* 90 (July 1993): 370–73.

1993k. "Putnam and the Relativist Menace," *Journal of Philosophy* 90 (September

1993): 443–61. (Previously published in French; see 1992c)

1994a. "Dewey Between Hegel and Darwin." In *Modernist Impulses and the Human Sciences*, ed. Dorothy Ross (Baltimore: Johns Hopkins University Press, 1994). (Previously published in French; see 1992o.)

1994b. "Does Democracy Need Foundations?" In *Politisches Denken: Jahrbuch 1993*, hrsg. Volker Gerhardt u.a. (Stuttgart and Weimar: Metzler Verlag, 1994), 21–23.

1994c. "Taylor on Truth." In Philosophy in an Age of Pluralism: The Philosophy of Charles Taylor in Question, ed. James Tully (Cambrifdge: Cambridge University Press, 1994), 20–36.

1994d. "Replies" (to Burzta and Buchowski, Dziemidok, Gierszewski, Kmita, Kwiek, Morawski, Szahaj, Zeidler, and Zeidler-Janiszewska), *Ruch Filozoficzny* 50, no. 2: 178–79, 183–84, 188–89, 194–95, 198–200, 205–7, 209–10, 214–16, 218.

1994e. Review of The Grandeur and Twilight of Radical Universalism, by Agnes Heller and Ferenc Feher. *Thesis Eleven* 37 (1994): 119–26.

1994f. "Sind Aussagen universelle Geltungsansprueche?" *Deutsche Zeitschrift furer Philosophie*, Band 42, Heft 6 (1994), 975–988.

1994g. "Tales of Two Disciplines." *Callaloo* 17, no. 2 (1994): 575–607.

1994h. Review of Willful Liberalism: Voluntarism and Individuality in Political Theory and Practice, by Richard Flathman. *Political Theory* 22, no. 1 (February 1994): 190–94.

1994i. "The Unpatriotic Academy," *New York Times*, 13 February 1994, op-ed page.

1994j. "Why Can't a Man be More Like a Woman, and Other Problems in Moral Philosophy." Review of Moral Prejudices: Essays in Ethics, by Annette Baier. *London Review of Books*, 24 February 1994, 3–6.

1994k. "Taylor on Self-Celebration and Gratitude," *Philosophy and Phenomenological Research* 54, no. 1 (March 1994): 197–201.

1994l. "Religion as Conversation-Stopper," *Common Knowledge* 3, no. 1 (Spring 1994): 1–6.

1994m. "Sex, Lies, and Virginia's Voters," *New York Times*, October 13, 1994, op-ed page.

1994n. "A Leg-Up for Oliver North (review of Richard Bernstein, *Dicatorship of Virtue: Multiculturalism and the Battle for America's Future*), *London Review of Books*, October 20, 1994, 13–14. (A revised version appeared in *Harper's* for Junuary, 1995, under the title "Demonizing the Academy.)

1994o. "Does Academic Freedom Have Philosophical Presuppositions?" *Academe* 80 no. 6 (November/December 1994): 52–63.

INDEX

RORTY AND PRAGMATISM

was electronically composed in 10 on 14 Adobe Galliard
with display type in Bureau Eagle;
printed on 60-pound, acid-free, Glatfelter Supple Opaque paper,
with 80-pound endsheets and dust jackets printed in 3 colors,
Smyth-sewn and bound over 88-point binder's boards
in Roxite A-grade cloth,
by Thomson-Shore, Inc.
Both book and jacket design are the work of Bonnie Campbell.
Published by Vanderbilt University Press,
Nashville, Tennessee 37235.